Banking on Health

Shiri Noy

Banking on Health

The World Bank and Health Sector
Reform in Latin America

Shiri Noy
Department of Sociology
University of Wyoming
Laramie, WY, USA

ISBN 978-3-319-87156-1   ISBN 978-3-319-61765-7 (eBook)
DOI 10.1007/978-3-319-61765-7

Cover credit: © Viorika/GettyImages

Printed on acid-free paper

This Palgrave Macmillan imprint is published by Springer Nature
The registered company is Springer International Publishing AG
The registered company address is: Gewerbestrasse 11, 6330 Cham, Switzerland

To my parents, Ori and Dalia Noy

Acknowledgements

One of the reasons I find sociology so useful is that it highlights the social nature of individual undertakings. This book would not have been possible without the support of so many people. I owe a great debt of gratitude to my dissertation committee, as this project began at Indiana University, Bloomington. Patricia McManus has been an incredibly generous and formidable mentor throughout the years. Together with the rest of my committee, Art Alderson, Clem Brooks, Bernice Pescosolido, and Brian Steensland, she has provided incisive and constructive feedback on this project. I am also indebted to Brian Powell, who has always made himself available for questions and comments. I have also been fortunate to count on the personal and intellectual support of many friends and colleagues: Aaron Ponce, Abby Shaddox, Alya Guseva, Ann McCranie, Anna Zajacova, Carly Schall, Carrie Larson, Casey Oberlin, Christi Smith, Claudia Geist, Dana Prewitt, Dave Messenger, Dee Redmond, Dean Noy, Donna Barnes, Emily Bowman, Emily Meanwell, Evie Perry, Fabio Rojas, Jaime Kucinskas, Jamie and Deb Prenkert, Jenn and Dave Chonowski, J.D. Wolfe, Jelena Radovic Fanta, Jenny Stuber, Joe DiGrazia, Joe Harris, John and Carrie Shandra, Julia Obert, Juliana Martinez Franzoni, Kevin and Kelly Doran, Kyle Dodson, Laura Hamilton, Mandy Stewart, Marina Gerbin Landau, Malcolm Holmes, Matthew Painter, Michael Vassuer, Rashawn Ray, Richard Machalek, Ronen Noy, Sarah Hatteberg, Sharon Hamilton, Tanja Vuckovic Juros, Tiffany Julian, and Tim O'Brien.

I am especially grateful to all of the people who were so kind to me in Lima, Buenos Aires, and San Pedro and San Jose where I conducted my country case-study research. I especially thank my respondents for their generosity with their time, experiences, and information. In Peru, I thank Mariana, Adam, and Orit Pollak as well as the dearly departed Eugene and Aurelia Farkas (who I lovingly knew as Tata and Bobbi) who so kindly hosted me and made my stay so comfortable and wonderful. They are my second family, and they graciously open their home to me each time I visit. I also thank José Alberto Castro Quiroz and Liliana Vasquez who were especially helpful and whose office in the Ministry of Health became my headquarters of sort. In Costa Rica, I thank the Instituto de Investigaciones Sociales (IIS) at the University of Costa Rica that graciously hosted me during my time there and especially Koen Voorend and Fran Robles. In Buenos Aires, I thank Nacho Bontempo who made me feel so welcome and Federico Tobar and Carlos Vassallo, who were among my first interviewees and opened many subsequent doors for me. I also thank the several transcriptionists in all three countries who helped me transcribe these interviews. I would not have been able to accomplish this research without funding from the Sociology department, the Center for Latin American and Caribbean Studies, and the Office for the Office of the Vice President for International Affairs at Indiana University. I am also thankful for the financial support from a National Science Foundation Dissertation Improvement Grant, an American Sociological Association Fund for the Advancement of the Discipline Grant, and a University of Wyoming Basic Research Grant.

I am grateful to my editor at Palgrave Macmillan, Alexis Nelson, and editorial assistant Kyra Saniewski who were extraordinarily helpful and gracious in shepherding this book to publication. I thank my family for being so encouraging, in particular my brothers, aunts, uncles, cousins, and grandparents. I dedicate this book to my parents who have always supported me in everything I do, and are responsible for nurturing my curiosity—academic and otherwise. Without this sense of adventure, the desire to know how things work, especially in other places, I never would have embarked on this research.

CONTENTS

LIST OF FIGURES

LIST OF TABLES

CHAPTER 1

The World Bank, Development, and Health

INTRODUCTION

Once upon a time economic development proceeded hand-in-hand with the development of state-sponsored systems to support a healthy, educated workforce. And countries like Germany, England, Sweden, and the United States developed social welfare programs that fit their distinctive histories, political ideologies, and internal economies. Today, things are quite different. Globalization is altering how states understand their responsibility in defining, providing, and ensuring their citizens' social rights, in both developing and developed countries. Developing countries, where existing welfare systems are typically limited in coverage and scope, are deciding on levels of social protections amidst the challenges of increasing and sustaining economic growth in an ever more globalized world. In this globalized reality, the fate and fortune of countries' economies are more closely tied to financial and economic crises in other countries and influenced by global actors. International financial institutions (IFIs), such as the International Monetary Fund and the World Bank, are active participants in the emergence of welfare states in the developing world, in contrast to the relative autonomy of welfare states that matured during the industrial era. Specifically, the World Bank—one of two "global ministries of health" (along with the World Health Organization)—has historically been the single largest external funder of health in the developing world, rendering it an important yet understudied actor in the field of global health.

© The Author(s) 2017
S. Noy, *Banking on Health*, DOI 10.1007/978-3-319-61765-7_1

This book examines the role of the World Bank in health sector reform in Latin America. Latin America boasts a long legacy of public health leadership, with the advent of social medicine in the 1930s. Health has often been a central concern in state development in the region. However, a complex history of economic stagnation, recession, and political instability in much of Latin America and the Caribbean has conspired to prevent the development of social protections established during this earlier period into universal health systems in many countries. Latin America's increased integration into the global economy, patchy democratic history, high levels of economic growth and inequality, and the heavy-handed influence of IFIs makes it a particularly interesting region in which to examine the dynamics of state-building, globalization, and health sector reform. I argue that we should take seriously the role of the World Bank in global health. As an important normative power and the largest single external funder of global health, it wields enormous influence. It affects which health issues come to be seen as problems, dictates they should be addressed, and delineates who should address them at the national level.

The Puzzle

This book addresses a central research puzzle: why has the World Bank, with its immense normative and financial power in health, not uniformly imposed a neoliberal turn in health in Latin American countries? This is especially surprising given the World Bank's emphasis on neoliberal structural adjustment policies and many Latin American countries' experiences of economic crisis and recession in the 1980s and beyond. During this time period these countries were desperately seeking outside funds and leadership, and especially vulnerable to IFIs' influence. I argue that the World Bank's effect on health policies and expenditures in Latin America since 1980 is contingent on countries' state capacity and autonomy in health, but also on the variable nature of the World Bank's approach to health across countries and over time.

The answer to this puzzle is then multi-faceted. The World Bank is seen as a neoliberal hegemon, using its financial and normative power to push national policies in the direction of privatization, marketization, and individualism. This book challenges this view. Indeed, the World Bank is neither hegemonic nor uniformly neoliberal in its involvement in health sector reform in Latin America. I argue that the World Bank's approach to health is contingent: it is mediated by national institutions, and has shifted from emphasizing neoliberal ends (a market-oriented approach that limited state involvement and emphasized individualism) to neoliberal means (programs and projects which use market tools and logics), sometimes in the service of more equitable and universalist goals. In doing so I draw on globalization, development, welfare state, and state-building theories that together help account for the trajectory of health sector reform in Argentina, Costa Rica, and Peru and the World Bank's changing approach to health in Latin America and beyond.

As I discuss in the following chapters and as detailed in the methodological appendix, the data for this book are based on fieldwork in Argentina, Costa Rica, and Peru, cross-national data on health expenditures, and research at the World Bank archives. I spent several weeks in 2009 in Lima, Peru and most of 2011 in Buenos Aires, Argentina, San Jose and San Pedro, Costa Rica, and Lima, Peru collecting government documents and interviewing key informants who were central to the health policy reform process since the 1980s in these three countries. The analysis presented here draws information from over 300 documents from national sources and World Bank projects in these three countries and over 100 interviews I conducted with policymakers, international organization personnel, experts, and social security personnel across these three countries. Finally, in 2015 I spent two weeks at the World Bank archives reviewing correspondence, drafts, and other material on health loans and projects in these countries and conducting interviews with several current and former World Bank personnel (see the Methodological Appendix for a complete list). Taken together, these data provide a rich and nuanced account of the ways in which the World Bank has interacted with domestic institutions and politics leading to distinctive outcomes in health sector reform.

GLOBAL GOVERNANCE AND THE CHANGING SHAPE OF NEOLIBERALISM

In an era of intensified globalization, neoliberalism has become an increasingly popular and prevalent policy approach, but the term lacks definitional and analytic clarity. Generally, neoliberalism posits that economic growth can best be achieved by relegating the distribution of goods, services, and resources to the market and private sector. Neoliberalism has been categorized as anything from an economic approach to an ideology or philosophy. Generally, however, neoliberalism is characterized by the idea that markets are the most efficient form of resource distribution, resulting in a healthier economy. Underlying this belief in the benefits of allowing the market to allocate resources is an emphasis on individuals, property, and contracts as means to rationalize the economy (Babb 2013). The natural continuity of this idea, then, is that the economy is best left to the private sector, rather than government. Neoliberalism is a central feature of global governance, where global governance is broadly conceived of as efforts by states, international organizations, and other actors to identify, understand, negotiate responses to, and address challenges and problems (Griffin 2009; Karns et al. 2015).

Neoliberalism replaced an era of embedded liberalism in the developed world, lasting from approximately the 1940s to the 1970s, which struck a compromise between the free markets espoused by liberalism and welfare policies following Keynesian principles of state intervention (Polanyi 1944; Ruggie 1982). The neoliberal liberalization model of the 1980s and 1990s also replaced years of inward-looking development in developing countries; largely import-substitution efforts in Latin America, which were strategies of the 1960s and 1970s (Meseguer 2005). IFIs, namely the International Monetary Fund (IMF) and the World Bank, have been identified as central movers in diffusing neoliberal ideas via loan agreements and structural adjustment programs (Simmons et al. 2007; Laurell 2000; Keshavjee 2014). This approach coalesced under the heading of the "Washington Consensus," embodying a suite of pressures to expand the role of the free market, constrain the state, and increase U.S. influence in domestic policies of developing nations, especially in Latin America (Guillén 2001).

Some scholars suggest that neoliberalism is being strengthened by the intensification of globalization and social scientists have become increasingly concerned with how economic and financial globalization (largely identified as the integration of countries into the world economy) has affected developing nations (Rodrik 1997; Portes 1997). This concern has arisen particularly out of recognition that now, more than ever, development, growth, and state-building are occurring in an interconnected world, with powerful actors which influence states' decisions (Mishra 2004). Existing research indicates that the relationship between openness to markets and social spending is largely negative (Simmons et al. 2007; Brady and Lee 2014), with arguments largely focused on a "race to the bottom" among developing countries. As developing countries compete for international investments, they are induced to create better incentives than their competitors for foreign firms (Beeson 2001; Esping-Andersen 1999; Glatzer and Rueschemeyer 2004; Huber and Stephens 2012; Navarro 2007). This global competition for investment and foreign capital creates downward pressures on wages, working conditions, social policies, and business taxation (Yeates 2002). In addition to economic competition creating downwards pressures on social policies and spending, international organizations can also exert neoliberal pressures, further pushing down social expenditures and weakening state-sponsored social protections.

More recently, scholarship has pointed to the changing shape of neoliberalism, rather than its supplantation. Central neoliberal concerns: the primacy of the market, free trade, and competition are now seen as correlated with a certain "stateness" (Hay and Marsh 2010). However, this is not a welfare state in its classic understanding; it is a regulatory state which regulates, among other things, public goods. A state characterized by its interaction with international organizations and a global technocracy in making decisions about social provision. Among the most important actors influencing state decisions about social protections are international organizations, among them the World Bank, which I argue should be conceptualized as a uniquely powerful policy advisor, especially in developing countries.

The World Bank as Policy Advisor

International financial institutions, such as the World Bank are core actors in contemporary global governance. I argue that the World Bank is best understood and analyzed as a powerful (rather than neutral or subordinate) policy advisor to states in contemporary processes of national policy reforms. The World Bank (and the IMF together with other international financial institutions) are uniquely positioned vis-à-vis states in that they loan money conditionally and can mandate structural adjustment and other changes in return for loans. Borrower countries are often required to enact policy change to access loans and technical assistance and IFIs have historically promoted particular types of, largely neoliberal, policies. As such, it is important to understand the World Bank's changing approach to health given its important position as policy advisor, and given its central role in framing, labelling, and proposing solutions for national and international problems, including global health challenges (see Harman 2010 for a detailed analysis of the World Bank's approach to HIV/AIDS). The World Bank, via its technical advice, in addition to the loan money it provides, becomes especially important in this process as ideas such as the ones it proposes reduce uncertainty in times of crisis (Blyth 2002; Béland and Cox 2010).

The World Bank was founded along with the International Monetary Fund (IMF) at the Bretton Woods, New Hampshire conference of the 44 nations in 1944. While the goal of the IMF was to promote international economic stability by helping countries manage their exchange rates, the mission of the World Bank (then the International Bank for Reconstruction and Development) was to promote economic development among poor countries and help the economies shattered by WWII rebuild (Babb 2009). By custom, the World Bank is headed by a US citizen whereas the IMF is headed by a European. The Executive Directors, representing the World Bank's member countries, constitute the Board of Directors, and usually meet twice a week to supervise borrowing and financing decisions as well as complete other administrative tasks (Driscoll 1995).

The World Bank currently comprises two major organizations: the International Bank for Reconstruction and Development (IBRD, originally the sole component of the World Bank) and the International Development Association (IDA), founded in 1960. The World Bank Group, which consists of the IBRD, IDA and several other organizations, has approximately 10,000 employees (about four times as many as the IMF) and maintains about 120 offices globally (Bank 2017c), though a large majority of its staff work at its Washington, DC headquarters (Driscoll 1995). The poorer the country, the more favorable its borrowing conditions (Bank 2017a). While only low and middle-income countries can borrow from the World Bank, all member nations, both wealthy and poor, have the right to financial assistance from the IMF (Driscoll 1995). IBRD loans carry an interest rate slightly above the market rate at which the Bank itself borrows and must generally be repaid within 12–15 years, whereas IDA loans are interest free and have a maturity of 35 or 40 years. While the World Bank is considered the IDA and IBRD, the International Finance Corporation (IFC) is a member of the World Bank Group. It is the largest development institution that focuses exclusively on the private sector in developing countries. It was established in 1956 and is owned by 184 member countries (IFC 2017). It operates as an autonomous financial entity, making independent investment decisions from the World Bank (that is, it is part of the World Bank group, but the IDA and IBRD comprise the World Bank). It lends to the private sector but also advises governments on building infrastructure and promoting private sector development.[1]

In making loans to developing countries, the World Bank does not compete with other sources of finance. It assists only those projects for which the required capital is not available from other sources on reasonable terms (Driscoll 1995). In its early years, the United States controlled 37.2% of the World Bank votes, which gave it control over changes to the Bank's articles of agreement, though decisions to modify individual loans require an 80% majority vote (Babb 2009). The World Bank and IMF have been criticized for acting as a vehicle for U.S. interests, and more generally for promoting developed country interests in its governance and decision-making structures, as voting shares are based on contributions (Clegg 2013). As such, the World Bank is subject to competing pressures: powerful governments, such as that of the U.S. and other industrialized countries, influence its work, the professional economists working within the bank, and the borrower governments to whom it lends, vis-à-vis whom the Bank's "influence is in part persuasive and in part coercive" (Woods 2006).

The Washington Consensus: Word and Deed

The term "Washington Consensus" was coined in 1989 to describe the typical reform package promoted by IFIs and the U.S. for developing countries in the 1980s and 1990s. These packages recommended trade and financial liberalization, privatization of state enterprises, and legal protection for property rights. According to Williamson (2002), the economist who coined the term, the Washington Consensus advocated "pro-poor and pro-growth" public expenditure, such as spending on basic health, education, and infrastructure rather than defense or administration. Naim (2000) has argued that there was never a consensus, with economists disagreeing not only about the content, but also about the pace and sequence of reforms. He concludes that "Washington Confusion" might be a better descriptor for the so-called consensus.

What is clear is that if there was a consensus, the reality was seemingly at odds with stated recommendations, at least as regards social expenditure. Weaver (2008) dubs this a "hypocrisy trap" the World Bank is caught in, where it rarely complies with its own stated policies. As

Williamson (2000) states: "the least progress had been made in implementing the second policy, redirecting public expenditure policies" and Kanbur (1999) is more direct, "the Washington Consensus became what it did, not what it said." However, the original Washington Consensus indicates that at least some economists were aware that spending on health and education were important as they might help reduce poverty and spur economic growth, presumably due to the increased productivity of a healthy, educated workforce and its attractiveness to foreign investors.

Neoliberalism has been critiqued for many reasons, but particularly for its single-minded focus on efficiency, often at the expense of equity. In the economic literature, equity and efficiency are largely seen as competing goals. Although equity is typically defined as distributional fairness rather than equality, it is often associated with a reduction in inequality. In mainstream economics, promoting equity in the form of equality is generally seen as harming overall economic production. As one popular economics textbook notes:

> Efficiency means that society is getting the maximum benefits from its scarce resources. Equality means that those benefits are distributed uniformly among society's members...When government policies are designed, these two goals often conflict...In other words, when the government tries to cut the economic pie into more equal slices, the pie gets smaller (Mankiw 2014).

Therefore, these two goals are seen as being at odds. It is then not surprising that IFIs would focus on efficiency rather than equity in the quest for economic growth and financial and fiscal stability.

IFIs emphasize efficiency, economic growth, and stability in their projects, programs, and structural adjustment loans. Generally, efficiency refers to the same or better outcome per given amount of resources invested. As it relates to health, efficiency is a reduction or maintenance of public spending and other resources devoted to health in return for similar levels of outcomes, whether in terms of services rendered or outcomes in morbidity and mortality. Along with the focus on economic growth in the 1980s—the Washington Consensus, the World Bank began to reconsider its approach to poverty in the 1990s—the so-called post-Washington Consensus. In the 1980s, the prevailing belief was that economic growth would reduce poverty as the benefits of growth trickled down to the population. However, by the early 1990s, the World Bank came to realize that economic growth might actually exacerbate inequality and poverty, at least in the short-term.

A Paradigm Shift? Human Rights, Poverty Reduction, and a Possible Post-Washington Consensus

The term "post-Washington Consensus" emerged in the late 1990s and suggested the importance of considering the role of governance institutions in any reform effort (Burki and Perry 1998; Clift 2003; Öniş and Şenses 2005; Stiglitz 1998, 2003; Radin 2008). The post-Washington Consensus emerged in response to "the growing role of parliaments, the courts, and NGOs [non-government organizations] in resisting the reform initiatives" (Naim 2000) and demand for reform with a human face (Ilon 1996). For health, the post-Washington Consensus framework may represent a paradigm shift, a return to the previous emphasis on health first introduced at Alma Ata. In 1978 the United Nations Development Program (UNDP) and WHO sponsored an International Conference on Primary Health Care which led to a document by a regional arm of the WHO, the Pan-American Health Organization (PAHO), to declare the intention of providing health care for all by the year 2000 in the Report of the International Conference on Primary Health Care, Alma-Ata 1978. The post-Washington consensus may, contrary to the Washington Consensus, focus on investment in health and education (human capital) as an end unto itself rather than only a means to economic growth.[2]

Counter intuitively in the context of broad development policy (because of its emphasis on markets) the Washington Consensus helped establish the primacy of the state due to its failures. Whereas previously the emphasis was on external factors influencing countries' level of development—the externally determined price of a main primary good export, foreign aid, etc.—the Washington Consensus established that national policymakers, by implementing "good" domestic policies, could make a difference for the health of the economy (Naim 2000). Some argue, however, that talks of moving beyond the Washington Consensus are overstated, because government intervention is still discouraged except in the case of "market imperfections" since the state remains suspect: driven by rent-seeking agents and prone to corruption (Bonal 2002; Fine 2002).

The World Bank's 1980 "Health Sector Policy Paper" first formally committed the World Bank to direct lending in the health sector, coinciding with the beginning of debt crises in many developing countries and leading to largely infrastructural projects, such as building hospitals. Since then, the World Bank's approach to health has evolved. In 1993, in its World Development Report "Investing in Health" the World Bank began to emphasize investment in human capital (Jamison et al. 1993). However, the ultimate goal remained economic growth, where greater human capital makes for a better labor force, which in turn attracts investment and stimulates economic growth.

Complementing this attention to poverty reduction is the commitment of the World Bank and other international organizations to the Millennium Development Goals (MDGs). The MDGs are eight international development goals that were established following the United Nations Millennium Summit in 2000, with targets set for 2015 (Di Leva 2004). In terms of health, the MDGs included combating HIV/AIDS and malaria, improving maternal health, and child mortality. The World Bank has been promoting the MDGs in its projects and policies, and since 2015 has focused on Sustainable Development Goals (SDGs) which also have health components. In addition, in 2004 the World Bank and the IMF started producing the annual Global Monitoring Report, "which focuses on how the world is doing in implementing the policies and actions for achieving the MDGs and related development outcomes" (Bank 2017b). The MDGs and SDGs represent a renewed focus on health and in particular, maternal and infant health. Together with other changes, detailed in the follow chapters, this is suggestive of a movement towards considering health promotion in its own right and tied to poverty reduction, rather than only as a tool for investment in human capital and in the service of economic growth. However, some argue that this is simply a repackaged neoliberalism, which interfaces with the state and society by offering "a less offensive way to address the question of poverty while at the same time perpetuating a relationship in which the poor are the objects of intervention" (Larner and Walters 2004).

The World Bank and Health

The World Bank has been dubbed one of two "global ministries of health" along with the World Health Organization (WHO) (Deacon 2007). Understanding national health policies then requires increased attention to global social governance and the role of international actors, such as the World Bank, in these processes (Kaasch and Martens 2015). While the WHO, its regional offices (for example, PAHO) and its role in health sector reform have attracted a large amount of scholarly interest (Chorev 2013; Meier and Ayala 2014; Hanrieder 2014), the World Bank's role in health has been surprisingly, comparatively understudied. Given its powerful status as an authority on global health and historically the largest external funder of health in developing countries (Ruger 2005) it is important to consider how the World Bank may influence countries' health sector reforms, both via loans and financial resources, often with strings attached, as well as via normative stances on health problems and solutions.

The World Bank's work in health has been criticized for focusing on human capital at the expense of health as a human right. For example, the World Bank's 1993 World Development Report states, "(s)uccess in reducing poverty requires two equally important strategies: promoting the use of the most important asset of the poor—their labor—and increasing their human capital through access to basic health care, education, and nutrition" (Jamison et al. 1993). The criticisms of this approach are compounded by the World Bank's problematic (non) treatment of identities (including gender, race, disability, etc.) which are so intertwined with health and require considerable attention in designing inclusive health policies and programs. Despite repeated assertions both in the popular media and in scholarly research that World Bank involvement via loans, especially structural adjustment loans (SALs), have had detrimental effects on welfare states and social policy more generally there has been little empirical study of the mechanisms, channels, and effects of World Bank and other IFI involvement in health policy (Hunter and Brown 2000; Navarro 2007; Huber and Solt 2004; Birn and Dmitrienko 2005; Willis and Khan 2009).

Health sector reform is a unique policymaking domain. It may be different than other policy areas for three reasons: the prevalence of ideas of rights to health access, the importance of health for identity, and the important role of technology and expertise in health care (Béland 2010; Carpenter 2012). In particular, the organization of health care is uniquely reliant on "the co-organization of expertise and state power" (Carpenter 2012). Existing research indicates that health spending patterns do not neatly map onto existing typologies of welfare states nor do their determinants necessarily mirror those of general social spending (Noy 2011;

Huber et al. 2008; Huber and Stephens 2012; Bambra 2007). Indeed, the development of national health systems is sometimes incongruous with that of other sectors of social provision and protections within the same countries, in both established welfare states and developing countries.

I define health sector reform as changes in health expenditure, policies, and programs. Health sector reform includes the creation of new institutions and programs (for example, a new public insurance system), the reform of existing policies (for example, expansion of benefits under public insurance), and changes in national health expenditures (for example, an increase in overall or public spending on health). Contained within the broader concept of health sector reform are changes in government health policy that have a major impact on health care delivery within a nation. I conceptualize government health policy broadly to include government expenditures on health and government-initiated rules, programs, regulations, and legislation that affect the organization of the health care sector.

Health sector reform is an inherently political process. Treating health sector reform as a process influenced by domestic actors such as governments, medical professionals, civil society groups, political parties, and global and regional actors such as the World Bank, helps clarify how countries negotiate these pressures and how they translate into policy reform. Health sector reform includes, therefore, not only changes in health policies, such as new health programs and institutions and agencies (which may provide, finance, or regulate health services), but also changes in health expenditures and the divide between private and public health expenditure and provision of health services.

Tools of Influence: Loans, Conditionality, and Structural Adjustment

How can we account for the World Bank's ability to influence national policy? IFIs can use their loans as clout to influence national policy in the face of countries' precarious economic positions, particularly during times of economic crisis, recession, and hyperinflation. One of the most criticized ways in which the World Bank attempts to influence social policy is by granting loans to governments conditional on their agreement to implement mandated reforms (Babb 2005; Kapur et al. 1997). These are often structural adjustment projects, which are closely coupled with neoliberal reforms (Harrison 2010; Wood 2012). The debt crisis at the end of the 1970s and beyond meant governments in developing countries were in especially vulnerable positions in the following decades. Many agreed to implement IFI reforms as these became a precondition to receiving bailout funds. Privatization was a particularly salient condition, as it generated revenues and satisfied multilateral lenders (Babb 2005).

Theoretically, scholars have argued that powerful international financial institutions work conditions into their loans, which are desperately sought by countries in economic crisis. It is these loans and their accompanying conditions that allow IFIs to dictate reductions in social spending as well as restructuring of social sectors. However, the stringency of these conditions is debated, with some arguing that the World Bank is not particularly concerned with countries meeting these conditions (Weyland 2005; see also Pribble 2013 who finds symmetry in the World Banks relationship with policymakers in Chile and Uruguay), which are often purposefully vague. Others suggest that these conditions may be driven by local policymakers who want to codify their preferred policies (Dreher 2004; Vreeland 2003; Weyland 2005). However, it is also possible that though IFIs might not exert much direct influence it is enough that they change the internal balance of political power to indirectly influence policy outcomes (Henisz et al. 2005). In addition, the influence of IFIs can be ideational: taking the form of ideas and recommendations for best practices, rather than only material (money via loans). In particular, the diffusion of other countries' experience via consultants hired by the World Bank and technical assistance loans to research and formulate policy is one such a channel of ideational IFI influence (Jordana and Levi-Faur 2005; Hall 2007). As far as empirical evidence, few studies have examined what these conditions consist of and how they are negotiated.

World Bank loans and projects are not an event; they are a process, involving national actors, often from varying agencies and ministries and with different interests and priorities (Dreher 2004; Weyland 2005). In addition, while the World Bank is a highly centralized and bureaucratized institution, World Bank staff varies across countries and over time, which suggests that their approaches and policy prescriptions may also vary. Taken together, the evidence on the effects of IFI conditionality on social policy, and health policy more specifically, remains inconclusive.

Empirically, existing studies provide little direct evidence that borrowing from the IMF and World Bank results in lower public spending on health. However, their detrimental effect on other social indicators and programs such as education, poverty, and pensions, has been documented (Bonal 2002; Hunter and Brown 2000; Ilon 1996; Easterly 2000; Mesa-Lago and Müller 2002; Mesa-Lago 2006, 2008; Deacon 1997). In terms of outcomes, recent research focusing on Sub-Saharan Africa finds that countries borrowing from the World Bank experienced negative effects on infant child mortality, though this appears to be the result of structural adjustment rather than health investments which appear to have opposite effects (Shandra et al. 2004; Coburn et al. 2015). In Latin America, existing accounts have noted that there is increased privatization that works in the interest of foreign corporations and insurance agencies (Armada et al. 2001; Barrientos and Lloyd-Sherlock 2000; De Vos et al. 2006; Homedes and Ugalde 2005). When directly studied, the effects of neoliberal pressures on public health spending have been mixed. Hunter and Brown (2000) find no correlation between World Bank lending in a given country and the resources devoted to education and health. Noy (2011) and Huber and Stephens (2012) find that in Latin America IFI presence is not associated with significantly lower levels of public health spending as a percent of GDP.

Case-studies of neoliberal pressures on health sector reform in Latin America have focused on two cases where reform was arguably the most extreme in its neoliberal bent: Colombia and Chile. In the 1980s in Chile, under the rule of Pinochet, medical care delivery was opened to the private sector and decentralized to the municipal level, largely aggravating existing inequalities (Unger et al. 2008). In 1993, Colombia, another major site of health care reform influenced by neoliberal ideas, replaced the public sector with one in which private and public providers compete for clients, insurance premiums are paid by employers, and the government covers the poor (Mesa-Lago 2008; Stocker et al. 1999). The analysis of the involvement and effects of the World Bank on health sector reform in these two countries is informative, but may overstate the World Bank's ability to influence countries' health sectors and misrepresent its role across Latin America (Noy 2015). Altogether, while the World Bank's work across domains has been well documented, in particular its involvement in pension reforms (Ragin 1994; Mesa-Lago and Müller 2002; de Mesa and Mesa-Lago 2006; Brooks 2005; Béland and Waddan 2000; Orenstein 2008), its work in and effect on gender equality, among others (Griffin 2009; Bedford 2007, 2009; Ferguson and Harman 2015; Calkin 2015), it is an understudied actor in global health. In addition to examining the World Bank's role in health sector reform in Latin America, this book makes a unique contribution in that it focuses neither solely on the World Bank nor its work in a single country, rather, tracing its overall evolving approach to health (Chap. 2) and examining its regional effects on health expenditures (Chap. 3) and its involvement among others actors in national health sector reform, which as country case-studies (Chaps. 4, 5, and 6) demonstrate are not uniformly apparent across places and projects nor over time.

Ends and Means: Policy Paradigms, Goals, and Instruments in Health Sector Reform

Any analysis of health sector reform must consider not only the particular reforms, their timeline, and the policy instruments used, but the context against which they operate and the goals which they seek to fulfill. Efficiency and equity have already been described as important goals in health sector reform: the former a neoliberal imperative, the latter emphasized in the approach which frames health as a right. It is important to distinguish not only between goals and instruments used to achieve them but also how these are framed and discussed. While *programmatic* ideas are concrete, precise, and policy-specific solutions to policy problems, *paradigmatic* ideas define the assumptions about how the world works more generally, operating at the cognitive background (Campbell 1998). As such, paradigmatic ideas are largely apparent at the discursive level, whereas paradigmatic ideas are policy tools and instruments. This distinction echoes Hall's (1993) discussion of first, second, and third order levels of policy change. First order change involves changes in the setting (or levels) of the instruments, second order change involves a change in the techniques or policy instruments used to attain the goals, and third order policy change involves changes in the overarching goals that guide policy in a particular field, akin to paradigmatic ideas.

Some policies and instruments may be more commensurate with particular goals: for example, a focus on targeting and means-testing of services in health is typically seen as enhancing efficiency, while movements toward universal access are seen as working in the interest of equity. Examining paradigmatic goals and instruments allows an investigation not just of the policy instruments utilized in health sector reform but also which goals these reforms aim to address. Systematically examining goals and instruments also allows for greater comparability across country cases, and allows me to distinguish between ends and means, where neoliberalism—an emphasis on the market and market mechanisms, individual responsibility, decreased state provision and involvement in health—on the part of both national governments and the World Bank can manifest in either goals, instruments, or both.

Paradigmatic Goals: Equity and Efficiency

A shift from a Washington Consensus to a possible Post-Washington Consensus or a more human-rights based approach suggests a fundamental alteration of the World Bank's approach to health. In contrast to neoliberalism which emphasizes efficiency as the ultimate goal, a human-rights discourse on health emphasizes equity. However, attention to the paradigmatic goals of equity and efficiency are often matters of emphasis rather than exclusion. Even governments pursuing neoliberal policies may pursue equity inasmuch as inequitable health outcomes might reduce the overall productivity of the labor force. Similarly, those discussing health as a human right may reference the importance of efficiency in ensuring public resources reach the largest number of people. Policy instruments, on the other hand, are referenced not only in discourse, justification, and intentions for reform (the case for paradigmatic goals), but are implemented (in policies, programs, new and changing roles of existing agencies, new agencies, etc.).

Policy Instruments in Health Sector Reform

Scholarship on neoliberalism and social policy suggests that IFIs have promoted particular policy instruments in the pursuit of efficiency, economic growth, and stability: *first,* decentralization and deconcentration, both geographically and institutionally. *Second,* separation of functions between government agencies in the quest for efficiency and transparency, to reduce corruption and other misuse of funds. *Third,* the use of a variety of tools to ensure that good performance is encouraged and rewarded, such as performance-based management and results-based financing. *Fourth,* attempts to reduce the size and reach of the public sector, in particular privatization, private sector involvement, and sub-contracting to the private sector. The *fifth* instrument is a focus on primary health care. *Sixth,* and finally, targeting in health policy. Each of these policy instruments was featured to varying degrees in health sector reform across the three countries and were discussed in World Bank projects, government and other national documents, and interviews with policymakers.

Decentralization and Deconcentration
Deconcentration typically refers to administrative deconcentration, or the delegation of administrative duties to lower levels within the government bureaucracy. Decentralization, on the other hand, most often refers to the transfer of decision-making ability (and responsibility) to sub-national (state, municipal) government units. However, while decentralization typically implies geographic delegation as compared with references to deconcentration, these terms are also often used interchangeably.

Decentralization and Deconcentration are argued by their proponents to enhance both efficiency and equity. When administration is decentralized it is more responsive to local needs and issues and is therefore more equitable. Decentralized management is also more efficient because it is tailored to local needs and eliminates an oversized centralized bureaucracy (Bossert 1998). Its critics, on the other hand, argue that it promotes inequality if the decentralized units are unequal at the beginning of the process, and serves to reduce central government accountability to both local governments and citizens alike (Mills 1994).

Separation of Functions
The idea of separating functions refers to the separation of the provision, purchasing, and financing of health care, whether these are relegated to the private or public sector, in the quest for efficiency. It is most closely associated with increased rationalization (and bureaucratization) of health care. Separating these functions, proponents argue, may also reduce corruption and allows market mechanisms to better dictate costs, prices, and expenditures. While it is discussed in the context of enhancing efficiency, its critics have argued that it is inefficient in that it often serves to increase administrative staff costs and bloat, in effect

negating its intended effect of streamlining the health system (Hammer and Berman 1995; Polidano and Hulme 1999).

Performance-Based Financing
Performance-based measures, particularly management contracts, are also discussed as a tool to increase efficiency, and indirectly, equity. In this conception, efficiency is enhanced by sub-contracting services to newly autonomous and self-managing hospitals and clinics, for example. Funding is allocated (via reimbursements) based on outcomes and performance, measured by a variety of health indicators (Aucoin 2002). Such contracts can also be applied to individual providers (e.g. doctors and nurses) rather than clinics or hospitals. The introduction of these kinds of contracts is consistent with the central tenets of neoliberalism, and while it does not directly introduce competition, it is more market based than simply funding centers without attention to specific outcomes (rather than holistic care). Additionally, in theory (though not always in practice), performance-based management and budgeting allows the government to ensure that citizens are getting the best possible services and remove "bad" providers, in this way enhancing equity by promoting equality in terms of quality of service across providers (Meessen et al. 2011; Polidano and Hulme 1999).

Privatization and Private Sector Involvement
Privatization is one of the most heavily criticized and controversial neoliberal policy prescriptions. However, much like other instruments of neoliberalism, it is more prevalent in discussions of issues of economic policy and state-owned enterprises than social policy, but it is increasingly favored in this domain as well. In health policy, privatization often proceeds hand in hand with reductions in public provision of health services, a downsizing of health facilities, or sub-contracting some services (direct provision or laboratory services) to private companies.

Privatization has been viewed as a tool for enhancing efficiency (the market knows best), cutting back on unnecessarily complex government bureaucracy, and providing better quality services in the face of declining public infrastructure and public deficits (Mehrotra and Delamonica 2005). Criticisms of privatization hinge on two main issues: *first*, by virtue of its typically being a profit driven enterprise, it does not have patients' best interests at heart and therefore, publicly run facilities and publicly provided services are preferable; *second*, and related, privatization often creates a tiered system where those with ability to pay, receive top of the line services in purely private, costly advanced facilities while the poor are relegated to a now even more underfunded public sector.

Primary Health Care Approach

An emphasis on primary health care has, like most policy instruments, been argued to enhance equity or efficiency by different people. Originally it was associated with universalism, increased access, and equity, and closely identified with the World Health Organization (WHO) agenda and the Alma Ata conference of 1978 (De Vos and Van der Stuyft 2015). Indeed, David Tejada de Rivero (interviewed for this book) served as the Deputy Director-General of the World Health Organization between 1974 and 1985 during the time of this conference and was subsequently Health Minister of Peru. This policy instrument became a regional priority in Latin America. Primary health care was advanced largely by the WHO and PAHO, in the early 1970s and received renewed interest from IFIs and national governments alike in the 1990s and beyond (Gwatkin et al. 2004; Starfield et al. 2005).

Since then primary health care has also been described as enhancing efficiency (Cueto 2004). In this line of reasoning providing primary care reduces the use of more complex facilities (namely hospitals) and prevents the escalation of health issues that are instead treated at the source. If coupled with preventative care, rather than only curative care, it is further seen as not only improving people's health but also preventing them from needing costly treatments in the future.

Targeting

Targeting involves the focusing of resources and service provision on a particular segment of the population. Targeting in social provision has been advanced as a tool for doing more with less, and channeling resources to the "deserving poor," ensuring that those that really need help are receiving it.

Beneficiaries may be defined by a status characteristic (e.g. mothers and children or those below a certain income), a location (e.g. a particular province or town), or a particular illnesss and health intervention (e.g. HIV/AIDS or tuberculosis). Targeting has become an increasingly popular policy instrument given austerity, a tool by which the state can correct market inefficiencies in the provision of social services (Mkandawire 2005).

Targeting has also been cited as a way to achieve equity by raising the standard of living of the poor and otherwise neglected groups (e.g. on the basis of geographical location, gender, or ethnicity). In this latter formulation, it is a way of ensuring that health services reach populations or areas that the market cannot, or will not, because of lack of accessibility, inability to pay, or other reasons. It therefore falls to the state to provide for these segments of the population via targeting and its associated tools such as means-testing and user fees. Importantly, targeting is the policy instrument, where means-testing, and sometimes user fees, are ways to ensure enforcement. Targeting has consistently been identified as one of the central tenants of neoliberal influence as applied to social service provision—standing in opposition to universalist policies—and as a tool especially advanced by the World Bank since the 1980s (Mkandawire 2005; Silva et al. 2011). Existing studies are largely critical of targeting, finding that it is often ineffective and subject to corruption and capture (Mkandawire 2005; Coady et al. 2004).

While all of these policy instruments were present across all three countries, they have been pursued, implemented, framed, and discussed in different ways and to differing extents in Argentina, Costa Rica, and Peru. Targeting, decentralization, separation of functions, performance-based management, and privatization as policy instruments are seemingly most closely aligned with efficiency; the latter three can be thought of as market-based mechanisms while targeting stands in contrast to universalism. A primary health approach is most closely aligned with equity and poverty-amelioration. However, as detailed above, each can be and has been discussed or implemented in the context of pursuit of equity, efficiency, or both. In my case-study analyses presented in Chaps. 4, 5, and 6, I pay particular attention to the ways in which these instruments are framed and discussed by the World Bank and national governments and their implementation. In this way, I am able to examine the timing of these reforms, analyzing how closely each of these instruments is aligned with the paradigmatic goals of equity and efficiency, and examining how they are promoted and implemented differently in health policies, projects, and programs by national governments and the World Bank.

HEALTH, DEVELOPMENT, AND THE STATE IN LATIN AMERICA

Although this book foregrounds the effect of the World Bank on health sector reform, the Bank exerts only one of a myriad of pressures on health sector reform in Latin American countries. Latin American countries, broadly, found themselves at a particular historical moment in the late 1980s and through the 1990s and early 2000s. Many of them were mired in and emerging from "the lost decade" of the 1980s, characterized by deep economic recession and crisis. A growing middle class (resulting from higher rates of education and urbanization), a loss of legitimacy of authoritarian regimes following economic failure, and an increasingly active civil society all contributed to democratic transitions. Latin American countries were, then, increasingly democratically governed, achieving financial stability, and recouping economic growth and development in the 1990s and early 2000s. Part of the challenge of these new democratic regimes was state-building and strengthening institutions, in particular welfare and social programs, which had often been neglected in the 1970s and 1980s.

Regional Context

The intensification of globalization, on the other hand, may exert opposite pressures. While democratization and emergence from the severe financial crises of the 1980s would induce a renewed commitment to social spending and social policy in Latin America, globalization might challenge this trend. A "race to the bottom" between developing countries' governments created by competition for global capital would lead to less social provision as countries cut taxes and reduce environmental and labor standards to attract foreign investors. In addition, powerful IFIs and other international organizations were espousing free markets as embodied in the neoliberal ideology of the Washington Consensus, leading to meager social programs. More recently, there is the suggestion that a human rights paradigm has replaced the neoliberal one in the influence of IFIs on health, suggesting reinvigorated welfare state development in Latin America and other developing regions.

An examination of health sector reform in Latin America requires an understanding of not only the regional but also the historical context. Most Latin American countries were colonized by the Spanish, which resulted in a particular set of institutional arrangements, distinct from those of other colonial powers (Lange et al. 2006). Spanish colonialism, because of its mercantilist nature from the eighteenth century onwards, focused on resource extraction. Institutions were established to oversee this economic transfer rather than promoting any local development (Lange et al. 2006). This reaffirms a regional focus, though the effects are not necessarily uniform across Latin America in that more extensive Spanish mercantilist colonialism is associated with subsequent higher inequality, and more predatory states (Lange et al. 2006). Of the three case-studies examined in this dissertation, Peru experienced the highest level of colonialism, and served as one of the two first and most important viceroyalties (the other in Mexico), whereas Argentina and Costa Rica experienced lower levels of colonialism (Lange et al. 2006; Mahoney 2003). Levels of colonialism are negatively correlated with subsequent levels of social development and with weaker state institutions. As I discuss below this is manifest in state capacity and autonomy in the health sector in the Peruvian state: where a generally weak state is also weak in its autonomy and capacity in health.

A regional focus on the effects of the World Bank remains valuable in the face of globalization because while IFIs are global in their reach, they have regional offices and regional goals. In addition, regional similarities in culture and history, broadly writ, allow an examination of IFI effects on national policies while holding comparatively constant these regional factors. While regions are not internally homogenous, strong regional economic, political, and other ties often result in more similar responses to globalization by countries within a single region than across regions (Hay 2000). That is, in order to conduct cross-regional analyses it is valuable to first understand regional trends and cross-national, intra-regional variation. This is supported by existing studies of public policy in Latin America that have focused on the importance of regional diffusion dynamics (Weyland 2005, 2006; Brooks 2005; Henisz et al. 2005).

The neoliberal focus on open markets and deregulation on the part of the state have often led to the assumption that general social spending and government-sponsored social safety nets will suffer (Glatzer and Rueschemeyer 2004; Simmons et al. 2006). In the health sector, scholars have found that globalization and neoliberalism have resulted in an increased role of for-profit private (often transnational) corporations and insurance companies (Waitzkin 2011; Lloyd-Sherlock 2005) but have provided little information on the effects of health spending and policies. Research on public spending in Latin America highlights the importance of political factors such as legacies of democracy and left party involvement (Avelino et al. 2005; Brown and Hunter 2004; Noy 2011; Huber and Stephens 2001, 2012). Other studies, namely case-studies, have largely highlighted global pressures by international organizations and the neoliberal model in Latin America (de Mesa and Mesa-Lago 2006; Mesa-Lago 2002, 2006; Mesa-Lago and Müller 2002; Silva et al. 2011). On the other hand, much of the theoretical literature based on the OECD context points to the importance of demographic, globalization, and domestic economic pressures for social spending and welfare states (Esping-Andersen 1999; Glatzer and Rueschemeyer 2004).

In all, these pressures combined to create a particular trajectory of welfare state development and domain-specific reforms in health in Latin America. This particular historical opening for the development of welfare states, increased regionalization, within-region diffusion, and IFI pressures have created a distinctive environment to examine variation in health sector reform. These circumstances allow me to examine the ways and extent to which national context and historical institutional legacies shape how these seemingly homogenous and homogenizing pressures have been borne out in the field of health care. Altogether, democratization and increased accountability to citizens, coupled with pressures from human rights discourse (including in health care) and increased demands for social services, create an unprecedented push towards welfare state development. Concurrently, Latin America and the Caribbean's increased integration into the global economy, patchy democratic history, high levels of economic growth and inequality, and the heavy presence of IFIs have often been cited as challenging the move towards more inclusive social protection.

Latin American Health Systems in Historical Perspective

In Latin America until the 1950s, most countries' health care systems were quite similar: public health insurance plans were available to employees in the formal labor market (financed via employer, employee, and sometimes government contributions), the poor had access to public services, and the wealthy had access to private services. While the levels of coverage varied depending on how much of the labor force worked in the formal market, the structure was similar. Charity organizations, largely religious, provided supplementary care. The legacy, therefore, was one of segmented and fragmented systems. Latin America also provides a particularly interesting context to examine neoliberalism and health because of its storied history in social medicine. Social medicine refers to an approach that emphasizes the social, environmental, economic, and political causes of illness, that is, its social rather than biological correlates (Waitzkin et al. 2001a). As such, it is a decidedly institutional and holistic, rather than solely medical, approach to health care. In the 1930s social medicine experienced its "golden age," under the influence of Allende in Chile, followed by the Cuban revolution in the 1960s (Waitzkin et al. 2001b). However, progress varied widely across countries in social medicine, partly owing to political instability in many Latin American countries in subsequent decades.

There have been a wide variety of trajectories since the 1950s in terms of health sector reform. As mentioned, in Chile in the 1980s under the rule of Pinochet medical care delivery was opened to the private sector and decentralized to the municipal level, largely aggravating existing inequalities (Unger et al. 2008). In 1993, Colombia, another major site of health care reform influenced by neoliberal ideas, replaced the public sector system with one in which private and public providers competed for clients, insurance premiums were paid by employers, and the government covered the poor (De Vos et al. 2006). The Costa Rican model, on the other hand, is distinct from all other Latin American countries. Costa Rica integrated its social security program with the Ministry of Health in 1993, resulting in a single-payer model managed by the social security program and financed by employers, employees, and the government (with subsidies by the government for the poor) (Clark 2004).

State Capacity and Autonomy in Health

Policies and state structures, interests, and decisions about health sector reform are the results of both the structure of the state and previous policies and existing institutions. Institutions are broadly defined as rule-like sets of regularized practices, which structure political and economic action and outcomes (cf. Hall and Taylor 1996; Thelen 1999). Historical institutionalist theory is sensitive to policy legacies, recognizing that early policy decisions constrain later policy options (Pierson 1993, 1994, 2000, 2004; Hall 1993; Skocpol and Amenta 1986; Skocpol 1992, 1995; Béland 2005). In particular, institutional analysis explains non-linear relationships and variations across (national) contexts, where "policy inputs and policy outputs may be linked together in different ways in different political systems" (Immergut 1992b). These state-centered and institutional approaches helped motivate the selection of Argentina, Peru, and Costa Rica for my case-study analyses of health sector reform, based on their differing levels of state capacity and autonomy in health.

I extend the classic concepts of state capacity and autonomy to develop ideas of states' capacity and autonomy in health. *State autonomy* is broadly conceived as "the ability [of the state] to formulate collective goals" (Evans 1995) and sometimes described as state cohesion and the extent that the state is characterized by Weberian bureaucratic structure, namely meritocracy (Evans and Rauch 1999; Evans et al. 1985; Skocpol 1988). Autonomy has been used primarily in analyses of state-industry relations (Evans 1995; Beeson 2001; Wade 1990), but I utilize it to explain different trajectories of health sector reform. I refine general understandings of state autonomy, applying this concept to health to refer to whether the state has a clear agenda for the health sector.

State capacity, on the other hand, is the ability of the state to implement its intended policies (and govern its population), which may be blocked because of opposition by other actors, lack of resources, institutional weakness, or a myriad of other reasons (Mann 1984). Existing research has focused on state embeddedness, rather than capacity, likely owing to the fact that many of the studies that use these concepts are focused on the relationship between the state and industry (Evans 1995; Wade 1990). However, when examining social service reform, the state's ability to implement policies becomes centrally important—this is what I call state capacity in health.

While they are distinct analytic concepts, capacity is often related to embeddedness, which is in turn related to autonomy. States that do not have strong bureaucracies will find it difficult to implement policies and set up or utilize existing infrastructures (Geddes 1994). Also, associations with other institutions in society—civil society, or in the case of health, the national medical association for example—are certainly related to the success of reforms. However, these are two distinct axes: states may have coherent plans but be unable to carry them out.

The state as a site for policy reform has received increased attention in recent decades. The historical institutionalist literature, with its emphasis on path-dependence and the importance of past events and structure for current processes and outcomes has been criticized for seeming actor-free. This culminated, within sociology, by a call in the mid-1980s to "bring the state back in" (Evans et al. 1985). State-centered theorists have in part addressed this gap by examining how the state, and how different actors within the state, follow and deviate from expected paths given existing structures. These considerations include both elements constraining and enabling state policy choices such as globalization, public opinion, and social movements but also the relationships between different elements of the state: different ministries, branches, agencies, and political administrations. Health sector reform is a particularly compelling area in which to examine how policy change occurs because of the diversity of alternatives and variation in institutional arrangements across countries.

The developmental state is a theoretical approach situated in the multi-disciplinary literature on development. The approach identifies the importance of a well-functioning, highly involved state in propelling countries' pursuit of economic and social development. In the 1970s and 1980s, there was much discussion of the malignant effect of government intervention (Evans and Rauch 1999). The IMF and the World Bank witness to the predatory states of the 1970s and 1980s, advocated free markets and structural adjustment programs in part as a response to these state failures (Portes and Landolt 2000). The performance of the Asian Tigers, and to a lesser extent Chile, served as an inspiration to many developing countries, promoted by IFIs as exemplars of the benefits of liberalization and deregulation. The welfare state literature reminds us that this support for market capitalism was revolutionary because the state they discussed was one upholding absolutist privilege, mercantilist protectionism, and corruption. During this time, in the developing world, the market was seen as an equalizer in response to a usurious and plundering state (Esping-Andersen 2013).

The attribution of the success of the Asian Tigers to market liberalism has been challenged by critics who argue that the economic success of these states owed to particular regional, cultural, social, political, and other unique characteristics, rather than liberalizing economic policy (Meseguer 2005). Most importantly, this research highlights the centrality of a strong government to these countries' economic success. In fact, since much of the literature on policy change from a global perspective has noted the intense increase in state (and other forms of) regulation in the 1990s (for discussions of the regulatory state in Latin America specifically see Levi-Faur and Jordana 2006; Jordana and Levi-Faur 2005). Previous research has found that IFIs' interactions with national institutions and governments pattern policy outcomes in the case of pensions, for example (Deacon 1997). This has reinvigorated the study of the role of the state in development and social provision and debates about the causes and consequences of developmental states. State-centric theories in the welfare state literature too emphasize the importance of state capacity, state structure, and policy legacies as well as the initiatives of state bureaucrats within the state (Amenta 2005; Immergut 1992a; Skocpol 1988; Orloff and Skocpol 1984).

Recent research on state autonomy and capacity has pushed scholars to disassemble states by domains. For example, scholars have identified "pockets of effectiveness" (Roll 2014) within otherwise ineffective and weak states while others have argued that we cannot think about state autonomy and capacity unitarily, rather arguing that these may vary across regions within countries, that is, spatially (Soifer 2012; Sánchez-Talanquer 2017). Together, this scholarship suggests that while the concepts of state capacity and autonomy are useful in thinking about states' abilities to formulate and implement policies, they need to be further refined. Importantly, the concepts of state autonomy and capacity have been utilized to understand national development, and have focused on internal, that is domestic, national outcomes. In this book, I argue that these concepts are also important for our understanding of states' relationships with external agents, such as the World Bank.

Many developing countries find themselves in a precarious situation: social provision was neglected by previous predatory state regimes, but new internal demands for the expansion of social services are constrained by neoliberalism and competition in global markets. A renewed attention to the role of the state in development has also been accompanied by a call to move beyond the dichotomy of strong and weak states to unpack the particular attributes of the state that are conducive to development, following the recognition that strong states can be predatory (Evans 1997; Jayasuriya 2005; Scott 1998; Weiss 1999). Most notably, Evans (1995) developed the concept of "embedded autonomy" arguing that states that are more autonomous (characterized by a strong and cohesive bureaucracy) and more embedded (characterized by positive state-society partnerships) are best able to positively foster economic growth. However, most of these studies on developing countries were concerned with the state's role in industry, with less attention to sectors more closely related to human development, namely health and education (Evans 1995; Geddes 1994; Doner 1992; Wade 1990).

In order to understand the ways in which the World Bank influences health sector reform across countries, I argue that we should consider states' autonomy and capacity in health. Broadly, if states have high autonomy in health it may limit the ways in which the World Bank can influence their agendas and otherwise affect change. Similarly, if states have limited capacity in health they might be more amenable to World Bank and other IFI funding, and therein influence, at least in terms of strategies for the provision of health services. However, I find that having low autonomy and capacity may also limit the World Bank's influence in interesting and sometimes unexpected ways: in weak states, there is not a durable stable central apparatus for IFIs to co-opt.

Case Selection

This book begins with an examination of how the World Bank's approach to health has changed over time (Chap. 2). I then turn my attention to a regional analysis of the trends and correlates of health expenditures in Latin America and the Caribbean (Chap. 3). I then focus on three countries to examine the World Bank's work in health in Argentina, Peru, and Costa Rica and how these countries' state capacity and autonomy in health influence how they interacted with the World Bank and whether and how they were able and willing to contest, negotiate, and resist World Bank pressure (Chaps. 4, 5, and 6). Argentina, Peru, and Costa Rica have all have experienced World Bank involvement and have responded very differently to World Bank and IFI recommendations, making them a particularly interesting site to examine the dynamics of health sector reform. In all three countries, the World Bank is said to have pursued a similar neoliberal agenda: promoting privatization, targeting (and the associated means-testing), and decentralization of the health sector (Haggard and Kaufman 2008; Huber and Stephens 2002, 2012). Indeed, all Latin American and Caribbean countries (with the exception of Cuba) have been under direct pressure from the World Bank and other IFIs via loan agreements and structural adjustment programs to reform their health sector in the context of broader public sector reforms. I have chosen Argentina, Peru, and Costa Rica because they vary along two dimensions that I argue are important in shaping interaction with the World Bank and health policy reform: state capacity and autonomy in the health sector.[3]

Figure 1.1 demonstrates how states vary along two dimensions that are analytically meaningful in terms of policy reform: state autonomy and capacity. I categorize these countries along these dimensions in 1980 which is the starting point for my analysis, though such categorizations can be quite durable. Argentina is among the most developed Latin American countries, and one of the countries hardest hit by the 1980s recession. Its current health system has its roots in mutual aid societies (*Obras Sociales*) dating back to the 1900s (Rivas-Loria and Shelton 2004). In Argentina, privatization in the form of user fees predated international pressure: they were imposed by the Ministry of Health during the military dictatorship of 1976–1983 (Lloyd-Sherlock 2006; Lloyd-Sherlock 2005). In 1994, efforts by the government to introduce full competition into the social health insurance market by allowing workers to select a private insurer—following World Bank pressure—was blocked by labor unions (Rivas-Loria and Shelton 2004). Therefore the Argentinian state is characterized by relatively high autonomy: while the bureaucracy is relatively meritocratic with a comparatively cohesive state apparatus (though political instability has certainly disrupted state building, see Melo 2007; Levitsky and Murillo 2009) though there have been several failed concerted efforts to reform the health sector by the state. In terms of capacity, unions are strong, have their own infrastructure, and have prevented the government from implementing state-mandated reforms. That is, the state has low capacity in health.

Peru is an Andean country, characterized by three geographic regions with different populations and health needs, and an irregular political history including rapid transitions between autocratic and democratic governments. Turnover in the health ministry has been high and existing accounts of health sector reform in Peru highlight how neo-populist leaders (Alberto Fujimori and Alejandro Toledo) aggressively promoted increased coverage, while continuing to receive generous World Bank loans (Weyland 2005). However, the health ministry and social security system struggled to implement these reforms, as much of the labor market still informal and little systematic organization and infrastructure in place. Peru is, therefore, characterized by relatively low state autonomy, especially as it relates to the health system's bureaucracy within the state,

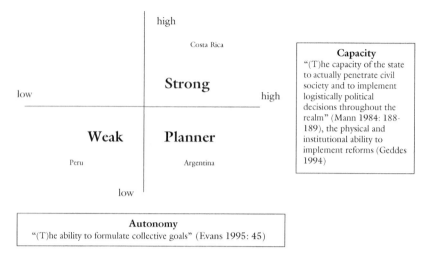

Fig. 1.1 Comparison of cases along the analytical dimensions of state capacity and autonomy in health

which is highly fragmented and segmented (Ewig 2006). In addition, Peru displays comparatively low capacity, with few resources devoted to the health sector, and infrastructure not extending across the country largely due to its geographical vastness and diversity. Therefore, Peru during this time period can be labeled a "weak state" in health—that is, the Peruvian government rarely had coherent and clear goals for the health sector, and the state has historically struggled to implement even the few reforms it has sought to carry out in an effective way.

Costa Rica has arguably the most advanced and established welfare state in Latin America (with the possible exception of Cuba). It is highly socialized and one of only a few countries in the world without a standing army, which frees up much of its budget for social spending. Following the economic crisis, the Costa Rican government, like many in the region, received international funding for health policy reform and was, therefore, among the first countries in the region to engage in health sector reform, largely implemented in the 1980s (Mesa-Lago 2008; Rivas-Loria and Shelton 2004; Unger et al. 2008). By the early 1990s, Costa Rica achieved near universal coverage managed by the social security program with the Ministry of Health maintaining an oversight role. The Costa Rican state is characterized by high autonomy—a meritocratic state bureaucracy that is well integrated, and the state historically had high infrastructural capacity to implement formulated policies—close engagement with civil society, industry, and extensive existing infrastructure (Clark 2004). This is the classic "strong state" in regards to the health sector: a state with clear goals and the ability to achieve them during this time period.

OUTLINE OF THE BOOK

The book proceeds in three parts: first, I focus on the World Bank's changing role in health, I then turn to examining regional trends and health expenditure analysis, finally turning my attention to the three country case-studies. In Chap. 2 I focus on the World Bank's approach to health. Given its heterogeneous involvement and work in health sector reform in Latin America, I use archival data from the World Bank and interviews with current and former World Bank health professionals to account for the World Bank's changing approach to health. I also discuss the shift from a public health approach involving investments in facilities such as hospitals in health lending and programming at the World Bank to a structural adjustment emphasis in the 1990s and an embrace of universalism more recently. I also trace the changing logic of neoliberalism, where neoliberal ends were replaced by a focus on neoliberal means to address equity and universalism.

In Chap. 3 I employ cross-section time-series regression models to examine the correlates of health expenditures in Latin America and the Caribbean. In particular, I focus on public, private, and overall spending on health (as a percent of GDP to capture changes in spending relative to the size of the economy), public health expenditure (both as a percent of total government spending—capturing government emphasis on health compared to other sectors and total health spending—examining how the distinction between public and private resources in health have changed over time), and per capita health spending in Latin America (to capture overall spending, weighted by population).

In Chaps. 4, 5, and 6, I examine health sector reform in Argentina, Peru, and Costa Rica. I highlight the World Bank's involvement in health sector reform in these countries. In these chapters, I draw from data from hundreds of government and World Bank and other IFI policy documents to examine the discourse and implementation of six prevalent policy instruments: targeting, decentralization, management-based contracts, performance-based financing, primary health care models, and privatization in Argentina, Peru, and Costa Rica. I also utilize data gleaned from interviews with key informants—policymakers, experts, and IFI personnel—to triangulate and contextualize the policy documents to provide a more comprehensive timeline of health reforms, as well as failed initiatives. In particular, data from interviews allow me to examine how reforms proceeded compared with the official plans and to highlight episodes of contention and conflict in health policy reform, both between national actors and with international organizations. In doing so I examine how state autonomy and capacity, as well as historical institutional health arrangements, have shaped subsequent health sector reforms in Argentina, Peru, and Costa Rica's health systems.

In Chap. 7, I synthesize my findings. In this chapter, I argue that only through the joint examination of the quantitative, regional and qualitative, case-study evidence can we make sense of the effect of the World Bank on health sector reform in Latin America. While quantitative models do not reveal a downward effect on health expenditures and indeed, trends indicate increased public health spending in the region I argue that it is not because the World Bank does not matter for health in Latin America, only that it matters differently across countries, effects not well captured by a regional quantitative analysis. I argue that state capacity and autonomy in health together with existing institutional legacies and the historical structure of the health sector pattern how the World Bank has affected reforms. Particularly, I show that in Costa Rica strong state autonomy and capacity have allowed the state to resist cutbacks in coverage and maintain centralized state funding, with some changes to the administration of services, that is, adoption of sometimes neoliberal tools in the service of universalist, inclusive ends in health. In Peru, low state capacity and autonomy have resulted in more neoliberal changes in tools but not ends (targeting and private sector involvement, albeit with slowly increasing coverage). This case suggests a paradox of the strength of weak states where the World Bank cannot co-opt or even enduringly influence the weak state apparatus in health because it is fragmented, small, and disorganized. In Argentina, high state autonomy but low capacity (blocked by strong regional and professional unions) has resulted in piecemeal reform. This chapter concludes by outlining the empirical and theoretical contributions of the book.

Finally, the book's Methodological Appendix contains information on how data were gathered and analyzed including the statistical models, interview instrument, list of interviews, and archives consulted in this research. Perhaps most usefully, the appendix details the challenges and utility of taking a multi-method, cross-national approach in social science research and practical advice for conducting interviews with high-ranking key informants.

NOTES

1. While the IFC has become involved in the education and health sector I do not focus on the IFC since it has only supported a couple of projects in health in my three country cases (Argentina, Costa Rica, and Peru) and is a separate entity from the World Bank though part of the World Bank group. In addition, while the IFC is an important actor that deserves additional attention because its work is vis-à-vis private companies it often has limited effects on health sector reform writ large (see Mehrotra and Delamonica 2005).
2. For example, starting in the late 1990s, the World Bank began to consider the Human Development Index (a measure developed by the United Nations Development Programme in 1990 which measures nutritional status, educational attainment, and health status) as an important indicator of poverty (Bonal 2002). As compared with the previous indicator, GDP per capita, this measure clearly incorporates the social dimensions of development. However, much like its predecessor, the post-Washington Consensus "remains imbued with confusion and theoretical grey areas" (Santiso 2004).
3. While I do not claim that the selected cases of Argentina, Peru, and Costa Rica are representative of Latin America, I believe that the findings about how countries interact with the World Bank and differentially respond and incorporate neoliberal reform pressures in the health sector—and how this is related to existing institutional configurations—will extend to our understanding of these processes in other developing countries. This study provides particularly important variation in examining health sector reform in Latin America, as Colombia, Chile, and more recently Brazil have been overstudied in comparison to other Latin American countries. Chile adopted IFI plans for reform almost wholesale in the 1980s involving the decentralization of primary care and privatization of health insurance, owing to a neoliberal dictator (Pinochet), and in Colombia, a modified plan of structured competition in health service provision was introduced in 1993 with the famous *Ley 100*. Finally, Brazil implemented a Unified Health System (*Sistema Único de Saúde*, SUS) in 1990 together with a massive effort to decentralize the health system through that decade.

REFERENCES

Amenta, E. (2005). State-centered and political institutional theory: Retrospect and prospect. *Handbook of Political Sociology*, 96–114.

Armada, F., Muntaner, C., & Navarro, V. (2001). Health and social security reforms in Latin America: The convergence of the World Health Organization, the World Bank, and transnational corporations. *International Journal of Health Services, 31*(4), 729–768.

Aucoin, P. (2002). Paradigms, principles, paradoxes and pendulums. *Public Management: Reforming Public Management, 3*(2), 26.

Avelino, G., Brown, D. S., & Hunter, W. (2005). The effects of capital mobility, trade openness, and democracy on social spending in Latin America, 1980–1999. *American Journal of Political Science, 49*(3), 625–641.

Babb, S. (2005). The social consequences of structural adjustment: Recent evidence and current debates. *Annual Review of Sociology*, 199–222.

Babb, S. (2009). *Behind the development banks: Washington politics, world poverty, and the wealth of nations.* Chicago: University of Chicago Press.

Babb, S. (2013). The Washington consensus as transnational policy paradigm: Its origins, trajectory and likely successor. *Review of International Political Economy, 20*(2), 268–297.

Bambra, C. (2007). Going beyond the three worlds of welfare capitalism: Regime theory and public health research. *Journal of Epidemiology and Community Health, 61*(12), 1098–1102.

Bank, W. (2017a). *How does the World Bank classify countries?* Accessed January 1, 2017 https://datahelpdesk.worldbank.org/knowledgebase/articles/378834-how-does-the-world-bank-classify-countries.

Bank, W. (2017b). *Millennium development goals.* Accessed January 1, 2017.

Bank, W. (2017c). *What we do.* Accessed January 1, 2017 http://www.world-bank.org/en/about/what-we-do.

Barrientos, A., & Lloyd-Sherlock, P. (2000). Reforming health insurance in Argentina and Chile. *Health Policy and Planning, 15*(4), 417–423.

Bedford, K. (2007). The imperative of male inclusion: How institutional context influences World Bank gender policy. *International Feminist Journal of Politics, 9*(3), 289–311.

Bedford, K. (2009). *Developing partnerships: Gender, sexuality, and the reformed World Bank.* Minnesota: University of Minnesota Press.

Beeson, M. (2001). Globalization, governance, and the political-economy of public policy reform in East Asia. *Governance, 14*(4), 481–502.

Béland, D. (2005). Ideas and social policy: An institutionalist perspective. *Social Policy & Administration, 39*(1), 1–18.

Béland, D. (2010). Policy change and health care research. *Journal of Health Politics, Policy and Law, 35*(4), 615–641.

Béland, D., & Cox, R. H. (2010). *Ideas and politics in social science research.* Oxford: Oxford University Press.

Béland, D., & Waddan, A. (2000). From thatcher (and pinochet) to clinton? Conservative think tanks, foreign models and US pensions reform. *The Political Quarterly, 71*(2), 202–210.

Birn, A.-E., & Dmitrienko, K. (2005). The World Bank: Global health or global harm? *American Journal of Public Health, 95*(7), 1091–1092.

Blyth, M. (2002). *Great transformations: Economic ideas and institutional change in the twentieth century.* Cambridge: Cambridge University Press.

Bonal, X. (2002). Plus ça change… The World Bank global education policy and the post-Washington consensus. *International Studies in Sociology of Education, 12*(1), 3–22.

Bossert, T. (1998). Analyzing the decentralization of health systems in developing countries: Decision space, innovation and performance. *Social Science and Medicine, 47*(10), 1513–1527.

Brady, D., & Lee, H. Y. (2014). The rise and fall of government spending in affluent democracies, 1971–2008. *Journal of European Social Policy, 24*(1), 56–79.

Brooks, S. M. (2005). Interdependent and domestic foundations of policy change: The diffusion of pension privatization around the world. *International Studies Quarterly, 49*(2), 273–294.

Brown, D. S., & Hunter, W. (2004). Democracy and human capital formation education spending in Latin America, 1980 to 1997. *Comparative Political Studies, 37*(7), 842–864.

Burki, S. J., & Perry, G. (1998). *Beyond the Washington consensus: Institutions matter.* Washington, DC: World Bank Publications.

Calkin, S. (2015). "Tapping" women for post-crisis capitalism: Evidence from the 2012 World development report. *International Feminist Journal of Politics, 17*(4), 611–629.

Campbell, J. L. (1998). Institutional analysis and the role of ideas in political economy. *Theory and Society, 27*(3), 377–409.

Carpenter, D. (2012). Is health politics different? *Annual Review of Political Science, 15*, 287–311.

Chorev, N. (2013). Restructuring neoliberalism at the World Health Organization. *Review of International Political Economy, 20*(4), 627–666.

Clark, M. A. (2004). Reinforcing a public system: Health sector reform in Costa Rica. *Crucial needs, weak incentives: Social sector reform, democratization, and globalization in Latin America,* 189–216. Washington: Woodrow Wilson Center Press and The Johns Hopkins University Press.

Clegg, L. (2013). *Controlling the World Bank and IMF: Shareholders, stakeholders, and the politics of concessional lending.* Berlin: Springer.

Clift, J. (2003). Beyond the Washington consensus. *Finance and Development, 40*(3), 9.

Coady, D., Grosh, M. E., & Hoddinott, J. (2004). *Targeting of transfers in developing countries: Review of lessons and experience* (Vol. 1). Washington, DC: World Bank Publications.

Coburn, C., Restivo, M., & Shandra, J. M. (2015). The World Bank and child mortality in sub-saharan Africa. *Sociology of Development, 1*(3), 348–373.

Cueto, M. (2004). The origins of primary health care and selective primary health care. *American Journal of Public Health, 94*(11), 1864–1874.

de Mesa, A. A., & Mesa-Lago, C. (2006). The structural pension reform in Chile: Effects, comparisons with other Latin American reforms, and lessons. *Oxford Review of Economic Policy, 22*(1), 149–167.

De Vos, P., De Ceukelaire, W., & Van der Stuyft, P. (2006). Colombia and cuba, contrasting models in Latin America's health sector reform. *Tropical Medicine & International Health, 11*(10), 1604–1612.

De Vos, P., & Van der Stuyft, P. (2015). Sociopolitical determinants of international health policy. *International Journal of Health Services, 45*(2), 363–377.

Deacon, B. (1997). *Global social policy: International organizations and the future of welfare.* Bistro: Sage.

Deacon, B. (2007). *Global social policy and governance.* Bistro: Sage.

Di Leva, C. E. (2004). Sustainable development and the World Bank's millennium development goals. *Natural Resources & Environment,* 13–19.

Doner, R. F. (1992). Limits of state strength: Toward an institutionalist view of economic development. *World Politics, 44*(03), 398–431.

Dreher, A. (2004). A public choice perspective of IMF and World Bank lending and conditionality. *Public Choice, 119*(3–4), 445–464.

Driscoll, D. D. (1995). *The IMF and the World Bank: How do they differ?* Washington, DC: International Monetary Fund.

Easterly, W. (2000). The effect of IMF and World Bank programs on poverty. *Available at SSRN 256883.*

Esping-Andersen, G. (1999). *Social foundations of postindustrial economies.* Oxford: Oxford University Press.

Esping-Andersen, G. (2013). *The three worlds of welfare capitalism.* US: Wiley.

Evans, P. (1997). State structures, government-business relations, and economic transformation. *Business and the State in Developing Countries,* 63–87.

Evans, P., & Rauch, J. E. (1999). Bureaucracy and growth: A cross-national analysis of the effects of "Weberian" state structures on economic growth. *American Sociological Review,* 748–765.

Evans, P. B. (1995). *Embedded autonomy: States and industrial transformation* (Vol. 25). Cambridge: Cambridge University Press.

Evans, P. B., Rueschemeyer, D., & Skocpol, T. (1985). *Bringing the state back in.* Cambridge: Cambridge University Press.

Ewig, C. (2006). Global processes, local consequences: Gender equity and health sector reform in Peru. *Social Politics: International Studies in Gender, State & Society, 13*(3), 427–455.

Ferguson, L., & Harman, S. (2015). Gender and infrastructure in the World Bank. *Development Policy Review, 33*(5), 653–671.

Fine, B. (2002). *Social capital versus social theory.* UK: Routledge.

Geddes, B. (1994). *Politician's dilemma: Building state capacity in Latin America* (Vol. 25). California: University of California Press.

Glatzer, M., & Rueschemeyer, D. (2004). *Globalization and the future of the welfare state.* Pittsburgh: University of Pittsburgh Press.

Griffin, P. (2009). *Gendering the World Bank: Neoliberalism and the gendered foundations of global governance.* Berlin: Springer.

Guillén, M. F. (2001). Is globalization civilizing, destructive or feeble? A critique of five key debates in the social science literature. *Annual Review of Sociology,* 235–260.

Gwatkin, D. R., Bhuiya, A., & Victora, C. G. (2004). Making health systems more equitable. *The Lancet, 364*(9441), 1273–1280.

Haggard, S., & Kaufman, R. R. (2008). *Development, democracy, and welfare states: Latin America, East Asia, and Eastern Europe.* Princeton: Princeton University Press.

Hall, A. (2007). Social policies in the World Bank: Paradigms and challenges. *Global social policy, 7*(2), 151–175.

Hall, P. A. (1993). Policy paradigms, social learning, and the state: The case of economic policymaking in Britain. *Comparative politics,* 275–296.

Hall, P. A., & Taylor, R. C. (1996). Political science and the three new institutionalisms. *Political Studies, 44*(5), 936–957.

Hammer, J. S., & Berman, P. (1995). Ends and means in public health policy in developing countries. *Health Policy, 32*(1), 29–45.

Hanrieder, T. (2014). Local orders in international organisations: The World Health Organization's global programme on AIDS. *Journal of International Relations and Development, 17*(2), 220–241.

Harman, S. (2010) *The World Bank and HIV/AIDS: Setting a global agenda.* UK: Routledge.

Harrison, G. (2010). *Neoliberal Africa: The impact of global social engineering.* London: Zed Books.

Hay, C. (2000). Contemporary capitalism, globalization, regionalization, and the persistence of national variation. *Review of International Studies, 26*(4), 509–531.

Hay, C., & Marsh, D. (Eds.). (2010). *Demystifying globalization.* Basingstoke: MacMillan Press.

Henisz, W. J., Zelner, B. A., & Guillén, M. F. (2005). The worldwide diffusion of market-oriented infrastructure reform, 1977–1999. *American Sociological Review, 70*(6), 871–897.

Homedes, N., & Ugalde, A. (2005). Why neoliberal health reforms have failed in Latin America. *Health Policy, 71*(1), 83–96.

Huber, E., Mustillo, T., & Stephens, J. D. (2008). Politics and social spending in Latin America. *The Journal of Politics, 70*(02), 420–436.

Huber, E., & Solt, F. (2004). Successes and failures of neoliberalism. *Latin American Research Review, 39*(3), 150–164.

Huber, E., & Stephens, J. D. (2001). *Development and crisis of the welfare state: Parties and policies in global markets*. Chicago: University of Chicago press.

Huber, E., & Stephens, J. D. (2002). Globalisation, competitiveness, and the social democratic model. *Social Policy and Society, 1*(01), 47–57.

Huber, E., & Stephens, J. D. (2012). *Democracy and the left: Social policy and inequality in Latin America*. Chicago: University of Chicago Press.

Hunter, W., & Brown, D. S. (2000). World Bank directives, domestic interests, and the politics of human capital investment in Latin America. *Comparative Political Studies, 33*(1), 113–143.

IFC. (2017). About IFC. http://www.ifc.org/wps/wcm/connect/corp_ext_content/ifc_external_corporate_site/about+ifc_new.

Ilon, L. (1996). The changing role of the World Bank: Education policy as global welfare. *Policy & Politics, 24*(4), 413–424.

Immergut, E. M. (1992a). *Health politics: Interests and institutions in Western Europe*. CUP Archive.

Immergut, E. M. (1992b). The rules of the game: The logic of health policy-making in France, Switzerland, and Sweden. *Structuring politics: Historical institutionalism in comparative analysis*, 57-89.

Jamison, D., Mosley, W., Measham, A., & Bobadilla, J. (1993). *World development report: Investing in health*. Washington, DC: World Bank.

Jayasuriya, K. (2005). Beyond institutional fetishism: From the developmental to the regulatory state. *New Political Economy, 10*(3), 381–387.

Jordana, J., & Levi-Faur, D. (2005). The diffusion of regulatory capitalism in Latin America: Sectoral and national channels in the making of a new order. *The Annals of the American Academy of Political and Social Science, 598*(1), 102–124.

Kaasch, A., & Martens, K. (2015). *Actors and agency in global social governance*. Oxford: Oxford University Press.

Kanbur, R. (1999, July 30). The strange case of the Washington Consensus. A brief note on John Williamson's "What should the Bank think about the Washington Consensus". New York: Cornell University.

Kapur, D., Lewis, J., & Webb, R. (1997). *The World Bank: Its first half-century*, Volume I: History, 2. Washington, DC: Brookings Institution.

Karns, M. P., Mingst, K. A., & Stiles, K. W. (2015). *International organizations: The politics and processes of global governance* (3rd ed.). London: Lynne Rienner Publishers.

Keshavjee, M. S. (2014). *Blind spot: How neoliberalism infiltrated global health* (Vol. 30). California: University of California Press.

Lange, M., Mahoney, J., & Vom Hau, M. (2006). Colonialism and development: A comparative analysis of Spanish and British colonies. *American Journal of Sociology, 111*(5), 1412–1462.

Larner, W., & Walters, W. (Eds.). (2004). *Global governmentality: Governing international spaces.* New York, NY: Routledge.

Laurell, A. C. (2000). Structural adjustment and the globalization of social policy in Latin America. *International Sociology, 15*(2), 306–325.

Levi-Faur, D., & Jordana, J. (2006). Toward a Latin American regulatory state? The diffusion of autonomous regulatory agencies across countries and sectors. *International Journal of Public Administration, 29*(4–6), 335–366.

Levitsky, S., & Murillo, M. V. (2009). Variation in institutional strength. *Annual Review of Political Science, 12,* 115–133.

Lloyd-Sherlock, P. (2005). Health sector reform in Argentina: A cautionary tale. *Social Science and Medicine, 60*(8), 1893–1903.

Lloyd-Sherlock, P. (2006). When social health insurance goes wrong: Lessons from Argentina and Mexico. *Social Policy & Administration, 40*(4), 353–368.

Mahoney, J. (2003). Long-run development and the legacy of colonialism in Spanish America. *American Journal of Sociology, 109*(1), 50–106.

Mankiw, N. (2014). *Essentials of economics.* US: Cengage learning.

Mann, M. (1984). The autonomous power of the state: Its origins, mechanisms and results. *European Journal of Sociology, 25*(02), 185–213.

Meessen, B., Soucat, A., & Sekabaraga, C. (2011). Performance-based financing: Just a donor fad or a catalyst towards comprehensive health-care reform? *Bulletin of the World Health Organization, 89*(2), 153–156.

Mehrotra, S., & Delamonica, E. (2005). The private sector and privatization in social services is the Washington consensus 'dead'? *Global Social Policy, 5*(2), 141–174.

Meier, B. M., & Ayala, A. S. (2014). The pan american health organization and the mainstreaming of human rights in regional health governance. *The Journal of Law, Medicine & Ethics, 42*(3), 356–374.

Melo, M. A. (2007). Institutional weakness and the puzzle of Argentina's low taxation. *Latin American Politics and Society, 49*(4), 115–148.

Mesa-Lago, C. (2002). Myth and reality of pension reform: The Latin American evidence. *World Development, 30*(8), 1309–1321.

Mesa-Lago, C. (2006). Private and public pension systems compared: An evaluation of the Latin American experience. *Review of Political Economy, 18*(3), 317–334.

Mesa-Lago, C. (2008). *Reassembling social security: A survey of pensions and health care reforms in Latin America*. Oxford: Oxford University Press.

Mesa-Lago, C., & Müller, K. (2002). The politics of pension reform in Latin America. *Journal of Latin American Studies, 34*(3), 687–715.

Meseguer, C. (2005). Policy learning, policy diffusion, and the making of a new order. *The Annals of the American Academy of Political and Social Science, 598*(1), 67–82.

Mills, A. (1994). Decentralization and accountability in the health sector from an international perspective: What are the choices? *Public Administration and Development, 14*(3), 281–292.

Mishra, R. (2004). Social protection by other means: Can it survive globalization. *A Handbook for Comparative Social Policy*. Cheltenham/Northampton: Edward Elgar Publishing, 68–90.

Mkandawire, T. (2005). *Targeting and universalism in poverty reduction*. Geneva: United Nations Research Institute for Social Development Geneva.

Naim, M. (2000). Fads and fashion in economic reforms: Washington consensus or Washington confusion? *Third World Quarterly, 21*(3), 505–528.

Navarro, V. (2007). *Neoliberalism, globalization, and inequalities: Consequences for health and quality of life*. Citeseer.

Noy, S. (2011). New contexts, different patterns? A comparative analysis of social spending and government health expenditure in Latin America and the OECD. *International Journal of Comparative Sociology, 52*(3), 215–244.

Noy, S. (2015). The Washington consensus and social policy: World Bank projects and health sector reform in Costa Rica. *Latin American Policy, 6*(2), 182–204.

Öniş, Z., & Şenses, F. (2005). Rethinking the emerging post-Washington consensus. *Development and Change, 36*(2), 263–290.

Orenstein, M. A. (2008). *Privatizing pensions: The transnational campaign for social security reform*. Princeton: Princeton University Press.

Orloff, A. S., & Skocpol, T. (1984). Why not equal protection? Explaining the politics of public social spending in Britain, 1900–1911, and the United States, 1880s–1920s. *American Sociological Review*, 726–750.

Pierson, P. (1993). When effect becomes cause: Policy feedback and political change. *World Politics, 45*(4), 595–628.

Pierson, P. (1994). *Dismantling the welfare state?: Reagan Thatcher and the politics of retrenchment*. Cambridge: Cambridge University Press.

Pierson, P. (2000). Increasing returns, path dependence, and the study of politics. *American Political Science Review, 94*(2), 251–267.

Pierson, P. (2004). *Politics in time: History, institutions, and social analysis*. Princeton: Princeton University Press.

Polanyi, K. (1944). *The great transformation: The political and economic origins of our time*. US: Beacon Press.

Polidano, C., & Hulme, D. (1999). Public management reform im developing countries: Issues and outcomes. *Public Management an International Journal of Research and Theory, 1*(1), 121–132.

Portes, A. (1997). Neoliberalism and the sociology of development: Emerging trends and unanticipated facts. *Population and Development Review*, 229–259.

Portes, A., & Landolt, P. (2000). Social capital: Promise and pitfalls of its role in development. *Journal of Latin American Studies, 32*(02), 529–547.

Pribble, J. (2013). *Welfare and party politics in Latin America.* Cambridge: Cambridge University Press.

Radin, D. (2008). World Bank funding and health care sector performance in Central and Eastern Europe. *International Political Science Review, 29*(3), 325–347.

Ragin, C. (1994). A qualitative comparative analysis of pension systems. *The comparative political economy of the welfare state*, 320–345.

Rivas-Loria, P., & Shelton, C. (2004). Analysis of health sector reforms. *Region of the Americas.* Washington, DC: Pan American Health Organization.

Rodrik, D. (1997). *Has globalisation gone too far?* Washington, DC: Institute for International Economics.

Roll, M. (2014). *The politics of public sector performance: Pockets of effectiveness in developing countries.* UK: Routledge.

Ruger, J. P. (2005). The changing role of the World Bank in global health. *American Journal of Public Health, 95*(1), 60–70.

Ruggie, J. G. (1982). International regimes, transactions, and change: Embedded liberalism in the postwar economic order. *International Organization, 36*(2), 379–415.

Sánchez-Talanquer, M. (2017). *Political cleavages and the development of fiscal capacity: Historical evidence from Mexico and Colombia.*

Santiso, C. (2004). The contentious Washington consensus: Reforming the reforms in emerging markets. *Review of International Political Economy, 11*(4), 828–844.

Scott, J. C. (1998). *Seeing like a state: How certain schemes to improve the human condition have failed.* Yale: Yale University Press

Shandra, J. M., Nobles, J., London, B., & Williamson, J. B. (2004). Dependency, democracy, and infant mortality: A quantitative, cross-national analysis of less developed countries. *Social Science and Medicine, 59*(2), 321–333.

Silva, H. T., De Paepe, P., Soors, W., Lanza, O. V., Closon, M.-C., Van Dessel, P., et al. (2011). Revisiting health policy and the World Bank in Bolivia. *Global Social Policy, 11*(1), 22–44.

Simmons, B. A., Dobbin, F., & Garrett, G. (2006). Introduction: The international diffusion of liberalism. *International Organization, 60*(4), 781–810.

Simmons, B. A., Dobbin, F., & Garrett, G. (2007). The global diffusion of public policies: Social construction, coercion, competition or learning? *Annual Review of Sociology, 33*, 449–472.

Skocpol, T. (1988). Social revolutions and mass military mobilization. *World Politics, 40*(02), 147–168.

Skocpol, T. (1992). *Protecting Mothers and Soldiers: The Political Origins of Social Policy in the United States.*

Skocpol, T. (1995). *Social policy in the United States: Future possibilities in historical perspective.* Princeton: Princeton University Press.

Skocpol, T., & Amenta, E. (1986). States and social policies. *Annual Review of Sociology,* 131–157.

Soifer, H. (2012). Measuring state capacity in contemporary Latin America. *Revista de Ciencia Política, 32*(3), 585–598.

Starfield, B., Shi, L., & Macinko, J. (2005). Contribution of primary care to health systems and health. *Milbank Quarterly, 83*(3), 457–502.

Stiglitz, J. E. (1998). *More instruments and broader goals: Moving toward the post-Washington consensus.* Finland: UNU/WIDER Helsinki.

Stiglitz, J. E. (2003). Democratizing the international monetary fund and the World Bank: Governance and accountability. *Governance, 16*(1), 111–139.

Stocker, K., Waitzkin, H., & Iriart, C. (1999). The exportation of managed care to Latin America. *New England Journal of Medicine, 340*(14), 1131–1136.

Thelen, K. (1999). Historical institutionalism in comparative politics. *Annual Review of Political Science, 2*(1), 369–404.

Unger, J.-P., De Paepe, P., Cantuarias, G. S., & Herrera, O. A. (2008). Chile's neoliberal health reform: An assessment and a critique. *PLoS Med, 5*(4), e79.

Vreeland, J. R. (2003). *The IMF and economic development.* Cambridge: Cambridge University Press.

Wade, R. (1990). *Governing the market: Economic theory and the role of government in East Asian industrialization.* Princeton: Princeton University Press.

Waitzkin, H. (2011). *Medicine and public health at the end of empire.* Paradigm: Paradigm Publishers.

Waitzkin, H., Iriart, C., Estrada, A., & Lamadrid, S. (2001a). Social medicine in Latin America: Productivity and dangers facing the major national groups. *The Lancet, 358*(9278), 315–323.

Waitzkin, H., Iriart, C., Estrada, A., & Lamadrid, S. (2001b). Social medicine then and now: Lessons from Latin America. *American Journal of Public Health, 91*(10), 1592–1601.

Weaver, C. (2008). *Hypocrisy trap: The World Bank and the poverty of reform.* Princeton: Princeton University Press.

Weiss, L. (1999). State power and the Asian crisis. *New Political Economy, 4*(3), 317–342.

Weyland, K. (2005). Theories of policy diffusion lessons from Latin American pension reform. *World Politics, 57*(2), 262–295.

Weyland, K. (2006). *External pressures and international norms in LatinAmerican pension reform.* Citeseer.

Williamson, J. (2000). What should the World Bank think about the Washington consensus? *The World Bank Research Observer, 15*(2), 251–264.

Williamson, J. (2002). Speeches, testimony, papers did the washington consensus fail? *Institute for International Economics.*

Willis, K., & Khan, S. (2009). Health Reform in Latin America and Africa: Decentralisation, participation and inequalities. *Third World Quarterly, 30*(5), 991–1005.

Wood, C. A. (2012). Adjustment with a woman's face: Gender and macroeconomic policy. *Struggles for Social Rights in Latin America*, p. 209.

Woods, N. (2006). *The globalizers: The IMF, the World Bank, and their borrowers.* Cornell: Cornell University Press.

Yeates, N. (2002). Globalization and social policy from global neoliberal hegemony to global political pluralism. *Global Social Policy, 2*(1), 69–91.

CHAPTER 2

Neoliberalism and the World Bank's Changing Approach to Health

Greater involvement by the Bank in the health sector is justified for several reasons. First, the Bank's expertise in country programming and in sector analysis is needed to help ensure the success of emerging national policies to expand the coverage of health care… Second, significant involvement in the health sector is an important element of the Bank's concern for alleviating poverty in the developing countries. An expanded policy for health operations is essential to deal effectively with the problems of poverty and low productivity among the poor.
—World Bank Health Sector Policy Paper 1980: 63–64, which formally committed the World Bank to lending in the health sector

As far back as 1980, the World Bank viewed itself as an expert in global health. The Bank viewed its work with developing countries in health falling squarely under its missions of poverty reduction and economic development, as demonstrated in this chapter's opening quote. Understanding the World Bank's evolving approach to health is central to unpacking the changing shape of neoliberalism in health sector reform. In this chapter, I examine the World Bank's changing approach to health since the 1980s. I argue that the World Bank is concerned with the overarching goals of both efficiency—doing the same or more work with fewer or the same resources—and equity—increased equality in access and outcomes in health. These goals are often discussed in tandem, though common understandings suggest that while not mutually exclusive, the pursuit of one may diminish the other. The policy

© The Author(s) 2017
S. Noy, *Banking on Health*, DOI 10.1007/978-3-319-61765-7_2

instruments promoted by the World Bank, and detailed in Chap. 1, are decentralization, separation of functions, performance-based management, privatization and private sector investment, a primary health care approach, and targeting. Each of these instruments may serve the goals of equity, efficiency, or both, but have traditionally, with the exception of a primary health care approach, been viewed as neoliberal and working in the service of efficiency more than equity. While the case-study Chaps. 4–6 demonstrate that the World Bank's approach is variable across countries, it remains useful to examine the World Bank's overall and changing approach to health. In this chapter, I provide a comprehensive discussion of World Bank operations and discourse surrounding health since 1980.

To accomplish this goal, I trace the World Bank's evolving approach to health, drawing from archival policy documents and interviews. Since the 1980s the World Bank has been discussing universal coverage in health however, its projects often focused on market approaches (i.e. private sector involvement in insurance markets) and a diminished, provisory, and advisory role of the state in health (i.e., targeted programs for the poor). Over time, however, its emphasis has shifted in two ways: first, in providing systemic, organizational support and recommendations both via its research and lending instruments rather than focusing only on standalone (as compared to system-wide) projects, and second, to emphasizing sometimes neoliberal means but increasingly embracing in practice its declared but neglected mission of increased access to health especially for the poor, even if it emphasizes neoliberal tools to achieve this task. The World Bank's 1980 health policy paper, quoted at the beginning of this chapter, which commits it to lending in health notes that "countries should be willing to devise a strategy for providing access to basic health services to all citizens over a reasonable period of time. Development of health planning capacity and of a long-term plan for the health sector will be encouraged" (65). From its earliest commitment to direct lending to the health sector in developing countries, the World Bank has been concerned with not only increased access but also expanded coverage. However, it has strayed from this mission over the years, often working in a piecemeal way on disparate projects without concerted attention towards increased access. More recently, however, it has circled back to its commitment to universal health care with research, publications, and official policy statements.

BANKING IN HEALTH: THE 1975 HEALTH
SECTOR POLICY PAPER

In 1975, the World Bank published its first policy statement linking health conditions and economic development with its *Health Sector Policy Paper* (Bank 1975; Coburn et al. 2015). This paper pointed to inequalities both between and within countries and discussed two options for the World Bank's involvement in health: begin lending separately for basic health services or incorporate health into its existing forms of lending. The World Bank chose to incorporate health into its existing projects, namely population projects, partly because of concerns with foreign governments' cooperation and ability to institute health reforms and infrastructure. The World Bank points to borrowing countries' weak health systems and cites the channeling of limited resources to hospitals and highly trained personnel, concentrated in urban areas, as an impediment to large-scale health reform and as obstacles to governments' implementing health reforms. Specifically, it notes that "effective political commitment to health care for the bulk of the population poses considerable problems for many governments" (60) and suggests that states are sometimes unwilling to consider significant reforms and that their health priorities "are inconsistent with equitable health programming approaches" (60). Interestingly, the report also raises questions about whether and how the World Bank should and could be involved in health sectors in developing countries.

The World Bank was hesitant to become involved in health because of its limited experience in this field, as well as the possible adverse effects on economic growth and poverty alleviation. The report states: "Paradoxically, health improvements may pose a threat to well-being if the net effect is to increase the rate of population growth significantly" (28). By reducing mortality and increasing fecundity, better health interventions may result in increasing populations and undermine economic growth, presumably due to a larger dependent population and strain on existing infrastructure. The World Bank further demurs from implementing large-scale health projects, partly because "the Bank would have to finance a very large share of the growth in total national government expenditure on health" (61). In the end, it was hesitant to invest in health because of the large amount of capital that would be necessary to support such a project portfolio across low- and middle-income nations. One of the primary reasons the Bank was hesitant to get involved in

health was because it viewed investment in health as squarely in the public domain, and the purview of governments. In retrospect, this approach
seems somewhat ironic given its emphasis on privatization in health
reforms among borrower countries in subsequent years.

In this early period, the Bank sought to support than supplant public
health investments. The World Bank would re-orient member government spending in health and emphasize the need for it to target the poor.
Interestingly, in the first public policy statement on health, the World Bank
rejects private market involvement in the sector, stating: "[t]he private
market cannot be expected to allocate to health either the amount of the
composition of resources that is best from a social perspective" (29).

The preference for government-led investments in health was justified in two ways: first, because "consumers of health services" are unable to choose rationally (i.e. the World Bank points to the consumer's
lack of experience as a patient and the complexity of medical problems
preventing the patient from necessarily choosing the best medication,
medical course of action, etc.) and second, due to positive externalities
generated by health interventions (i.e., preventing the spread of infectious diseases have benefits for communities and the broader population
and should therefore not be left only to patients acting in their own individual interest). Therefore, because of these issues of information asymmetry and the related principal-agent problem (whereby doctors make
decisions that impact the patient), and owing to externalities the World
Bank supports public interventions in health. Importantly, though the
Bank's stance is for government involvement it still follows an economic
logic: governments should subsidize care for the poor and principles of
cost-effectiveness to should guide decisions about which interventions to
pursue (e.g., the decision on how to treat cholera should consider cost
of immunizations as compared with sanitation measures at reducing the
rates of cholera, 31).

During this time period the World Bank's increasing involvement in
health is a proposed collaboration with the WHO. The report notes that
while the WHO has technical expertise, it has limited strength in conducting economic analyses and does not finance large capital expenditures. As such, the World Bank viewed the WHO as a complementary
agency and collaboration as mutually beneficial. Despite these arguments
for the World Bank's increased involvement in health, the 1975 report
ultimately favors the option of including health components and considering health effects in existing projects rather than pursuing direct

lending in health but leaves open the option of direct lending in health for the future.

WORLD BANK DIRECT LENDING IN HEALTH: 1980 HEALTH POLICY PAPER

The World Bank changed its official policy with the publication of its 1980 *Health Policy Paper*, moving away from considering health in existing projects to supporting stand-alone health investments. In this report, health is treated as a basic need as well as a means to economic development, citing a shift "in the emphasis of development from economic growth to meeting basic needs" (30). The economic costs of ill health include lost labor productivity, wasting resources (namely nutrients consumed by diseases), possible limits on exports and tourism because of fear of disease, inability to utilize resource-rich land (due to the presence of diseases that cannot be eradicated in these areas), and possible effects of human diseases on animals. This paper echoes the sentiments of the 1975 report (and indeed incorporates revised portions of that paper), noting that the private market cannot effectively provide health. Notably, this report criticizes low government expenditures in health in developing countries, noting that private health expenditure outpaces public spending. However, the report notes that not only are government commitments to health low, even these scarce resources are utilized inefficiently, focusing on hospitals and failing to provide coverage to large swathes of the population.

This report also reinforces and sets the stage for establishing more partnerships with other multilateral organizations (i.e., WHO, UNICEF, UNDP) working in health including bilateral agencies. The report notes that while the WHO in particular has expertise in health management it has "little experience, compared with the Bank, in identification, appraisal, or supervision of health care programs" and points to the WHO's "modest financial resources" (Bank 1980). In all, the World Bank seeks to "complement the activities of the WHO" (66) and reasserts a focus on family planning (as part of a primary health care strategy) because of the relationship between health and population. In this report, the World Bank sets itself up as an important, if not the most important, player in global health, willing to work cooperatively but bringing unique resources, both financial and institutional, to this arena.

The focus as outlined in this report is squarely on primary health care and assisting countries in their planning capacity.

DEBT CRISIS AND STRUCTURAL ADJUSTMENT: WORLD BANK INTERVENTIONS

The debt crisis of the 1980s and beyond, resulting in what some have called the "lost decade" in Latin America, rendered many developing countries unable to pay their foreign debts in the face of rising oil and other commodity prices and plagued by hyperinflation. The World Bank, along with the IMF, responded by rescheduling loan payments and providing borrowing nations with a new lending instrument: structural adjustment loans. These structural adjustment loans were intended to assist countries in their resolving balance-of-payment issues by requiring a borrowing nation to implement macro-economic policy reforms. The reforms included export promotion, reduction in state expenditures and sizes, and privatization (Coburn et al. 2015; Bryant and Bailey 1997). Importantly, these were originally seen as a short-term solution: "Adjustment lending was originally expected to be a short-lived diversion from the Bank's central mission, the promotion of economic and social development through well-designed investment activities" (Chhibber et al. 1991). However, they became a staple of World Bank lending and operations in the 1980s and 1990s, and among the most heavily criticized aspect of the Bank's work.

Structural adjustment loans and programs were somewhat successful in stimulating economic growth which allowed, among other things, the generation of funds for debt repayment. Debt repayment and economic growth and stability have, since their founding, been central concerns of both the Bank and in particular the IMF. In the quest for economic growth, however, social development and outcomes were sometimes compromised. Empirically, structural adjustment programs have been shown to adversely affect health outcomes, at least in Africa (McMichael 2016; Coburn et al. 2015). As my analysis in Chap. 3 demonstrates, World Bank conditions on loans do not appear to be significantly related to health expenditures in Latin America, calling into question the effect of structural adjustment policies on health expenditures, if not all public expenditures. Nonetheless, the World Bank received fierce criticism for its structural adjustment lending due to mounting evidence that structural adjustment programs have a negative impact on health outcomes. This research has largely been limited to maternal and infant health outcomes in Sub-Saharan Africa (Shandra et al. 2004, 2010, 2011, 2012; Coburn et al. 2015) which may account for a lack of effect on health expenditures that I find in Chap. 3, nor does my analysis focus exclusively on structural adjustment loans. Importantly, while this research on Sub-Saharan African suggests a negative effect of structural adjustment loans on health outcomes, this same research also suggests that health loans more generally (as compared with structural adjustment loans) have a positive effect on health outcomes including child and maternal mortality rates. However, the negative outcomes of adjustment programs observed during the 1980s led to fierce criticism of the Bank, and in particular its work in health.

Structural Adjustment "with a Human Face"? The Social Dimensions of Adjustment

The World Bank itself admits that structural adjustments require tough decisions, and may have an adverse effect on safety nets in the short-term. However, it argues they are required for growth and development in the long-term. Others have been more critical. A 1987 report by the United Nations Children's Fund (UNICEF) criticized the World Bank's adjustment policies, noting that they had hampered the expansion and maintenance of not only health, but also education, sanitation, and housing, rendering children especially vulnerable (Cornia et al. 1987). The report led to increased scrutiny and pressure on the World Bank. The World Bank's response to this report was initially dismissive of such concerns noting that such short-term "growing pains" were necessary to ensure economic growth in the long-term (Coburn et al. 2015). However, the Bank redoubled its efforts in health investment shortly thereafter. In particular, its investments sought to build hospitals and clinics, immunize the population, and train medical personnel (Peet 2003; Fair 2008). However, the focus on systemic reforms in the sector remained and, perhaps, intensified. Fair (2008: 9) notes: "Whereas in the early 1980s less than one-fifth of health projects included explicit reforms or systematic objectives, this number quickly multiplied to approximately one-third of all health projects in the late 1980s and continued to grow to nearly one half of all health projects by the late 1990s." In direct response to the effects of structural adjustment loans, during this time period, the World Bank also concerned itself with the "social dimensions of adjustment," supporting small-scale projects to offset the negative social effects of adjustment projects (Jayarajah et al. 1996). In doing so, the World Bank argued that "[s]ocial safety net provisions, intended to enable beneficiaries to meet their immediate basic needs, are income transfers received by individuals in addition to what might be expected from economic growth channels or general (untargeted) expenditures for human resource development" (104). Safety nets were appropriate, according to the Bank, for two groups of people: those rendered "vulnerable" by structural adjustment and those already living in poverty prior to adjustment. The World Bank has supported some "government-sponsored safety net programs" since 1987 (133). Later, however, the Bank moved away from this approach with the rise of antiwelfarism (a broader political current evident with the Thatcher and Raegan administrations, and subsequent state approaches inspired by them) towards empowering the poor via market integration, rather than focusing on social and public provision of assistance (Hutchful 1994). This approach, while it has been tempered, is evident to this day in the World Bank's discourse: an emphasis on incorporating the poor into decision-making and program processes as active agents, rather than as recipients of benefits. On the one hand, such efforts at enhancing agency among the poor are commendable, in practice, however, this often means burdening them with additional responsibility and limiting their access to basic needs in a timely manner—a goal more easily achieved via the safety net approach.

Addressing the social dimensions of adjustment, according to the World Bank, involved strengthening national data and information systems (also described in Chaps. 4–6 in projects in Argentina, Peru, and Costa Rica as facilitating targeting in identifying poor and needy populations) and via training and institutional capacity building, to allow social dimensions to be integrated into government policy plans. In 1987, the World Bank underwent internal reorganization, where two new objectives were introduced: improving health financing in terms of efficiency and equity and engaging in the systemic reform of health systems. These reforms sought to address the social and institutional barriers to health care, and engage the poor. The Bank's reformed approach was centrally concerned with equity, in a way that it had not been previously, however, it continued to rely on policy prescriptions considered neoliberal including targeting (typically means-tested), decentralization, and following an economic, quantitative logic. In particular, World Bank personnel developed a wealth index, which measured household wealth using assets rather than income or consumption. While this time period saw increased and increasingly careful attention to health by the World Bank, these projects were overall rated less positively than projects in other (non-health) sectors (Fair 2008) and were often smaller-scale and limited in scope. Altogether, many of these projects appeared to be providing band-aid solutions to systemic issues brought on by structural adjustment. By the early 1990s, therefore, the World Bank had undergone several shifts in its approach to health, grappling with incorporating health into larger, multi-sectoral projects and addressing it in standalone efforts, against the backdrop of structural adjustment loans.

The 1993 World Development Report: Individualism, Human Capital, and DALYs

It is hard to overstate the importance of the 1993 World Development Report (WDR) for cementing the World Bank's global leadership in health. It crystallized what may now be considered the neoliberal "turn" in health—economic analyses, a baseline service package, a focus on individualism in health, and circumscribing government's role in the sector—in a single, widely disseminated report. In particular, the World Bank identifies strategies by which governments could improve health systems and health outcomes. It takes as its primary unit of analysis households and individuals and suggests competition in the health services market to improve equity and efficiency in the distribution of resources, particularly public expenditures. Therefore, while there is still room for public action in health (owing to externalities), there is a clear focus on health systems and competition from private providers.

The report argues that health matters not only for well-being as an end in itself, but can be justified on "purely economic grounds" (Bank 1993) as it prevents worker illness, allows better use of natural resources and land, increases the enrolment of children in school, and frees alternative resources that would otherwise be spent on treating illnesses. This reasoning echoes the cost of ill-health identified in the 1980 World Bank Policy Paper, but instead of enumerating the cost of disease, reframes them (slightly altered) as benefits for investments in health.

The report continues by noting that the gains are relatively larger for the poor. The role of government as described in the WDR is twofold: provider but only of essential clinical services, and promoter and regulator of greater diversity and competition in the financing and delivery of health services (iii).

Of particular note, however, the World Bank calls for private sector involvement as a cornerstone for improving health: "Government regulation can strengthen private insurance markets by improving incentives for wide coverage and for cost control. Even for publicly financed clinical services, governments can encourage competition and private sector involvement in service supply and can help improve the efficiency of the private sector by generating and disseminating key information" (iii). This entails a preference for insurance schemes rather than single-payer public provision and often involved the utilization of user-fees and the incorporation of NGOs as service providers. The report reads: "Public finance of essential clinical care is thus justified to alleviate poverty. Such public funding can take several forms: subsidies to private providers and NGOs that serve the poor; vouchers that the poor can take to a provider of their choice; and free or below-cost delivery of public services to the poor." (5). Importantly, however, the report does not ignore the problems associated with unregulated private markets: escalating costs for clients because of the "moral hazard" of insurance (i.e., insurance reduces the incentives for individuals to avoid risk and expense) and the issue of asymmetrical information (i.e., health providers income depends on advice given, perhaps leading to excessive treatment given patients' lesser information) and the presence of externalities meaning that private markets provide less than optimal levels of public goods. However, the report also notes that private providers are sometimes more technically efficient and offer higher quality service. The role of government appears to be primarily of regulation of a more efficient, but flawed, private, competitive market in health, and only secondarily of public financing (including subsidies and subcontracting) of health.

Despite the limited role of public financing of health in the 1993 WDR the issue of how to allocate such funding remained central. The 1993 WDR introduced the idea of the global burden of disease framework in order to allow governments to better allocate health spending based on estimations of the extent to which populations suffer from diseases via Disability-Adjusted Life Years (or DALYs). DALYs are to be used as a tool to prioritize particular health interventions and accounts not only for premature mortality but also disability (Anand and Hanson 1998). DALYs are intended to provide a summary measure of population health and allow a comparison of the cost of treatment and prevention across diseases. They seek to capture the impact of both premature mortality (quantity of life) and morbidity or disability (quality of life) and measure the number of life years lost. When the burden of disease is high and cost-effectiveness of intervention is high the intervention can be considered a priority (Bank 1993). Overall, the report focused on investing in health and education, especially among poorer segments of the population to achieve the dual objectives of economic and social development, particularly in the form of economic growth and poverty reduction. In using this tool, the focus shifted to cost effectiveness via the reduction of DALYs. Though the emphasis of the report is firmly on efficiency and economic growth, it also turns its attention to poverty reduction in its own right. This may be seen as a promotion of direct intervention in the health sector in the service of equity, which is quite different than the previous approach of allowing economic growth to trickle down and in this way ameliorate poverty (Bank 1997).

The methodology and creation of the DALYs metric was subject to much debate. On the one hand, it was said to have "greatly facilitated scientific and political assessments of the comparative importance of various diseases, injuries and risk factors, particularly for priority-setting in the health sector, and has led to strategic decisions by some agencies, e.g. the WHO, to invest greater effort in program developments to address priority health concerns such as tobacco control and injury prevention" (Lopez 2005). As such, the WDR then did not only establish some priorities but introduced a methodology by which more specific priorities could be established at international and national levels.

On the other hand, the report was also referred to as a "prescription for health disaster" (Antia 1994). Criticisms can be categorized along three broad themes: first, the Western ahistorical approach implicated in the report, second, the lack of attention to solutions and instead the focus on DALYs as a diagnostic, and third, the lack of attention to equity and the assumption of equality across DALYs. Related to the first criticism, the WDR was criticized for prioritizing a Western approach to health including hospitals, technologies, and medical doctors without accounting for local cultures and customs. In addition, there is no attention to social and political context, and DALYs take a piecemeal approach to health and illness. Further, the WDR did not consider some of the inequalities and conditions in developing countries that the report and the Bank seek to address are the result of the systemic inequality inherent in global economic relationships, some of which are enhanced by the World Bank's own practices, including structural adjustment (Antia 1994). Second, some argue that while the DALYs were systematically applied the same could not be said for the cost-effectiveness of interventions to address these issues, that is, solutions seeking to address the identified priorities were sometimes costly with little payoff (Paalman et al. 1998). Finally, a third criticism centers on issues of equity. That is, a DALY gained is treated equally net of whom it is gained for whether they be generally healthy or not, as well as the fact that at basic package of service stands in opposition to comprehensive care.

Understanding the World Bank's changing approach to health and criticisms of such is central therefore not only because of the financial power it wields and conditions it can impose on government spending and behavior, but also because of its normative power in outlining appropriate measurements, priorities, and policy instruments in health. This role has become even more important as other international organizations have entered the global health arena, reducing the World Bank's relative financial commitments to health but arguably not its ideational, technical sway. The World Bank has consistently devoted several billion dollars to health assistance from the mid-1990s and beyond as demonstrated in Fig. 2.1.

While the Bank's involvement in health has not diminished it has been far outpaced by the growth in spending by bilateral agencies, international and domestic NGOs, and new foundations, namely the Bill & Melinda Gates Foundation. However, through the 1990s the World Bank was the single largest external funder of global health (Ruger 2005) and as such, as a single institution was a leader in global health norms and policies. In addition, as consistently mentioned since its official commitment to lending in health in the 1980s, its comparative advantage in financial and economic domains has allowed it to retain its important role despite its falling share of expenditures in global health.

These patterns, however, also vary across regions. Figure 2.1 obscures both cross-regional and cross-national variability in the sources of

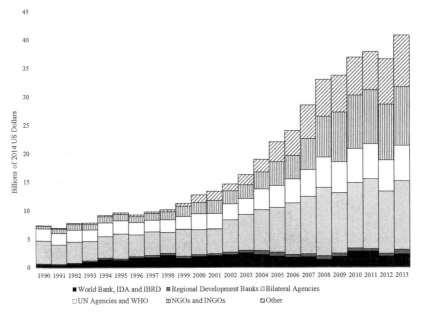

Fig. 2.1 Development assistance for health globally, 1990–2013. *Source* Institute for Health Metrics and Evaluation (IHME). *Notes* Other includes public–private partnerships (for example, the Global Fund to Fight AIDS, Tuberculosis, and Malaria), US Foundations, the Bill & Melinda Gates Foundation, the European Commission

development assistance for health. Figure 2.2 presents this same data on sources for Development Assistance in Health regionally in Latin America and the Caribbean. In this region, the World Bank's spending on health comprises a much larger share of overall development assistance in health, and indeed in some years far outpaces each of the other sources. Therefore, while Fig. 2.1 suggests that the World Bank may be losing its financial clout as a funder of health in some countries or regions, there is reason to expect that it continues to be especially if not increasingly important in some countries and regions, including Latin America and the Caribbean, as suggested by Fig. 2.2. This variation further motivates the regional focus of this book.

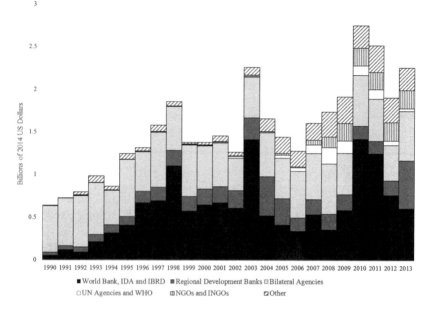

Fig. 2.2 Development assistance for health in Latin America and the Caribbean, 1990–2013. *Source* Institute for Health Metrics and Evaluation (IHME). *Notes* Other includes public–private partnerships (for example, the Global Fund to Fight AIDS, Tuberculosis, and Malaria), US Foundations, the Bill & Melinda Gates Foundation, the European Commission

THE LATE 1990S, EARLY 2000S: HEALTH OUTCOMES AND SYSTEMS

In the 1990s the World Bank largely followed the lead it had established in the 1980s and 1990s, focusing on governments establishing a basic package of services (including in Argentina and Peru, as described in Chaps. 4 and 5) and increasing government regulation in health and primary care and essential services, with some targeted programs aimed at poverty alleviation. Fair (2008) calls this the "health outcomes and systems" phase where the objectives were to improve outcomes for the poor and better the performance of health systems. While ostensibly concerned with systems, the World Bank is less concerned with what a health care system is than what it does—especially compared to other international organizations such as the World Health Organization (Kaasch 2015). In its 1997 *Health, Nutrition, and Population Sector Strategy Paper* the World Bank focuses on outcomes, again discussing health in the context of growth and poverty reduction: "Investing in people is at the center of the World Bank's development strategy as it moves into the twenty first century, reflecting the fact that no country can secure sustainable economic growth or poverty reduction without a healthy, well nourished, and educated population" (Bank 1997).

This renewed focus on the poor and their health outcomes corresponded to an organizational shift in the World Bank: In 1996, Richard Feachem directed the newly created Health, Nutrition, and Population Sector, which subsequently became more sympathetic to public health, as compared with health economics, approaches (Deacon 2007; Abbasi 1999). Improving health outcomes was to be achieved via stimulating demand for health services and promoting client-generated and driven strategies and via intersectoral collaboration. This approach was motivated in part by an emerging understanding among World Bank personnel that the focus on user fees, emphasized in the early 1990s, needed to be revisited as it was having a devastating effect on health and economically on families (Irvine et al. 2013). The clients in this formulation are governments, though the Bank recognizes the complexity of health sectors in borrowing countries: "it is necessary to reconcile the divergent views of the various interest groups—the Bank's clients (typically the ministries of health and finance), stakeholders (local communities, health care providers, and insurance companies), beneficiaries (patients, the poor, women, children, and other vulnerable groups), and other development partners" (10). The report also highlights the importance of the Bank's collaborative work with other organizations and self-describes the Bank as a "global knowledge broker" (12) in health. Given that its share of financial commitments to health is falling (Fig. 2.1), this emphasis on partnerships is strategically advantageous to the Bank. Partnerships then take on a new meaning for the World Bank: It continues to provide loans in health and becomes a knowledge broker, related not only to its partnerships with governments, beneficiaries, and other organizations, but also to its ability to collect, compile, and disseminate data. This statistical contribution began with the DALYs, cost-effectiveness calculations, and burden of disease data but it has continued with the provision of the World Development Indicators among other data. This self-concept as a knowledge broker has also seemingly created an opening for the Bank to be more self-critical than before. For example, the report notes that the Bank has not paid "sufficient attention to the political economy of reform and its economic, regulatory, and institutional underpinnings" (13).

The World Bank's commitment to health outcomes and data collection were combined and crystallized with the Millennium Development Goals (MDGs). The MDGs were established at the Millennium Summit in September 2000, a series of targets to be reached by 2015 to address extreme poverty. Of the eight goals, five (Goals 1, 4, 5, 6, and 7) dealt with health, in particular: eradicating extreme poverty and hunger, reducing child mortality, improving maternal health, combating HIV/AIDS, malaria and other diseases, and ensuring environmental sustainability including halving the proportion of people without access to safe drinking water. While the MDGs reinforced the Bank's commitment to health outcomes, they did not focus on distribution. As such, there was concern that health outcomes would improve overall but not focus specifically on the poor (Fair 2008). While the World Bank's approach to health varied across countries (as detailed in the case-study Chaps. 4–6 and further examined in Chap. 7) the next WDR to address health in a major way did not come until over 10 years after the 1993 WDR, with the 2004 WDR: *Making Services Work for Poor People*.

The 2004 World Development Report: Pursuing Accountability and a Pro-growth, Pro-poor Agenda

The 2004 WDR provided a sharp refocusing of the World Bank's agenda on poor people and revisited the original goal of the "Washington Consensus," which had not quite materialized in the 1980s and 1990s: pro-growth and pro-poor policies (Williamson 2000). Then World Bank President Wolfensohn, in the foreword to the 2004 WDR discusses health in terms very different than those of the 1993 WDR and the MDGs. In direct response to the focus on numbers, the World Bank sought with this WDR, a more "human" approach: "Development is not just about money or even about numerical targets to be achieved by 2015, as important as those are. It is about people. The WDR focuses on basic services, particularly health, education, water, and sanitation, seeking ways of making them work for poor people. Too often, services fail poor people. These failures may be less spectacular than financial crises, but their effects are continuing and deep nonetheless" (xv). The recommendations are threefold: first, individual-oriented clinical services, population-oriented outreach, and family-oriented services. While the focus is still on individuals: as purchasers, coproducers, and monitors of health services this WDR does discuss not only individuals and families but also community programs. The long-standing emphasis on health as a basic need remains a running theme in the 2004 WDR, and while community programs are discussed, the framework is still market-oriented, characterized by individuals making choices, which was also the underpinning of earlier, market-oriented, individualist, and consumerist approaches such as user fees.

The logic remains decidedly economic and utilizes neoliberal tools: private sector involvement (especially via public–private partnerships), separation of functions, decentralization, and targeting. Government financing of services remains justified on the grounds of market failures, though there is an opening for its justification on human rights grounds in the 2004 WDR. More centrally, this WDR foregrounds accountability to poor people of social, including health, policies, and programs. However, while the 2004 WDR seeks to empower the poor by bringing them into the policy process, it also places additional responsibilities, and therefore burdens, on this already disadvantaged group to make sure that services are allocated and working appropriately.

2005 AND BEYOND: BACK TO BASICS IN HEALTH?

With the hiring of Jim Yong Kim as the World Bank's 12th president in 2012, there was much anticipation, especially for the Bank's work in health. Kim, a physician, and anthropologist, was a cofounder of a non-profit organization which sought to bring advanced medical care to the poorest areas of developing countries. As Fig. 2.1 demonstrates, while many other organizations have entered into the global health financing arena the World Bank has maintained its commitments to health in absolute terms, and often works in cooperation with bilateral and other agencies, allowing it to maintain its status as a normative, technical, and financial authority in health. Since 2007, the World Bank has focused on health systems strengthening, further emphasizing its focus on institutional development and the connection between systems and outcomes.

Altogether, the World Bank has circled back in its discourse: in the 1980s, it focused on government involvement in health, though this was never truly implemented in deed. It then espoused a more individualist, market-oriented approach to health, and is reaffirming its commitment to promoting universalism. Importantly, this universalism is to be achieved not only by governments but still with the participation of the private sector and in particular, public–private partnerships (Stephens 2007). The World Bank has consistently argued that this is where its expertise lies, and where it has the most to offer: in cost-effectiveness and the financial aspects of health sector reform. Together with the case–study analyses presented in the following chapters, this suggests that the World Bank is now promoting universalist ends, but via policy tools that many consider neoliberal: separation of functions, targeting, decentralization, etc.

Today, the World Bank champions universalism. A review piece published as part of its "Universal Health Coverage Studies Series" notes that "universal health coverage (UHC) interventions in low- and middle-income countries improve access to health care. It also shows, though less convincingly, that UHC often has a positive effect on financial protection, and that, in some cases, it seems to have a positive impact on health status." (Giedion et al. 2013). Universalism is also clearly emphasized in the third of the seventeen Sustainable Development Goals (SDGs) for 2030, which replaced the MDGs which themselves expired in 2015 (UN 2015b), The SDGs consist of 17 goals with 169 global targets, spearheaded by the UN through a deliberative process involving member states, civil society, and other organizations. Among the targets of the third goal are: "Achieve universal health coverage, including financial risk protection, access to quality essential health-care services and access to safe, effective, quality and affordable essential medicines and vaccines for all" (UN 2015a). Universal access to health is a cause also generally championed by Kim, as he states in a speech given in 2016: "The evidence tells us there is no better prescription for health, wealth, and security as a health care system that provides equal coverage to every single person" (Bank 2016). The World Bank then appears to be circling back to its original goals as outlined in its 1980 health policy paper, where it embraced the goal of universal access to basic health services and committed to providing help towards that goal. However, how and whether these intentions will materialize into implementation by the World Bank, as well as where and how, remains to be seen.

REFERENCES

Abbasi, K. (1999). The World Bank and world health: Interview with Richard Feachem. *BMJ (Clinical Research ed.), 318*(7192), 1206–1208.

Anand, S., & Hanson, K. (1998). DALYs: Efficiency versus equity. *World Development, 26*(2), 307–310.

Antia, N. (1994). The World Development Report 1993: A prescription for health disaster. *Social Scientist, 22*, 147–151.

Bank, W. (1975). *Health.* Washington, DC: World Bank.

Bank, W. (1980). *Health sector policy paper* (World Bank). Washington, DC.

Bank, W. (1993). *World development report: Investing in health.* Washington, DC: World Bank.

Bank, W. (1997). *Sector strategy: Health, nutrition, & population.* Washington, DC: World Bank Group.

Bank, W. (2016). Remarks by World Bank Group President Jim Yong Kim at the Universal Health Coverage in Africa Side Event. August 26, 2016. http://www.worldbank.org/en/news/speech/2016/08/26/remarks-by-world-bank-group-president-jim-yong-kim-at-the-universal-health-coverage-in-africa-side-event. Accessed 14 Jan 2017.

Bryant, R. L., & Bailey, S. (1997). *Third world political ecology.* New York: Psychology Press.

Chhibber, A., Batemen, D., Hutcheson, T., Krumm, K., Oliveros, G., Rocha, R., et al. (1991). *The use of bank lending instruments: The inter-relation between adjustment and investment lending annual review of development effectiveness,* February 7, 1991. World Bank Archives.

Coburn, C., Restivo, M., & Shandra, J. M. (2015). The World Bank and child mortality in Sub-Saharan Africa. *Sociology of Development, 1*(3), 348–373.

Cornia, G. A., Jolly, R., & Stewart, F. (1987). *Adjustment with a human face. Vol. 1: Protecting the vulnerable and growth.* Oxford.

Deacon, B. (2007). *Global social policy and governance.* Thousand Oaks: Sage.

Fair, M. (2008). *From population lending to HNP Results: The evolution of the World Bank's strategies in health, nutrition and population.* Washington, DC: World Bank.

Giedion, U., Alfonso, E. A., & Díaz, Y. (2013). *The impact of universal coverage schemes in the developing world: A review of the existing evidence.* Washington, DC: World Bank.

Hutchful, E. (1994). 'Smoke and mirrors': The World Bank's social dimensions of adjustment (SDA) programme. *Review of African Political Economy, 21*(62), 569–584.

IHME. (2016). *Development assistance for health database 1990–2015.* Seattle, United States: Institute for Health Metrics and Evaluation.

Irvine, A., Drew, P., & Sainsbury, R. (2013). 'Am I not answering your questions properly?' Clarification, adequacy and responsiveness in semi-structured telephone and face-to-face interviews. *Qualitative Research, 13*(1), 87–106.

Jayarajah, C., Branson, W., & Sen, B. (1996). *Social dimensions of adjustment: World Bank experience, 1980–1993.* Washington, DC.

Kaasch, A. (2015). *Shaping global health policy: Global social policy actors and ideas about health care systems.* New York: Springer.

Lopez, A. D. (2005). The evolution of the Global Burden of Disease framework for disease, injury and risk factor quantification: Developing the evidence base for national, regional and global public health action. *Globalization and Health, 1*(1), 1.

McMichael, P. (2016). *Development and social change: A global perspective.* Thousand Oaks: Sage.

Paalman, M., Bekedam, H., Hawken, L., & Nyheim, D. (1998). A critical review of priority setting in the health sector: The methodology of the 1993 World Development Report. *Health Policy and Planning, 13*(1), 13–31.

Peet, R. (2003). *Unholy trinity: The IMF, World Bank and WTO.* London: Zed Books.

Ruger, J. P. (2005). The changing role of the World Bank in global health. *American Journal of Public Health, 95*(1), 60–70.

Shandra, C. L., Shandra, J. M., & London, B. (2011). World bank structural adjustment, water, and sanitation: A cross-national analysis of child mortality in Sub-Saharan Africa. *Organization & Environment, 24*(2), 107–129.

Shandra, C. L., Shandra, J. M., & London, B. (2012). The international monetary fund, structural adjustment, and infant mortality: A cross-national analysis of Sub-Saharan Africa. *Journal of Poverty, 16*(2), 194–219.

Shandra, J. M., Nobles, J., London, B., & Williamson, J. B. (2004). Dependency, democracy, and infant mortality: A quantitative, cross-national analysis of less developed countries. *Social Science and Medicine, 59*(2), 321–333.

Shandra, J. M., Shandra, C. L., & London, B. (2010). Do non-governmental organizations impact health? A cross-national analysis of infant mortality. *International Journal of Comparative Sociology, 51*(1–2), 137–164.

Stephens, N. (2007). Collecting data from elites and ultra elites: telephone and face-to-face interviews with macroeconomists. *Qualitative Research, 7*(2), 203–216.

UN (2015a). Sustainable development goal, goal 3: Ensure healthy lives and promote well-being for all at all ages. http://www.un.org/sustainabledevelopment/health/. Accessed 11 Feb 2017.

UN (2015b). Sustainaible development goals. http://www.un.org/sustainabledevelopment/sustainable-development-goals/. Accessed 11 Feb 2017.

Williamson, J. (2000). What should the World Bank think about the Washington Consensus? *The World Bank Research Observer, 15*(2), 251–264.

CHAPTER 3

The State of Health in Latin America: Trends and Correlates of Health Expenditures

INTRODUCTION

Understanding the effect of the World Bank on Latin American health systems and expenditures requires a bird's-eye view of regional trends and the factors influencing public commitments to health in the region. This chapter contributes to an ongoing scholarly debate about the effect of globalization on the welfare state. However, much of the existing research has focused on mature welfare states and has pooled all domains of social spending together. Consequently, there has been little attention paid to how IFIs influence health expenditures in developing countries. In this chapter, I situate the effect of the World Bank on health spending in Latin America within the literature on social spending and globalization, asking (1) How has health expenditure changed over time in the region? (2) What factors account for changes in health spending in Latin America—is it primarily domestic demographic factors as highlighted by public health scholars, or is it also domestic political and economic conditions as highlighted by political scientists and sociologists? (3) Finally, to what extent can regional trends in health spending be explained by powerful international actors and the integration of Latin American countries into the global economic and political system, as suggested by the globalization literature?

In this chapter, I examine the trends and correlates of public and private expenditures on health care in Latin America and the Caribbean between 1995 and 2009. I *first* examine trends in health expenditure in

© The Author(s) 2017
S. Noy, *Banking on Health*, DOI 10.1007/978-3-319-61765-7_3

the region over this time period. *Second*, I investigate the applicability of national political, economic, and demographic explanatory factors identified by existing welfare state research, which has focused on the developed country context, to Latin American and Caribbean countries. *Third*, I examine whether economic globalization creates downward pressures on health spending in Latin America, as suggested by "race to the bottom" arguments or whether globalization might push citizens to demand more social protections of their government. *Fourth*, I use data on World Bank conditions on loans to empirically test suggestions of IFIs as neoliberal, coercive institutions which use conditioned loans to mandate reductions in public health spending. This analysis engages with assertions that while the World Bank may have pushed neoliberal reductions in public spending in the 1980s and early 1990s this approach has been replaced by a new human rights and poverty-alleviation paradigm. More information on data limitations and decisions can be found in the Methodological Appendix.

BACKGROUND

Examining the predictors and correlates of health expenditure in Latin America and the Caribbean is important for several reasons: *first*, it provides an opportunity to examine whether the predictors of overall social spending apply to the health sector; *second*, it allows us to compare the predictors of health spending in more developed countries, the site of most of the research on health systems and spending, to a developing region; *third*, much of the research on health systems in the developing is typically conducted in the context of single country or small-N comparative studies. An examination of the entire region of Latin America and the Caribbean over 15 years allows a systematic examination of the correlates of health spending in the entire region. *Fourth*, the use of several health spending measures, capturing overall, public, and private spending as well as the public-private mix in health financing, provides a more nuanced account of how globalization and international financial institutions as well as national demographic and economic changes are affecting different dimensions of health expenditure. I preface the regional analysis presented in this chapter by elaborating on the relevant theoretical approaches and literatures discussed in Chap. 1 which form the basis of the empirical expectations for this quantitative, regional analysis of health expenditures in Latin America.

Extending Welfare State Theories to Latin America

Latin American countries are assembling and reconfiguring their social policies in a markedly different context than the mature welfare states of Europe and other developed countries. Welfare state development in most developed countries occurred in the absence of IFIs, and under very different circumstances than those faced by developing countries. Nonetheless, the long tradition of research by sociologists, political scientists, and policy scholars has sought to understand the origins and consequences of state-sponsored social protections and government social spending may help illuminate the process of health sector reform in developing countries (Marshall 2009; Moore 1993; Esping-Andersen 1990, 1999).

This literature outlines three main theoretical approaches to the welfare state development: (1) the *logic of industrialism* approach which posits that differences in welfare state efforts and welfare state development are by-products of economic development and its demographic and social organizational consequences; (2) the *power resources* approach which identifies the distribution of organizational power between labor organizations and left parties on the one hand and center and right-wing political forces on the other hand as primary determinants of differences in the size and distributive impact of the welfare state; and finally, (3) the *state-centric* approach which is focused on the policy-making role of bureaucrats (Amenta et al. 2001; Huber and Stephens 2001; Ragin 1994). Of these, the logic of industrialism arguments and the power resources approach have been most successful in explaining changes in social expenditures, while the state-centric approach has aided scholars in examining the development of specific policies.

Pressures that have been identified as contemporary "threats" to the welfare state include globalization, global competition, and the continuing change in family and demographic structure. These influences are global in their reach but might be most strongly felt in Latin America and other developing countries given their precarious economic position and political instability (Rudra 2007). States are adapting their policies in response to these new conditions, and developing countries are increasingly pursuing more expansive welfare programs (Pierson 2004; Mesa-Lago 2006). The logic of industrialism approach which highlights the importance of economic growth and demographics together with the power resources approach which suggests that left party power is important to social spending merit attention in the Latin American context. While these theories were developed based on mature welfare states, investigations of the effects of globalization and global pressures require comparative consideration: are they truly global in their influence on social spending cross-regionally? While the welfare state literature has traditionally focused on developed countries, more recent work has begun examining welfare state development in Latin America and other developing regions (Brooks and Manza 2008; Pierson 2005; Pribble 2008; Rudra 2007; Franzoni Martínez 2008; Noy 2011; Huber et al. 2008; Huber and Stephens 2012).

The process of building welfare states in developing countries may be markedly different than that of European and other developed countries: *first*, in many Latin American countries, governments are developing their social policies amidst national political instability. *Second*, welfare states in developing countries are being built in an era of globalization and economic openness, with domestic policy being heavily influenced by international financial institutions, namely the World Bank and the IMF (de Mesa and Mesa-Lago 2006).

Scholars question whether it is possible for welfare states, of which health policy and spending is an increasingly large component, to be assembled in developing countries given these adverse conditions. For instance, much of the population is not yet commodified—that is, integrated into the formal labor market—where early welfare states typically developed in an effort to decommodify labor. Furthermore, many governments in developing nations are weak and unstable. *Third*, globalization is associated with free markets, which may hinder state social provision. Rudra (2007) suggests several reasons why we should expect governments to build welfare states in developing countries despite adverse conditions: first, risk and uncertainty are present in all countries, not only developing ones, and developing countries are in a position of "maximum uncertainty," which welfare states can help address and attenuate. Second, social reactions to the market and market instability are present in all countries including developing countries, not only in the OECD context. Third, the recent spread of democracy may encourage demand for welfare states among citizens. In addition, the lack of commodified status is not necessarily a barrier to the construction of welfare states as developing country governments and citizens look to the example set by developed countries. Further, while organized labor played an important role in the development of welfare states in many Organization for Economic Co-Operation and Development (OECD) countries, labor is often weakly organized in less developed countries (LDCs), and there is no minimum income. This, rather than discouraging state involvement, may push the state to take center stage in decommodification.[1] As a response to their increased vulnerability to the vagaries of the market in the face of increased economic openness, we may witness an increase in social programs and spending across sectors (e.g. health, unemployment, education, pensions, etc.) (Brooks and Manza 2008; Rodrik 1997).

When extending classic theories of welfare state development to developing country contexts, where these limited welfare states are sometimes labeled welfare regimes (Franzoni Martínez 2008), the "logic of industrialism" approach is seemingly the most appropriate as it relates to processes of economic development and the accompanying demographic changes. It proposes that we witness convergence between countries as they industrialize, as evidenced by lower fertility rates, higher divorce rates, and more opportunities for minority groups. This in turn increases demand for welfare states and the likelihood that states will supply social protections. With the preponderance of "democratic capitalism" in developing countries, Glatzer and Rueschemeyer (2004) argue we can expect a third transformation—the addition of social welfare to economic liberalization and political democratization. This is likely because social welfare policies are correlated with economic growth (as posited by the "logic of industrialism" welfare state theory). In addition, the classic welfare states in Europe flourished in countries that were economically open. Furthermore, welfare state policies have historically been associated with the trajectory of democratization.

The "power resources" approach, which has gained ascendancy in welfare state theory, focuses on the importance of left parties and veto points (Huber and Stephens 2001; Noy 2011), may also be important to understanding the dynamics of health systems and health policy reform. However, the dynamics of democratization and authoritarian-democratic oscillations in Latin America in the 1980s and 1990s have hampered the establishment of long-term left-party influence and traditions in many countries. Finally, the third major theory in the welfare state canon, together with the "logic of industrialism" and "power resources" approaches, is a "state-centric" approach that focuses on bureaucrats and state autonomy in shaping different trajectories of welfare state development. This approach, which focuses on the states' role in shaping reforms, may be particularly important for understanding the ways in which states reform their health systems in light of recommendations and pressures from the World Bank and IFIs.

The current state of public social spending and welfare state reform in Latin America provides an exciting arena for welfare state research. According to Huber (2005), who defines "welfare state" as a system of social protection that provides some form of social security coverage to at least 60% of the economically active population, only six Latin American countries (Argentina, Brazil, Chile, Costa Rica, Cuba, and Uruguay) and three Caribbean countries (the Bahamas, Barbados, and Jamaica)[2] could boast a welfare state as of 1980 and may be better described as welfare regimes. While Latin American countries do not typically have large welfare states, countries in the region "have long had occupational based welfare systems modeled along European lines, with defined-benefit pension plans, health services, and family allowances" (Kaufman and Segura-Ubiergo 2001). In addition, welfare state building has a long history in several Latin American countries beginning in the 1920s (in Argentina, Chile, and Uruguay), with a second wave in the 1930s and 1940s (including Brazil, Colombia, Costa Rica, Mexico, Panama, and Venezuela).

Latin America offers a unique opportunity to examine welfare state development and the determinants of government social spending due to the conditions of the so-called "lost decade" of the 1980s coupled with a legacy of social protection and a more recent history of social medicine. Marked by economic crisis and recession, and followed by inflation in many instances, the 1980s were a period of political instability in the form of democratic-authoritarian transitions and neoliberal pressures from international financial institutions. Furthermore, social policy in Latin America has undergone profound changes in the 1980s and 1990s, largely in the direction of state retrenchment and market expansions in the financing, delivery, and administration of social services and transfer payments (Huber and Stephens 2012; Mesa-Lago and Müller 2002; de Mesa and Mesa-Lago 2006).

Previous considerations of social spending and welfare states in Latin America suggest that there are important demographic, political, economic, and global factors that systematically influence social spending. Particularly, integration into global markets, left party influence, level of economic development, and trajectories of democratization have been identified by different theoretical, case-study, and quantitative analyses as being important influences on social spending. The systematic quantitative analyses of the determinants of health spending presented in this chapter serve to set up the case study research in subsequent chapters.

In particular, this chapter helps clarify the World Bank's effect on health expenditures alongside an analysis of which domestic economic, social, and political conditions as well as which facets of globalization are important for health spending at the regional level.

Development and Comparative Health Systems

The comparative health systems research highlights that national health care systems have evolved in the context of specific political, economic, and social histories and, as a result, the ways they finance, organize, and deliver health care vary widely. Yet, this literature also underscores the fact that many countries face remarkably similar health challenges (Mesa-Lago 2008; McGuire 2010). These universal challenges are largely economic and demographic. *First*, economic changes associated with development result in demographic changes which require different health responses. Overall, as countries develop population growth slows, fertility declines and life expectancy increases. As infectious diseases are increasingly controlled (with increased urbanization, the improvement of public health and sanitation systems, and vaccination) and people live longer, chronic and degenerative diseases become more salient causes of death. This shift in demographic and disease profiles, a shift in countries' epidimeological profiles, is currently under way in most developing nations and is seen as being completed in developed countries who continue to adapt to these changing conditions. Chronic diseases are significantly more costly to treat than acute ailments and changing family structures also pose challenges for elder care. *Second*, globalization may affect health given the shared economic challenges associated with global interconnectedness (economic crises, the so-called "race to the bottom," health and its relationship to labor pools and economic productivity via human capital investments) but also the spread of disease across borders with increased travel and transport cross-nationally, possibly spawning new pandemics.

Globalization, Neoliberalism, International Financial Institutions, and Health Spending

Globalization scholars have argued that neoliberal policies propelled by international financial institutions have had detrimental effects on welfare states and social—and by extension health—spending. However, this claim has been subject to little empirical scrutiny when compared to the wealth of research on the implications of neoliberalism for trade, monetary, and fiscal policy (Babb 2005; Fourcade-Gourinchas and Babb 2002; Portes and Hoffman 2003; Weyland 2005, 2006; Murillo 2002; Teichman 2004). Scholars have argued that powerful international financial institutions (IFIs), most notably the World Bank and IMF, work conditions into their loans to push national governments to reduce social spending (Armada et al. 2001; Birn and Dmitrienko 2005). These loans, desperately sought by countries in economic crisis, and their accompanying conditions, allow IFIs to dictate reductions in social spending and restructuring of social sectors. However, some existing research has argued that conditionality is not always unilaterally dictated by IFIs, in part because IFIs have limited ability to enforce compliance (Weyland 2005; see also Vreeland 2003).

While scholars have asserted that loan conditionality drives down public spending and particularly social spending in developing countries this claim has received comparatively little empirical attention (Babb 2005; see Vreeland 2006 for a discussion of IMF conditionality; and Weyland 2006 for some discussion of IFI involvement in social sector reforms in Latin America). There is some evidence that the World Bank and the IMF, largely via loan conditionality, have pushed for privatization of public companies and holdings (Babb 2005) but little information about their impact on health. Limited existing research indicates that engagement with IFIs has no effect on social spending in Latin America, and may even boost health spending (Noy 2011). However, no research has examined whether conditions on health loans may limit public health expenditures, despite the fact that this has been identified as one of the primary pathways of IFI influence.

Convergence in Health

One pervasive question in the study of global health is whether we will witness greater convergence in health expenditures and outcomes across countries with the intensification of globalization. Convergence in health outcomes suggests possible convergence in underlying health systems, which are themselves influenced by political, economic, and social changes and globalization (Kawachi and Kennedy 1997, 1999; Kawachi et al. 1999; Noy and Sprage-Jones 2016). Therefore, there is a tension between suggestions of globalization as promoting convergence and the continued particularity of national approaches to social protection.

While recognizing the distinctive features of national health systems, some scholars have proposed that health care systems in developing countries are converging (Elling 1994; Mechanic 1975; Mechanic and Rochefort 1996; Beckfield et al. 2013). The literature on health systems in the developing world has also suggested convergence, with some scholars citing globalization as largely responsible (Armada et al. 2001; Berman 1995; Noy and McManus 2015; for a more general argument about convergence across sectors in Latin America see Murillo 2002). The examination of health systems is especially timely in Latin American countries, given increased industrialization, modernization, and urbanization. More recently, integration into the world economy and expansion of markets and economic growth following deep recession in the 1980s also motivates such research. In particular, research on the ways in which health systems are adapting to and coping with shifting epidemiological burdens associated with development (the rise in non-communicable diseases such as heart disease and cancer), in addition to the traditional challenges associated with communicable diseases and malnutrition (such as high rates of infant mortality, dysentery, and tuberculosis), affects our understandings of the relationship between health sector reform, globalization, and health outcomes.

Previous Research on Social and Health Spending in Latin America

Research to date on social and health spending in Latin America has largely focused on the implications of democratization for social spending, with some attention to convergence (cf. Avelino et al. 2005; Brown and Hunter 2004; Huber and Stephens 2012; Huber et al. 2008). Some studies have found that democratization increases social spending (see Avelino et al. 2005 on social spending; Huber and Stephens 2012 on health, education and social spending; Huber et al. 2008 on health and education as well as health and social security expenditure; Brown and Hunter 2004 on education spending) while others have not found such an effect (Noy 2011; Kaufman and Segura-Ubiergo 2001). This research largely relies on data through the 1990s and focuses on social spending as a whole.

This chapter innovates and extends these existing studies in two important ways: *first*, few studies have examined the effects of IFIs on health spending and to my knowledge, this is the first study to examine the effect of loan conditionality on health spending in Latin America. *Second*, I use a later time period which is characteristic of increased involvement of the World Bank in developing countries' health sectors. This decision of time period is motivated largely by data reliability and availability. While there is data on public health spending as a percent of GDP for earlier time periods (even dating back to the 1970s for some countries) from Economic Commission for Latin America and the Caribbean (ECLAC/CEPAL) it provides only a limited number of measures and it is only available for some countries and is somewhat unreliable as elaborated in the book's Methodological Appendix. *Third*, I examine several measures of health expenditures which capture various dimensions of health expenditures and systems. Public spending on health as a percent of GDP has been an especially popular measure but it delivers only a partial picture of the dynamics of health spending, and provides little information on how health is prioritized relative to other social spending by the government and what proportion of spending is private, both potentially influenced by IFI pressures.

DATA AND MEASURES OF HEALTH EXPENDITURES

The analyses that follow rely on six measures of health expenditures: (1) total health spending per capita, (2) total health spending as a percent of GDP, (3) public health spending as a percent of GDP, (4) private health spending as a percent of GDP, (5) public health spending as a percent of total health spending and (6) public health spending as a percent of total public spending. Each of these measures taps a different dimension of state involvement in health and provides different information about the government's role and relationship to the provision of health. The measures include absolute expenditures, expenditures relative to national income and other social policy domains, and public expenditures as a share of all health expenditures. Descriptive statistics for all variables used in the analysis can be found in the Methodological Appendix.

Health Spending Per Capita

The first measure of health expenditure I utilize is total health expenditure per capita, adjusted for purchasing power parity (PPP). Total health expenditure is the sum of public and private health expenditure and covers the provision of health services (preventive and curative), family planning activities, nutrition activities, and emergency aid designated for health. It does not include the provision of water and sanitation. Establishing purchasing power parity, where one dollar purchases the same quantity of goods and services in all countries, allows for cross-country comparisons free of price and exchange rate distortions. Total health expenditure per capita is a general measure of the size of the health sector, and it is especially useful as an indicator of whether overall health expenditures are increasing or remain stable over time, weighted by population, which varies widely across Latin American countries, therefore providing a more comparable measure.

Total Health Spending as a Percent of GDP

The second measure of health expenditure also begins with the sum of public and private health expenditures but is then divided by the size of the economy. This is the conventional measure of total health spending as a percent of GDP, widely used in studies of health expenditures. This measure has several advantages as an overall indicator of the size of the health sector. First, trends in this measure indicate how fast the health sector is growing relative to overall economic growth. Second, this measure is especially useful for cross-national comparisons in Latin America and the Caribbean, because GDP varies widely but the proportion of GDP accounted for by the health sector is much more comparable.

Public Spending on Health as a Percent of GDP

Third, I examine public spending on health as a percent of GDP, which provides an indicator of public resources devoted to health relative to the size of the economy. Public health expenditure consists of spending from government (central and local) budgets, external borrowings and grants (including donations from international agencies and non-governmental organizations), and social (or compulsory) health insurance funds.

Private Spending on Health as a Percent of GDP

Fourth, I examine private spending on health as a percent of GDP. This provides an indication of private spending on health relative to the size of the economy, and it serves as a complement to the analysis of public spending on health as a percent of GDP. Private health expenditure includes direct household (out-of-pocket) spending, private insurance, charitable donations, and direct service payments by private corporations. Taken together, public and private spending on health as a percent of GDP provide an indication of the allocation of private and public resources to health as compared to the size of the economy and how these are changing over time.

Public Health Expenditure as a Percent of Total Health Expenditure

Fifth, I examine public health expenditure as a percent of total health expenditure. This measure provides information on the public-private mix of health care financing. The public share of health spending is arguably the most direct indicator of government commitment to the public provision of health care. In addition, information about the share of health spending that is public provides important information in light of findings about increased privatization in European nations and suggestions of such a trend in Latin America and other developing countries by those proposing "race to the bottom" globalization.

Spending on Health as a Percent of Total Government Spending

Sixth, and finally, I examine public spending on health as a percent of total government spending. This measure is an important indicator of how health is prioritized relative to public spending in other domains and allows an assessment of the state's commitment to health relative to other public spending domains and the status of the health sector among the government's priorities. That is, it might be that overall spending on health is increasing but at a slower rate than other domains of social spending (e.g. education). This measure then provides additional insight on how Latin American governments view their role in health provision compared to other policy domains. Examining the share of total government spending devoted to health along with the share of health spending that is public, the third measure, allows us an assessment of the status and structure of government participation in the health care system.

TRENDS IN SPENDING

Trends in health expenditure are displayed in Fig. 3.1. Figure 3.1 indicates that average health spending per capita has increased in Latin America and the Caribbean between 1995 and 2009, doubling over this time period from $362 to $740. Private health expenditure kept pace with economic growth over this time period, fluctuating between 2.9 and 3.1% of GDP. Public health spending as a percent of GDP as well as total health spending as a percent of GDP increased over this time period: from 3.2% to 3.9% and 6.1% to 7% respectively. Public health spending as a percent of total public expenditure decreased, but this has not been a linear process: it begins at 13.8%, showing variability but an overall decreasing until its low point at 12.2% in 2006 and increasing to 13% in 2009. Finally, public health expenditure as a percentage of total health expenditure shows a slight increase beginning in 2004: between 1995 and 2004 it is at around 52%, increasing to 55.6% by 2009.

Figure 3.1 demonstrates rapidly rising health expenditures per capita and growth in the health sector in Latin America during this period. Increases in public sector expenditures are outpacing increases in private

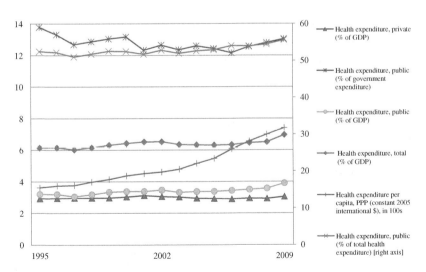

Fig. 3.1   Trends in health spending in Latin America and the Caribbean. *Data Source* World Bank Health, Nutrition and Population (HNP) Statistics

expenditures, resulting in an increase in the public share of the health sector. In addition, public spending increased faster than GDP during this period, and the share of total government expenditures allocated to health fluctuated between 12% and 14%, and was at its highest point in 1995, at the start of this period. As for the public-private mix, over half of total health spending is public and shows a slight increase over this time period. This is contrary to assertions of state retrenchment in social and health spending in the context of neoliberalism (cf. Glatzer and Rueschemeyer 2004). These trends suggest that health expenditure is rising, and in particular, public resources devoted to health have increased in Latin America. This provides cause to doubt the prevailing narrative of neoliberal IFIs limiting government expenditures on health and other social services though it does not provide direct evidence as to their effect. In the following section, I investigate the correlates and drivers of health expenditures.

REGRESSION SAMPLE AND METHOD

I use time-series cross-section models in order to examine the effect of IFI activity and the other economic, political and globalization indicators on health spending. The Methodological Appendix contains more detailed information on the sample, and corrections for autocorrelation and Methodological Appendix Table A.1 contains detailed information on the country-years included in the analysis.

EXPECTATIONS

In my expectations for the regression analysis, I draw from the literature on welfare state development, health sector reform in developing countries and globalization. The Methodological Appendix Table A.2 provides descriptive statistics for the variables in the regression analysis.

Economic and Demographic Conditions

Following the logic of industrialism approach, economic and demographic variables are most closely associated with trajectories of development arguments. I expect country wealth, elderly population and unemployment to positively affect overall health (both per capita and as a percent of GDP) and private health spending as a percent of GDP.

I expect elderly population and unemployment to positively affect all spending measures, but especially overall and public health spending.

Political Structure

I expect both democratization and left party seat share to be positively associated with public health spending across measures: as a percent of GDP, as a percent of total health spending and as a percent of total government expenditure. In particular, I expect a larger left party presence to be associated with an increase in public health spending as a percent of total health expenditure given left party concerns with social protections.

Economic Globalization

Given race to the bottom arguments, I expect globalization in the form of trade openness and foreign direct investment to be associated with a reduction in public health spending as a percent of total health spending but also public health spending as a percent of GDP. Relatedly, economic globalization might be associated with higher overall health spending and private health spending as it may create markets for more expensive medical treatments for those who can afford to pay for them.

World Bank Loan Conditionality

The literature on the effect of IFIs, namely the IMF and the World Bank, on social spending suggests two conflicting expectations: on the one hand, the globalization literature and especially the literature examining IFIs has focused on the homogenizing effects of globalization, operating both economically and financially (via "race to the bottom" competition for foreign investment and trade competitiveness) and politically and ideologically (via neoliberalism in the form of downwards pressures on the size of the public sector and public program diffused in loans and IFI projects). IFIs are also concerned with investment in human capital in the quest for prolonged economic development, necessitating a healthy and educated workforce which could be achieved by increasing public social spending, particularly on education and health. Given that loan conditionality has been identified as an important tool for the World Bank's effect on national social spending I expect conditions on World Bank loans and World Bank health-related loans to be associated with

lower public spending on health, both as a percent of GDP but especially for public health spending as a percent of total health spending.
In addition, given discussions of IFIs including recommendations and
conditions of economic openness in their loans this may translate to the
presence of additional private providers and insurers in health. Therefore
I expect World Bank conditions to be associated with higher private
health spending as a percent of GDP.

REGRESSION RESULTS

Table 3.1 displays results from the first time-series cross-section regressions. The autocorrelation parameter indicates that there is trending in
these data, which is expected given the slow change in national policies
and expenditures—that is, spending levels are path-dependent and durable. The results provide support for the logic of industrialism approach
within the welfare state literature and the economic and demographic
shifts in the health system literature, especially for overall health expenditure as a percent of GDP and per capita and private and public spending
as a percent of GDP. These literatures both point to the importance of
economic performance and demographic composition. Richer countries
show higher spending per capita (note that this variable, along with left
party is lagged by one year) but as a percent of GDP, their spending is
lower, on average, all else equal.

Economic and Demographic Conditions

Per capita spending on health is higher in richer countries in Latin
America and the Caribbean. Though the effect on health spending
as a percent of GDP is negative, supplementary analyses reveal that at
the bivariate level richer countries spend more on health as a percent of
GDP. However, when including the effect of elderly population then
the effect of national wealth per capita is associated with lower spending. In addition, this negative effect of GDP on total health spending
as a percent of GDP is not apparent in the fixed effects model presented
in Table 3.A.2 (in Appendix A of this chapter) either. Similarly, higher
GDP per capita is associated with lower public health expenditure as a
percent of total government expenditure, which might appear counter
intuitive. Once again, however, this effect is not robust and undiscernible
in Table 3.A.1 (in Appendix A of this chapter).

Table 3.1 Results for time-series cross-section regressions with panel corrected standard errors with an AR(1) correction of health expenditure in Latin America and the Caribbean, N = 226

	Health expenditure per capita	Total health expenditure as a % of GDP	Public health expenditure as a % of GDP	Private health expenditure as a % of GDP	Public health expenditure as a % of total health expenditure	Public health expenditure as a % of government expenditure
Economic and Demographic Conditions/Logic of Industrialism						
GDP per Capita $_{t-1}$	5.233***	−0.008+	−0.002	−0.004	−0.007	−0.019+
	(0.393)	(0.004)	(0.004)	(0.002)	(0.028)	(0.010)
Unemployment	−2.066	0.044	0.033	0.021	−0.077	−0.119
	(1.891)	(0.027)	(0.021)	(0.015)	(0.158)	(0.081)
Elderly Population	51.909***	0.424***	0.193+	0.211**	0.142	0.357
	(9.048)	(0.105)	(0.111)	(0.081)	(0.737)	(0.263)
Political Structure/Power Resources						
Democracy score	0.125	0.051	0.053+	−0.024	0.568+	0.159
	(3.61)	(0.047)	(0.029)	(0.028)	(0.327)	(0.160)
Left Party Seats $_{t-1}$	0.305	0.007	0.003	0.002	0.018	−0.025
	(0.618)	(0.007)	(0.005)	(0.004)	(0.045)	(0.021)
Globalization						
Trade openness	−0.049	−0.001	0.004	−0.006*	0.080*	0.012
	(0.227)	(0.003)	(0.003)	(0.003)	(0.037)	(0.011)
Foreign direct investment	0.687	0.007	0.001	0.004	−0.025	−0.018
	(0.759)	(0.008)	(0.004)	(0.006)	(0.054)	(0.034)
Autocorrelation (ρ)	0.85	0.80	0.85	0.86	0.85	0.76

Notes: *Source* World Bank Health, Nutrition and Population Statistics. Sources for the explanatory variables are detailed in the methodological appendix ***p < 0.001, **p < 0.01, *p < 0.05, + p < 0.10 (two-tailed tests). Each cell reports the unstandardized coefficient, with the standard error in parentheses. Constants calculated but not reported All models were estimated in Stata 12.1

The effect of unemployment on health expenditures is neither statistically significant nor is it consistent in its direction in Table 3.1 though it does have a positive effect on total and public health spending as a percent of GDP in the fixed and random effects models (see Tables 3.A.1 and 3.A.2 in this chapter's appendix).

A higher percentage of people 65 years and older, that is, a higher proportion of elderly population, is associated with higher spending across measures (see also Tables 3.A.1 and 3.A.2 in this chapter's appendix). This effect is statistically significant for per capita spending and makes sense given the higher costs of care, on average, for this segment of the population. Table 3.1 indicates a one percent increase in the percentage of elderly population is associated with an additional $52 (PPP, 2005 International$) in per capita spending, all else equal. A higher proportion of elderly population is also associated with higher total health spending as a percent of GDP and private spending as a percent of GDP but also marginally statistically significant (at the 0.10 level) for public health spending and is positive (though not always statistically significant) across outcomes, all else equal.

Political Structure

In terms of the effects of political factors, and those predicted to matter based on the power resources welfare state approach, I find a positive, but not statistically significant, relationship between left party seats and most of the health spending outcomes. The exception is a negative (again, not statistically significant—indeed the standard error is almost the size of the coefficient) effect of left party seats on health expenditure as a percentage of total government expenditure. Democratization, on the other hand, is found to have a marginally and statistically significant effect on public health expenditure as a percent of GDP and on public health expenditure as a percent of total health expenditure, all else equal. Democratization appears to, therefore, be associated with higher public spending (both as a percent of GDP and as a percent of total health spending), all else equal, as suggested by existing health systems research and by the power resources approach in the welfare state literature for general social spending.

Economic Globalization

Interestingly trade openness is associated with lower private health spending as a percent of GDP (in Table 3.1 but also in Table 3.A.1), a statistically significant effect. However, trade openness is also associated with higher public health spending as a percent of total health spending (also apparent in Table 3.A.2) but also with higher public health spending as a percent of GDP and public health spending as a percent of total public spending, though its effect on the latter is not statistically significant (and neither are significant in the fixed and random effects models, Tables 3.A.1 and A.2). This provides some support for contentions of governments upping social provision in the face of globalization. Foreign direct investment does not appear to have an effect on health spending across outcomes.

World Bank Loan Conditionality

Table 3.2 provides results for models which examine the effects of conditions on all World Bank loans and followed by conditions only on health and social sector loans on these same health outcomes, with and without controls (that is, in bivariate and multivariate models). The expectation is that the World Bank, with its neoliberal approach, will drive down public spending. However, given the refocusing of World Bank discourse on investment in human capital in the 1990s and beyond, the time period of these data, we may not see such an effect. Surprisingly, I find no evidence that conditionality affects health expenditures. None of the coefficient estimates for the two covariates measuring the total number of conditions and the number of conditions on health and other social sector loans are statistically significant, whether in the bivariate or multivariate context. The estimates are not consistently positive or negative, and all are small in magnitude. Overall, therefore, contrary to the expectations of the World Bank as a neoliberal, coercive behemoth, leveraging conditions on loans to drive down social expenditures. World Bank conditions do not appear to be driving down health spending (again, in contrast to accounts of neoliberal, coercive IFIs) nor are they associated with higher health spending (more consistent with discourse about World Bank pushes to increase health spending as investment in human capital and/or in line with the Millennium Development Goals).

Table 3.2 Results for World Bank conditions[a] for time-series cross-section regressions with panel corrected standard errors with an AR(1) correction of Health Expenditure in Latin America and the Caribbean, N = 226

		Health expenditure per capita	Total health expenditure as a % of GDP	Public health expenditure as a % of GDP	Private health expenditure as a % of GDP	Public health expenditure as a % of total health expenditure	Public health expenditure as a % of government expenditure
World Bank conditions on all loans	Bivariate	−0.151	<0.001	−0.001	0.001	−0.01	−0.005
		(0.197)	(0.002)	(0.001)	(0.001)	(0.009)	(0.005)
	Multivariate	−0.112	<0.001	−0.001	0.001	−0.007	−0.004
		(0.152)	(0.002)	(0.001)	(0.001)	(0.010)	(0.005)
World Bank conditions on health and other social sector loans	Bivariate	−0.495	0.002	−0.001	0.003	−0.042	−0.023
		(1.085)	(0.008)	(0.005)	(0.004)	(0.039)	(0.018)
	Multivariate	0.667	−0.001	−0.003	0.002	−0.037	−0.017
		(0.706)	(0.007)	(0.005)	(0.005)	(0.049)	(0.019)

Source World Bank Health, Nutrition and Population Statistics. Sources for the explanatory variables detailed in the methodological appendix

Notes ***p < 0.001, **p < 0.01, *p < 0.05, +p < 0.10 (two-tailed tests). Each cell reports the unstandardized coefficient, with the standard error in parentheses. All models were estimated in Stata 12.1

[a]The reported coefficients for World Bank conditions on all loans versus on health and other social sector loans were estimated separately. The bivariate models include only each of the above measures in turn. The multivariate models include all the predictors in Table 3.1 in addition to the globalization measures. These coefficients were calculated but are not reported. The inclusion of the World Bank loan conditions measures does not alter the conclusions reached from Table 3.1 about the effects of the other covariates

CONCLUSION

This chapter examined trends and correlates of health expenditures in Latin America and the Caribbean over time. The results suggest three conclusions. First, models of the welfare state developed to account for variation in social expenditures in developed countries have limited ability to account for variation in health expenditures in Latin America. My results indicate that it is largely demographic and economic factors that are associated with overall increases in health spending, consistent with development theories citing a changing epidemiological profile associated with an aging population and modernization. I find little evidence for the importance of left parties, though democratization is associated with higher levels of public spending (as a percent of GDP and in the private-public mix), consistent with previous findings (Huber and Stephens 2012; Huber et al. 2008).

Second, economic globalization appears to be associated with increases in public financing of health. Trade openness, interestingly, appears to be driving down private spending all else equal but is associated with higher public health expenditure as a percent of total health expenditure (this coefficient is also negative and statistically significant at the bivariate level). This suggests that global economic integration is associated with higher public health spending as a share of total health spending in Latin American countries, possibly owing to the fact that both are associated with a strategy of economic openness and investing in human capital on the part of many of these governments. Globalization has created increased risks and uncertainty, and these relationships may be the result of citizens demanding additional coverage where governments have responded by increasing their protection of citizens' from the vagaries of these more open economies and markets, at least in health.

Third, I find that World Bank conditions on loans, both health-sector specific and overall loans, have no effect on health expenditures. These null results are puzzling given the World Bank's heavy involvement in social sectors Latin America, previous literature pointing to conditioned loans as a mechanism for IFIs to advance neoliberal reforms, and the World Bank's important status as the largest external funder of global health (Ruger 2005).

The absence of any effects of World Bank conditions may be due to any of several factors: *first*, it may be possible that World Bank conditions suppress public spending in other domains, while government spending on health is resilient to IFI pressures or that World Bank conditions promote spending in health. However, if the latter were the case we would expect to see a positive relationship between World Bank conditions and the health share of public expenditures. We do not: the coefficient estimates are negative and insignificant. In addition, these measures are specifically related to conditions in health. *Second*, it may be that any negative effects of conditionality on social expenditures were concentrated in the period prior to the period under study. By the late-1990s, the utility of neoliberal policies had been called into question. This data are not well-suited to address this question. *Third*, it may be that the effects of World Bank projects, loans, and conditions are highly variable and country-specific, and cannot be captured using the models and measures presented here. This speaks to a need for increased country-level analyses of Latin American health systems in order to further explore the role that global pressures may play in government spending. Given the extent of discussion in the theoretical and some empirical literature on the effects of IFIs on social spending, it is possible that their effects are more nuanced, and ill captured by regression models and at the regional level.

The systematic, over-time comparison of the determinants of health spending in Latin America and the Caribbean presented in this chapter provides insight into how economic, demographic and political domestic factors as well as global integration influence public, private and overall health spending. These results serve to motivate a case-study analysis of changes in health policy—how are governments choosing to spend their money in the health sector in Latin America? What are their priorities? Does the World Bank matter for health policies and how public spending is allocated rather than just changes in expenditures? Working against the backdrop of the regional trends discussed in this chapter I now turn towards case-study analyses. In the three chapters that follow I present case studies of World Bank engagement and health reform in Argentina (Chap. 4), Peru (Chap. 5), and Costa Rica (Chap. 6), respectively. In the analyses that follow, I focus on the content of World Bank recommendations in the context of health sector reform in these three countries and the factors that account for government actions in accepting, resiting, and negotiating the World Bank's recommendations for the health sector.

Notes

1. Rudra's (2007) argument about developing countries finds a parallel in Orloff (1993) gendered analysis of welfare states: in OECD contexts, welfare states developed before a large segment of the population (women) was commodified, and therefore we should not assume that the non-commodified status of large segments of the population in developing countries would hinder the development of welfare states there.
2. With the exception of Costa Rica, these pioneer countries introduced their first social security schemes in the 1920s and 1930s (Huber 2005; Pierson 2005).

Appendix A

Tables 3.A.1 and 3.A.2 present fixed and random effects with an AR(1) correction. The preferred model for each of the six outcomes is selected on the basis of the Mundlak test and is highlighted in gray across Tables 3.A.1 and 3.A.2.

Table 3.A.1 Results for time-series cross-section random effects regressions with an AR(1) correction of health expenditure in Latin America and the Caribbean, N = 226

	Health Expenditure per Capita	Total Health Expenditure as a % of GDP	Public Health Expenditure as a % of GDP	Private Health Expenditure as a % of GDP	Public Health Expenditure as a % of Total Health Expenditure	Public Health Expenditure as a % of Government Expenditure
Economic and Demographic Conditions/Logic of Industrialism						
GDP per Capita$_{t-1}$	5.920***	0.001	0.006+	−0.002	0.039	0.007
	(0.555)	(0.005)	(0.003)	(0.003)	(0.034)	(0.014)
Unemployment	−0.706	0.066**	0.047*	0.026	−0.022	0.04
	(2.273)	(0.025)	(0.018)	(0.016)	(0.171)	(0.082)
Elderly Population	35.205	0.326**	0.114	0.176*	0.004	−0.251
	(26.068)	(0.116)	(0.098)	(0.084)	(1.122)	(0.369)
Political Structure/Power Resources						
Democracy Score	−2.592	−0.001	0.013	0.036	0.662	0.212
	(6.304)	(0.062)	(0.039)	(0.041)	(0.396)	(0.177)
Left Party Seats$_{t-1}$	−0.005	0.007	0.007	0.001	0.056	0.011
	(0.524)	(0.006)	(0.004)	(0.004)	(0.041)	(0.020)
Globalization						
Trade Openness	−0.691	−0.006	<0.001	−0.008**	0.051	0.001
	(0.524)	(0.004)	(0.003)	(0.003)	(0.033)	(0.014)
Foreign Direct Investment	0.222	0.002	−0.001	0.002	−0.019	−0.005
	(0.831)	(0.010)	(0.008)	(0.007)	(0.067)	(0.037)
Mundlak test Result	X²(7)=11.08	X²(7)=19.53	X²(7)=10.14	X²(7)=6.88	X²(7)=5.83	X²(7)=13.56
	(p>0.13)	(p<0.001)	(p>0.18)	(p>0.44)	(p>0.55)	(p<0.10)

Notes: *Source* World Bank Health, Nutrition and Population Statistics. Sources for the explanatory variables are detailed in the methodological appendix
***$p < 0.001$, **$p < 0.01$, *$p < 0.05$, +$p < 0.10$ (two-tailed tests). Each cell reports the unstandardized coefficient, with the standard error in parentheses. Constants calculated but not reported. All models were estimated in Stata 12.1

Table 3.A.2 Results for time-series cross-section fixed effects regressions with an AR(1) correction of health expenditure in Latin America and the Caribbean, N = 205

Health Expenditure per Capita	Total Health Expenditure as a %of GDP	Public Health Expenditure as a % of GDP	Private Health Expenditure as a % of GDP	Public Health Expenditure as a % of Total Health Expenditure	Public Health Expenditure as a % of Government Expenditure
Economic and Demographic Conditions/Logic of Industrialism					
GDP per Capita$_{t-1}$	5.500***	0.006	0.006	−0.003	−0.011	0.01
	(0.344)	(0.007)	(0.004)	(0.005)	(0.044)	(0.019)
Unemployment	−2.004	0.107***	0.054*	0.045**	−0.103	0.092
	(1.947)	(0.027)	(0.021)	(0.016)	(0.180)	(0.095)
Elderly Population	49.887***	0.839*	0.366+	0.548*	5.953**	0.186
	(7.763)	(0.339)	(0.193)	(0.240)	(2.076)	(0.844)
Political Structure/Power Resources					
Democracy Score	−2.592	0.012	0.026	−0.036	0.456	0.193
	(6.304)	(0.077)	(0.053)	(0.046)	(0.499)	(0.232)
Left Party Seats$_{t-1}$	−0.005	−0.001	0.004	−0.005	0.06	0.001
	(0.524)	(0.006)	(0.005)	(0.004)	(0.041)	(0.021)
Globalization					
Trade Openness	−0.691	−0.012+	−0.004	−0.008*	0.03	0.035
	(0.524)	(0.006)	(0.005)	(0.004)	(0.041)	(0.022)
Foreign Direct Investment	0.222	0.001	−0.002	0.002	−0.024	<0.001
	(0.831)	(0.010)	(0.008)	(0.006)	(0.066)	(0.037)
Mundlak test Result	X²(7)=11.08	X²(7)=19.53	X²(7)=10.14	X²(7)=6.88	X²(7)=5.83	X²(7)=13.56
	(p>0.13)	(p<0.001)	(p>0.18)	(p>0.44)	(p>0.55)	(p<0.10)

Notes: *Source* World Bank Health, Nutrition and Population Statistics. Sources for the explanatory variables are detailed in the methodological appendix
***$p < 0.001$, **$p < 0.01$, *$p < 0.05$, +$p < 0.10$ (two-tailed tests). Each cell reports the unstandardized coefficient, with the standard error in parentheses. Constants calculated but not reported. All models were estimated in Stata 12.1

REFERENCES

Amenta, E., Bonastia, C., & Caren, N. (2001). US social policy in comparative and historical perspective: Concepts, images, arguments, and research strategies. *Annual Review of Sociology*, 213–234.

Armada, F., Muntaner, C., & Navarro, V. (2001). Health and social security reforms in Latin America: The convergence of the World Health Organization, the World Bank, and transnational corporations. *International Journal of Health Services, 31*(4), 729–768.

Avelino, G., Brown, D. S., & Hunter, W. (2005). The effects of capital mobility, trade openness, and democracy on social spending in Latin America, 1980–1999. *American Journal of Political Science, 49*(3), 625–641.

Babb, S. (2005). The social consequences of structural adjustment: Recent evidence and current debates. *Annual Review of Sociology*, 199–222.

Beckfield, J., Olafsdottir, S., & Sosnaud, B. (2013). Healthcare systems in comparative perspective: Classification, convergence, institutions, inequalities, and five missed turns. *Annual Review of Sociology, 39*, 127–146.

Berman, P. (1995). Health sector reform: Making health development sustainable. *Health Policy, 32*(1), 13–28.

Birn, A.-E., & Dmitrienko, K. (2005). The World Bank: Global health or global harm? *American Journal of Public Health, 95*(7), 1091.

Brooks, C., & Manza, J. (2008). *Why welfare states persist: The importance of public opinion in democracies.* Chicago: University of Chicago Press.

Brown, D. S., & Hunter, W. (2004). Democracy and human capital formation education spending in latin america, 1980–1997. *Comparative Political Studies, 37*(7), 842–864.

de Mesa, A. A., & Mesa-Lago, C. (2006). The structural pension reform in Chile: Effects, comparisons with other Latin American reforms, and lessons. *Oxford Review of Economic Policy, 22*(1), 149–167.

Elling, R. H. (1994). Theory and method for the cross-national study of health systems. *International Journal of Health Services, 24*(2), 285–309.

Esping-Andersen, G. (1990). *The three worlds of welfare capitalism.* Cambridge: Policy Press, Cambtidge.

Esping-Andersen, G. (1999). *Social foundations of postindustrial economies.* Oxford: Oxford University Press.

Fourcade-Gourinchas, M., & Babb, S. L. (2002). The rebirth of the liberal creed: Paths to neoliberalism in four countries1. *American Journal of Sociology, 108*(3), 533–579.

Franzoni Martínez, J. (2008). Welfare regimes in Latin America: Capturing constellations of markets, families, and policies. *Latin American Politics and Society, 50*(2), 67–100.

Glatzer, M., & Rueschemeyer, D. (2004). *Globalization and the future of the welfare state.* Pittsburgh: University of Pittsburgh Press.

Huber, E. (2005). Globalization and social policy developments in Latin America. *Globalization and the Future of the Welfare State,* 75–105.

Huber, E., & Stephens, J. D. (2001). *Development and crisis of the welfare state: Parties and policies in global markets.* Chicago: University of Chicago press.

Huber, E., & Stephens, J. D. (2012). *Democracy and the left: Social policy and inequality in Latin America.* Chicago: University of Chicago Press.

Huber, E., Mustillo, T., & Stephens, J. D. (2008). Politics and social spending in Latin America. *The Journal of Politics, 70*(02), 420–436.

Kaufman, R. R., & Segura-Ubiergo, A. (2001). Globalization, domestic politics, and social spending in Latin America: A time-series cross-section analysis, 1973–97. *World Politics, 53*(04), 553–587.

Kawachi, I., & Kennedy, B. P. (1997). The relationship of income inequality to mortality: Does the choice of indicator matter? *Social Science and Medicine, 45*(7), 1121–1127.

Kawachi, I., & Kennedy, B. P. (1999). Income inequality and health: pathways and mechanisms. *Health Services Research, 34*(1 Pt 2), 215.

Kawachi, I., Kennedy, B. P., & Glass, R. (1999). Social capital and self-rated health: a contextual analysis. *American Journal of Public Health, 89*(8), 1187–1193.

Marshall, T. (2009). Citizenship and Social Class [in:] Inequality and Society. In J. Manza & M. Sauder (Eds.), *Social science perspectives on social stratification*. New York.

McGuire, J. W. (2010). *Wealth, health, and democracy in East Asia and Latin America*. Cambridge: Cambridge University Press.

Mechanic, D. (1975). The comparative study of health care delivery systems. *Annual Review of Sociology*, 43–65.

Mechanic, D., & Rochefort, D. A. (1996). Comparative medical systems. *Annual Review of Sociology*, 239–270.

Mesa-Lago, C. (2006). Private and public pension systems compared: an evaluation of the Latin American experience. *Review of Political Economy, 18*(3), 317–334.

Mesa-Lago, C. (2008). *Reassembling social security: A survey of pensions and health care reforms in Latin America*. Oxford: Oxford University Press.

Mesa-Lago, C., & Müller, K. (2002). The politics of pension reform in Latin America. *Journal of Latin American Studies, 34*(03), 687–715.

Moore, B. (1993). *Social origins of dictatorship and democracy: Lord and peasant in the making of the modern world* (Vol. 268). Beacon Press, Boston.

Murillo, M. (2002). Political bias in policy convergence: privatization choices in Latin America. *World Politics, 54*(04), 462–493.

Noy, S. (2011). New contexts, different patterns? A comparative analysis of social spending and government health expenditure in Latin America and the OECD. *International Journal of Comparative Sociology, 52*(3), 215–244.

Noy, S., & McManus, P. A. (2015). Modernization, globalization, trends, and convergence in health expenditure in Latin America and the Caribbean. *Sociology of Development, 1*(2), 113–139.

Noy, S., & Sprague-Jones J. (2016). Comparative dynamics of public health spending: Re-conceptualizing delta convergence to examine OECD and Latin America. *International Journal of Comparative Sociology, 57*(6), 425–448.

Orloff, A. S. (1993). Gender and the social rights of citizenship: The comparative analysis of gender relations and welfare states. *American Sociological Review*, 303–328.

Pierson, P. (2004). *Politics in time: History, institutions, and social analysis*. Princeton: Princeton University Press.

Pierson, P. (2005). The study of policy development. *Journal of policy history, 17*(01), 34–51.

Portes, A., & Hoffman, K. (2003). Latin American class structures: Their composition and change during the neoliberal era. *Latin American Research Review*, 41–82.

Pribble, J. E. (2008). *Protecting the poor: Welfare politics in Latin America's free market era*. Ann Arbor: ProQuest.

Ragin, C. (1994). A qualitative comparative analysis of pension systems. *The Comparative Political Economy of the Welfare State*, 320–345.

Rodrik, D. (1997). *Has Globalisation gone too far?*. Washington DC: Institute for International Economics.

Rudra, N. (2007). Welfare states in developing countries: Unique or universal? *Journal of Politics, 69*(2), 378–396.

Ruger, J. P. (2005). The changing role of the World Bank in global health. *American Journal of Public Health, 95*(1), 60–70.

Teichman, J. (2004). The World Bank and policy reform in Mexico and Argentina. *Latin American Politics and Society, 46*(1), 39–74.

Vreeland, J. R. (2003). *The IMF and economic development.* Cambridge: Cambridge University Press.

Vreeland, J. R. (2006). *The International Monetary Fund (IMF): Politics of conditional lending.* UK: Routledge.

Weyland, K. (2005). Theories of policy diffusion lessons from Latin American pension reform. *World Politics, 57*(02), 262–295.

Weyland, K. G. (2006). *External pressures and international norms in Latin American pension reform.* Citeseer.

CHAPTER 4

Argentina: Mixed Outcomes While Coping with Crisis in a Planner State

"[In the 1980s and 1990s] we went through a crisis of foreign debt, inflation and strong battles over distribution…The discussion of a national health insurance, in which, while the trade unions were still involved as important players, would mean a power cut for them, and at that time conditions made their resistance very effective…We did not manage to implement national health insurance"
—interview with Dr. Aldo Neri, Minister of Health of Argentina between 1983–1986 and the architect of a failed plan for national health insurance on reasons for its failure (Interview #74)

In 1985 then Argentinian health minister Dr. Aldo Neri attempted to introduce national health insurance to consolidate a disjointed system. This reform failed, and the Argentinian system remains fragmented and dominated by trade union run social security, rendering it especially vulnerable to unemployment and other changes in the labor force participation. Access to the social security health system depends on a person's (or their spouse's, for children their parent's) position in the formal labor market, though health care at public facilities is free in Argentina. This has created an opening for several World Bank projects in health that have been responsive to this fragmentation and economic crisis.

National economic crises and pressures render the Argentinian system particularly problematic and yet potential reformers in government are up against immense opposition to any change from the entrenched trade

S. Noy, *Banking on Health*, DOI 10.1007/978-3-319-61765-7_4

union run social security. Despite having high health coverage and free public health care, albeit concentrated in the capital of Buenos Aires, there remain persistent inequalities. These inequalities have been exacerbated by the foreign debt crisis, inflation, the convertibility crisis, and other financial woes. Argentina's national government had a reform agenda for the health system in the early 1980s, but failed to carry out its own proposals. Indeed there were several initiatives between 1980 and 2005 but these were stymied by financial crises and resistance and opposition by powerful domestic actors, as indicated in this chapter's opening quote. As such, this "planner state" in health was both open to World Bank recommendations and desperately in need of external funding for much of the period between 1980 and 2005. Given Argentina's weak position vis-à-vis IFIs we might expect this to be a period of radical reforms in line with a neoliberal policy paradigm despite any government plans to the contrary.

Radical, neoliberal change did not materialize in Argentina's health system for several reasons, as I detail in this chapter. Government autonomy and capacity in health are important for how countries work with the World Bank and subsequent health sector reform because they shape the patterns of interaction and constrain the direction of reforms. They are also important for how projects, loans, and their accompanying conditions are subsequently implemented in national health policies and programs. Argentina is characterized by relatively high state autonomy—the state has an agenda and is able to formulate collective goals—however, it is also characterized by low capacity. This is related to lack of resources but also the dispersion of power among a variety of key actors, especially in the health sector.

How can we account for the lack of sweeping neoliberal health reforms in Argentina during this time period? The Argentinian health system (segmented as it is) consists of three poorly-coordinated sectors: the social security system (*Obras Sociales*) which is itself comprised of multiple actors, the public sector, and the private sector. Therefore, power is dispersed and dramatic change unlikely given the multiplicity of actors and systems each with different interests and agendas, and the ability to oppose reforms. Second, there is little evidence that the World Bank was pushing a uniformly neoliberal agenda, indeed one of its largest and most successful projects involves providing care and services for mothers and children. While this is a targeted program it does not prize the market over the state, and when reformers have sought to unify the system, the World Bank remained agnostic, rather than pushing for or against increased state intervention (Interview #50; Interview #74).

Argentina's status as a planner state in health shapes the discourse surrounding and implementation of policies concerned with equity and efficiency. In addition, its planner state status affects the relative emphasis on the policy instruments used to achieve these paradigmatic goals. The fact that Argentina experienced a failed reform early in this time period led to a subsequent focus on efficiency over equity in health. These goals were pursued via targeted government projects to maintain and expand basic health services for women and children. This focus was driven by the national agenda, but that agenda was itself influenced by international discourse about the prioritization of mothers and children, especially in the context of the Millennium Development Goals.

GOVERNMENT AUTONOMY AND CAPACITY IN HEALTH IN ARGENTINA: THE PLANNER STATE

State autonomy in the health sector refers to the ability of the state to construct an agenda for the health sector. This definition recognizes that there are a multiplicity of actors that constitute the state. Indeed, the relationship between different actors within the state and their ability to come to an agreement on an agenda is precisely at the heart of this concept. Argentina, in 1980 and throughout the period between 1980 and 2005 (though certainly not at all time points), had relatively high state autonomy in that leaders were able to formulate clear goals for the health sector. This was the case during the time that Aldo Neri (one of my respondents, quoted at the beginning of this chapter) was health minister during the presidency of Raúl Alfonsín (1983–1986). There was also a strong agenda for health towards the end of this period, and at some moments in between, but particularly when Gines González García, another of my respondents, worked as health minister under President Néstor Kirchner (2002–2007).

Many of these plans did not come to fruition and indeed, most of the reforms that did take place were piecemeal and responsive (rather than proactive) to financial and economic crisis that plagued Argentina throughout this time period. As McGuire (2010) notes: "What constrained the effectiveness of the Argentine health care system was not a shortage of talented leaders, but the power of the social forces that the leaders confronted and the political situation that the people who appointed them faced." That is, it is the state's low capacity in health rather than low autonomy that prevented it from successfully implementing reforms. This however, had the benefit of also limiting the ability of not just the state to solidify a public system, but also of private insurance and other actors to compete with social security. During this time period, the World Bank does not promote neoliberal ends but rather remains is agnostic about the government's effort to develop a unitary public health insurance. The World Bank's work in the Argentinian health sector since 1980 supports the government in creating and expanding public programs, most notably an insurance program aimed at pregnant women. However, the World Bank seeks to accomplish this via some tools that can be characterized as neoliberal: decentralization and deconcentration, a separation of functions, performance-based management, privatization, and targeting.

Overall, progress in health reform was limited with mixed results. Trade unions were resistant to any changes that would require them to relinquish control over the union-based *Obras Sociales* social security system in the country. The government introduced piecemeal programs and reforms, often with the help of the World Bank, in an effort to patch coverage issues. Together, this indicates that Argentina had relatively low capacity in implementing health reforms conceived by the national government. This is due in part to the resistance of other important actors in the health system to planned reforms but is also due to a lack of state financial resources following economic crises.

Argentina's Health Sector: History, Structure, and Challenges

Argentina is a politically decentralized country and this structure is echoed in the institutions of the health sector. Provincial governments are largely responsible for their own health policies. Broadly, the Argentinian health system is composed of three sectors: public, social security, and private. The public sector is financed through state funds at the national and provincial level and provides free care to its citizens. The social security sector falls along trade and occupation lines and is funded through compulsory insurance contributions, providing a full range of health services. The private sector provides services to those that can afford to purchase private insurance or pay for private services.

The Public Sector

The public sector is run by national and provincial governments and is accessible to anyone requiring health care. It is intended primarily for those people not affiliated with the social security system and those unable to afford health care. The public sector is financed by public monies and occasionally is reimbursed by the social security system when its patients are attended at public facilities. The public system provides services to a little over 40% of the population (a figure that has remained stable since the late 1990s) and government health expenditure is about one-fifth of total health expenditure in Argentina (Cavagnero 2008).

Social Security: Obras Sociales

The social security system, *Obras Sociales* (literally translated as social works), is obligatory and is largely organized along broad occupational lines or industrial sectors. The public employees in each province are affiliated with their own *Obra Social* (OS) and there are 24 provincial OS, one in each province. The other *Obras Sociales* are organized along occupational and trade lines and created by professional associations and employee unions. There are over 300 *Obras Sociales*, which have their root in health insurance funds for workers created by trade unions (Teixeira and Fleury 2000; Belmartino 2000).

The *Obras Sociales* has a long history dating back to the early nineteenth century. In 1970 the *Obras Sociales* system was further institutionalized with the passing of Law 18.610 which made both inscription in an *Obra Social* along trade lines and employee contributions mandatory (Devoto and Cetrángolo 2002; Munck 1998). This law also created the National Institute of OS (*Instituto Nacional de Obras Sociales*, INOS) to regulate the OS, guarantee some baseline provision, and address the inequalities in size between the OS (Devoto and Cetrángolo 2002). INOS was responsible for administering a newly established fund, the Redistribution Fund (*Fondo de Redistribution*, FDR) which was intended to redistribute funds from wealthier to less wealthy OS, though this task has remained pending with little redistribution in practice (Lloyd-Sherlock 2000; Belmartino 2000; Báscolo 2008).

In addition, Law 19.032 of 1970 mandated the creation of separate coverage for pensioners. The Integral Medical Attention Program, *Programa de Atención Médico Integral* (PAMI), administered by the

National Institute for Social Services for Retirees and Pensioners, *Instituto Nacional de Servicios Sociales para Jubilados y Pensionados* (INSSJP) covers the elderly and retired populations. Approximately 50% of the population has some coverage from *Obras Sociales*, and around 30% of total health expenditure in Argentina is in the OS system (Belló and Becerril-Montekio 2011).

The Private Sector

The private sector includes private clinics and facilities, often subcontracted by OS. Some OS have agreements with these clinics, which also offer private insurance plans (called "Empresas de Medicina Prepaga", EMP or *prepagas*) that can be paid by individuals or companies with resources negotiated with the OS. Private health insurance accounts for about 15% of total health spending and covers between 10 and 15% of the population (Cavagnero 2008).

HEALTH POLICY REFORM, 1980–2005

By the 1980s the Argentinian health sector was characterized by much fragmentation. A lack of coordination and integration between the public, private and *Obras Sociales* sectors prevented it from functioning as a coherent health system (Devoto and Cetrángolo 2002). Early in this period, there was an attempt to integrate the entire health system. However, subsequent reforms focused on one of the three sectors at a time: public, private or social security, rather than attempting to unify or simultaneously implement policies across these sectors, as I discuss in detail below.

Failed Attempt to Integrate the Health System, 1984–1991

In 1985 there was an attempt to unify public health financing with the drafting of a Health Insurance Bill that would have universalized coverage (McGuire 2010). However, because funding for this bill would come from a combination of government funds and payroll deductions from the OS it was opposed both by medical personnel and labor unions. Medical personnel were worried about how the government intended to finance this scheme and how it would affect their wages while labor unions did not want to cede control of the OS (Interview #74). This attempt at reform was neither opposed nor supported by the World Bank and occurred prior to major involvement of the World Bank in the health sector. This is the only major overhaul of the system proposed during this 25 year period though there were other less ambitious but important reform efforts, and is an indication of Argentina's planner state status–big plans with diluted follow through.

In 1989, Laws 23.660 and 23.661 were passed. In keeping with the previous reform effort, this legislation sought to integrate the highly fragmented system in order to overcome the inequality between the services provided by the different OS (Interview #74). Law 23.661 attempted to legislate the development of a national health insurance plan which never came to fruition. Law 23.600 created the National Administration of Health Insurance (*Administration National del Seguro de Salud*, ANSSAL) (Belmartino 2000). This reform built on Law 22.373 of 1981 which had created a Federal Health Council (*Consejo Federal de Salud*) which coordinates meetings between the regional health authorities and the national Ministry of Health at least twice a year. The Council's goal is to increase regulation, coordination, and communication between the different health providers: regional and national both public and union-based (Giovanella et al. 2012). Law 23.661 was never fully implemented in practice (Interview #51). A national health insurance was never created that incorporated the uninsured population. The government was unable, in effect, to wrest any control from the labor unions over the OS and combine this with government funding to create a single revenue stream (McGuire 2010).

Introducing Competition Between Obras Sociales, Deconcentration, and Self-managed Hospitals, 1993

Only after the failed attempt in the late 1980s to unify the health system did the World Bank become actively engaged in health reform in Argentina. The World Bank becomes an important actor in an attempt to increase efficiency in Argentina via two interrelated reforms. Both reforms introduce neoliberal tools: first, increased competition between OS driven by newly granted consumer choice and second, decentralization of administrative authority to hospitals in the public system. According to Argentinian academic and prominent authority on health reform Susana Belmartino (2000) this initiative "centered on eliminating the 'captive population' of the *obras sociales* by allowing union members

freedom of choice between institutions administering social security contributions. In this way, it was hoped to stimulate competition, to generate incentives to reduce administration costs, and to offer better quality
healthcare."

In 1993, Decree 9/93 established that formal labor market employees
can choose which OS they are affiliated with. This means that formal sector workers are still required to affiliate with an OS, but are now able to
choose which one and OS compete for affiliates. This was subsequently
extended to all OS by Decree 1.141 of 1996 with the stipulation that
people can switch between OS once a year (Decree 84 of 1997). This
decree also gives the OS freedom to contract with private and other providers of health services, which promotes price competition among sup-
pliers.

This effort to increase efficiency was implemented in the public sector as well as the OS sector. Since 1993 public hospitals have been given
greater control over their operations in that they can be legislatively and
legally self-managed (*Hospitales de Autogestión*, also known as autonomous public hospitals) (Cavagnero et al. 2006; Cavagnero 2008). This
is included in the same Decree 9/93 which introduces choice among OS
to affiliates. Public hospitals had been shouldering the cost of providing
services, free of charge, not only to those relying exclusively on the public sector but also those that had OS or private insurance or capacity to
pay for the hospital's services (Belmartino 2000). Therefore, this reform
ensured that hospital financing was no longer based on a general budget
but rather on the services rendered to patients with an attempt to recoup
costs of services provided to the insured, a form of performance-based
financing. While these reforms have increased efficiency they may have
also exacerbated inequalities between hospitals and complicated things
administratively as hospitals try (not always successfully) to recoup payments from private insurance or social security when utilize hospitals
(Iriart et al. 2001).

The partial success of these reforms to enhance efficiency was due to
the weakening of the *Confederación General del Trabajo* (General Labor
Confederation, CGT) the body representing unions including the management of the OS system. The weakening of the CGT was the result
of a combination of the changing structure of the economy (collective
agreements by specific company rather than by trade/sector and infight-
ing among labor leaders themselves), the onset of economic crisis (which
on the one hand strengthened union position popularly but also created

an opening for government to enact change), and negotiations with the World Bank for loans, where the World Bank pushed for increased efficiency in the administration of expenditures (Interview #68). In addition, control of OS was sometimes leveraged vis-à-vis unions when negotiating other economic matters. Ultimately, in the face of economic crisis, the administration of the OS was less salient than other issues of employment policy such as salaries and unemployment benefits: "Control of the *obras sociales* is frequently used as a bargaining chip in the face of other issues that are perceived as more pressing to—or less reconcilable with—the reform process being carried out by the Ministerio de Economía de la Nación [Ministry of the Economy]" (Belmartino 2000).

Baseline Coverage and Programa Medico Obligatorio, 1995–1996

Amidst economic crisis, in 1995 Decree 292/95 mandated a reduction in employer contributions to the OS social security system from 6 to 5% where employees continued to contribute 3% of salary. This decree also officially eliminated hitherto existing double-coverage, due either to having more than one job or being the dependent of someone affiliated with another OS (Tobar 2001). Partly in response to the reduction of employer contributions, Decree 492/95 was passed in September which establishes a basic package of services all OS must cover. Decree 492/95 was motivated by pressure from trade unions opposed to the reduction of employers' contributions (that was passed in August with Decree 292/95). However, its main objective is to define a package of services that each *Obra Social* must supply and raises the minimum guaranteed contribution to US$40 per beneficiary (where this was previously US$30). According to Belmartino (2000):

> The resolution calls for the Ministerio de Salud y Acción Social de la Nación (MSAS, ministry of health and social action) and the Confederación General del Trabajo (CGT, general labour confederation) to designate a commission to be entrusted with establishing the package of services and setting the rules for its application…Once the package has been approved, an *obra social* that finds itself unable to finance it has 60 days in which to propose a merger with one or more other organizations. Otherwise, the Administración Nacional del Seguro de Salud (ANSSAL, national health insurance administration) has the power to order a compulsory merger

In practice, the ability to choose between OS provided affiliates with more choice but has also exacerbated inequality. Better off affiliates, that is, those that contributed more, often chose to migrate to OS that provides better services which reinforce their status and furthered inequality between the different OS. In 1996, in response to this issue, the Argentinian government introduced Decree 257/96 which establishes a baseline level of coverage that all OS must provide, updating the 1995 decree: the Obligatory Medical Program (*Programa Medico Obligatorio*, PMO) (Cavagnero 2008; Belmartino 2000). With this decree, the government establishes a basic package of services that all providers, namely OS but also private insurers, must provide with the goal of establishing minimum health services. The Superintendencia de Servicios de Salud (SSS) or Health Services Superintendency is the regulatory body which enforces this, replacing ANSSAL, also in 1996.

Responding to Crisis and a Renewed Concern with Equity, 1998–2003

In 2002, following the onset of another economic crisis, the government enacted some reforms in the context of the National Health Emergency Decree (Lloyd-Sherlock 2005). Employer contributions were once again set at 6% (following their reduction to 5% in 1995) and the PMO was revised. However, some have noted that because many OS and private insurers alike had failed to comply with the previous baseline it is unclear what the exact impact of this update to the PMO was (Cavagnero 2008; Lloyd-Sherlock 2005). Therefore, there is a concern with making access to basic health services equitable and there has been work on deciding what is to be included in this list of services. However, this move towards equity in service provision is not heavily enforced. This is another feature of the fragmented system with weak state capacity, where the national government is unable to ensure that providers comply with established rules.

The government also started a campaign for the use of generic medication (Cavagnero 2008). Law 25.649 was passed in 2002 and guaranteed access to essential medicine in the public sector through direct distribution of these medications to primary health care centers. In addition, this law requires that all packaging have the generic in addition to any brand names on it which has led to demand for the cheaper brands (Lloyd-Sherlock 2005). The subsequent implementation of this program in 2003 also provided essential medications for those below the poverty line. This program, *Plan Remediar,* was financed by the Inter-American Development Bank (IDB) but not the World Bank, ostensibly since this would interfere with the medications market (Interview #79), and possibly pharmaceutical interests. The World Bank sees such projects as outside its purview, but again, did not interfere in these plans (Interview #73).

The use of private contracts in IFI financed projects, both for technical assistance and consulting, is a common feature. This private subcontracting is especially apparent in infrastructural programs, for example in water supply projects (Water Supply Project Implementation Report 1998: 8). Therefore while the World Bank and IDB have stepped in repeatedly in order to assist Argentina in coping and ameliorating the effects of economic crisis on health access their tools of choice are consistently market-oriented. These tools promote competition and are focused on individual concerns (e.g. in the case of OS choice), though ostensibly in the interest of equity as well as efficiency.

National Maternal and Child Health Insurance—Plan Nacer, 2004

Plan Nacer ("the Birth Plan") is a national targeted health program established in 2004 which provides health insurance to mothers and children without other coverage. Its precursor, the Maternal and Infant Nutrition Program (*Programa Materno Infantil y Nutrición,* PROMIN), was established in 1993 by the government with World Bank and UNICEF support. This program trained health personnel and helped equip health facilities as well as manage the system of referrals from primary to secondary and tertiary care. A previous program (established in 1937), the National Mother and Infant Program (*Programa Nacional Materno Infantil,* PNMI), covered costs for mother and children's nutrition and health care (McGuire 2010). In late 2004 economic recovery together with an international focus on the Millennium Development Goals reinvigorated national thinking about maternal and infant health and saw the launch by the Ministry of Health, with World Bank funds, of *Plan Nacer.* The program was aimed at pregnant women and children under six that lacked insurance and was limited to nine of the poorer provinces in the Northern part of the country. While it was launched by the national Ministry of Health with the help of the World Bank it was implemented by provincial governments.

Plan Nacer provides a package of basic services, including checkups, medications, and obstetric services, that provincial governments purchase from both public and private providers for those inscribed in the program. It has been largely hailed as a success, as McGuire (2010) notes:

> The strong economic recovery from 2003 to 2006 surely helped to accelerate the pace of infant mortality decline throughout the country, but the much greater percent decline in the nine provinces in which the Birth Plan was initially implemented strongly suggests that the improvement of maternal and child health services among the most vulnerable segments of the population contributed significantly to the acceleration over these four years in the pace of infant mortality decline across Argentina as a whole.

The World Bank issued its first loan for this project (the antecedent to *Plan Nacer*) in 1993 and as the staff appraisal report states, the World Bank believed that the best way for the government to proceed was by focusing on health outcomes via targeting in the interest of efficiency: "The overarching goal of health policy should be the improvement of health status, within the existing financial constraints, through better targeting and more efficient resource use" (Maternal and Child Health and Nutrition Project Staff Appraisal Report 1993: 14).

Ends and Means in World Bank Health Projects in Argentina, 1980–2005

The trajectory of government programs and health sector reform in Argentina suggests that both the World Bank and the IDB were important for some phases of policy reforms in Argentina. However, despite the expectation that the World Bank would aggressively push a neoliberal agenda it appears that it played a non-trivial but certainly not a massive role in Argentina's health reforms, despite being positioned to do so vis-à-vis a national government in desperate need of loans in the midst of economic crisis. Indeed, the reforms overall sought to expand access, and improve both equity and efficiency, albeit via the use of some tools traditionally considered neoliberal.

Of the three country cases examined in this book, Argentina was in some ways the most vulnerable to World Bank and other IFI influence. It arguably experienced the most severe economic crises during this time period and certainly relied most heavily on IFI funding in an effort to deal with these crises and restore economic stability. Therefore, it is somewhat surprising that during this time the World Bank was not able to compel the government to implement more neoliberal reforms in health, especially given the plethora of projects it was involved in, listed in Methdological Appendix Table A.5. The World Bank began 31 projects in health between 1980 and 2005, the largest number across the three cases examined in this book (in comparison, the World Bank financed 8 projects in Costa Rica and 19 in Peru during this time period). About one in four projects by the World Bank in Argentina during this time had a health component, and the average project cost projects with health components was $354.23 million (with total project costs at $10,980.99 million). Of this amount, the World Bank contributed approximately 72% of the financing to these projects, with national and regional governments in Argentina and other aid agencies providing additional financing (see Table A.4 in the Methodological Appendix).

My evidence from both historical documents and interviews with policymakers and other key informants indicates that this is primarily because the World Bank did not seek to influence the government to implement far reaching neoliberal reforms, that is, the reduction of state involvement in health. The World Bank in addition to being concerned with the classically neoliberal principle of efficiency and its accompanying policy instruments of private sector involvement, targeting, etc. was also concerned with issues of equity and access. This is in the context of its goal of poverty reduction, social development, and investment in human capital as it described them in its Country Assistance Strategy (Aids and Sexually Transmitted Diseases Control Project Implementation Report 2004: 70). Having discussed the direction of health sector reform in Argentina I now turn my attention to examining the discourse and framing of national as compared with World Bank goals for health sector reform as well as programs and projects, focusing on differences and similarities in priorities and tools.

Paradigmatic Goals: Problem Definition and National Priorities

Scholarship on the coercive neoliberal agendas of IFIs and draconian structural adjustment projects suggests that the World Bank will frame and discuss efficiency and equity as competing principles and that we will witness the World Bank and IFIs primarily promoting efficiency. However, though efficiency is primary there is notable attention to equity, though the World Bank's approach to equity is decidedly formulaic. Equity is especially a geographic concern because of the decentralized structure of the health and broader political system in Argentina. Equity is even more salient a concern in the context of large inequalities in resources and services between the OS health insurance funds and across public facilities. Efficiency is identified as an important goal in health sector reform in the context of several economic crises Argentina weathered between 1980 and 2005, which raise concern with spending existing, and sometimes shrinking, resources more efficiently. This inefficiency is not limited to the relationships between the three different systems (public, social security, and private) in the health system, but also to issues within each sector. For example, the World Bank notes that "low internal efficiency characterizes the public hospital network. Largely this results from deficient administrative and management practices and the deteriorated condition of facilities" (Provincial Health Sector Development Project Staff Appraisal Report 1995: 6).

Equity as a goal is repeatedly discussed in World Bank documents, though it is often invoked in tandem with efficiency concerns. For example, one World Bank project diagnoses inequity and inefficiency in the health system:

> [there exist a m]ultiplicity of social insurance and public and private health subsystems adding up to an intricate, inequitable and ineffective financing and delivery of health services; [there is a n]eed for institutional development in national and provincial Ministries of Health (MoHs) to reinforce their capacity to regulate and control health care system (Aids and Sexually Transmitted Diseases Control Project Appraisal Document 1997: 4).

In that project, focused on reproductive health, the World Bank conceptualizes the state in a more regulatory role, consistent with neoliberal ideas that limit direct public provision. *Plan Nacer*, with its focus on mothers and children, is also justified on the grounds of both equity and efficiency: "In the short run, the highest priority on grounds of equity and efficiency is to address the health and nutritional needs of poor mothers and children. This should be done by progressively improving efficiency and effectiveness of maternal and child care services" (Maternal and Child Health and Nutrition Project Staff Appraisal Report 1993: 14). The central goal, therefore, is to streamline the system by helping the "deserving" and minimize access of the "undeserving," especially as it relates to those utilizing multiple social programs:

by cross-checking against other programs, the likelihood of awarding these benefits to non-deserving persons is substantially reduced. Through cross-checking as well, an estimated 20,000 cases of double coverage (national vs. provincial social programs) will be detected in the first participating province alone (Social and Fiscal National Identification System Project Appraisal Document 1999: 6).

Therefore, equity here will be achieved by channeling resources more effectively and cutting off those who are "undeserving" or double-dipping into programs via the use of means-testing and eliminating double coverage. This is different than a more comprehensive idea of equity which would reach the underserved in the context of a universalist approach rather than limiting access for some. Typically, the World Bank in its project documents will assert that it is pursuing equity and efficiency simultaneously. Equity is not explicitly defined in World Bank documents but it is operationalized as a more equal distribution of resources and particularly, helping the poor or groups that are "vulnerable." For example, in the Health Insurance Project meant to help with regulation of social health insurance and the definition of the PMO notes: "the objectives of the proposed project would be to improve the efficiency and equity of Argentina's social health insurance system, and to contain the already high level of health spending in the country" (Health Insurance Reform Loan Project Information Document 1995: 1).

Equity is often coupled with targeting, and performance-based management, as is the case in *Plan Nacer*. Indeed, the strategy is to help the "deserving" poor—those that are unable, but actively trying, to secure employment-based health insurance or health care for themselves. There is only a single national government health plan during this time period. But it allows an examination of stated, national goals for the health sector during this time period. This plan provides important insights into differences between how the World Bank and the national government discuss health officially. The World Bank coupling of equity and efficiency stands in contrast to the federal government's standalone emphasis on equity, the Federal Plan for Health in 2004 notes:

> Argentina faces two major challenges in health: in the short term, is necessary to overcome the ongoing health emergencies, protecting the gains made in the last twenty years and at the same time guaranteeing access to services and essential medicines to the entire population. In the long term,

the objective is to close those gaps that statistical averages obscure and that define the margins of inequity (3).

Overall, there is more attention to equity by the World Bank than expected. Nor can this be said to be a recent development inspired by the Millennium Development Goals or the result of a post-Washington consensus. Discussions of equity date back to documents published in the early 1990s. However, the only health-related project begun in the 1980s was a water supply project, which prevents a more fine-grained historical analysis of how health was discussed by the World Bank in loan and project documents during the 1980s in Argentina. This also speaks to the intensification of the World Bank's involvement in health starting in the 1990s, important because it points to the Bank's growing commitment to health and its emergent role as a normative and financial leader in developing countries' health systems.

Policy Instruments and Levels

The World Bank and the Argentinian government identify several policy instruments that may help achieve equity and efficiency. Due to Argentina's relatively high autonomy and low capacity in health—its status as a planner state—and because the national government is nearly constantly managing economic crisis during this period, targeting and performance-based management feature prominently as policy instruments in reforms during this time period. These instruments are utilized by the government in an effort to maintain and expand basic care (but without overhauling the system entirely) and promoted by the World Bank.

Six policy instruments introduced in Chap. 1 have been advanced by the World Bank and the Argentinian government in health during this time period: (1) decentralization and deconcentration, (2) performance-based management/financing, (3) separation of functions, (4) targeting, (5) private sector involvement, and (6) strengthening primary health care. These instruments are often employed in tandem and are purportedly mobilized in the interest of equity, efficiency, or both despite the fact that the first five are viewed as particularly neoliberal due to their emphasis on individualism, competition, bureaucratization, and rationalization as elaborated in Chap. 1. I examine targeting and performance-based financing together since they are often mentioned in tandem in Argentinian health sector reform. I then focus on private sector involvement followed by the primary care approach. Finally I examine decentralization and deconcentration together with separation of functions in World Bank and government discourse surrounding health policies and programs in Argentina as these were often coupled in reform efforts.

Targeting and Performance-Based Management
Of the six policy instruments, the ones that are most emphasized during this time period in Argentina are targeting, largely in tandem with performance-based financing, and private sector involvement. The focus on targeting and performance-based financing is most apparent in the implementation of *Plan Nacer*. In the face of economic crisis and poor performance in infant and maternal mortality regionally, especially when compared with high health spending levels (among the highest in the region), the World Bank notes that:

> In the short run, the highest priority on grounds of equity and efficiency is to address the health and nutritional needs of poor mothers and children. This should be done by progressively improving efficiency and effectiveness of maternal and child care services (Maternal and Child Health and Nutrition Project Staff Appraisal Report 1993: 14).

This concern with the allocation of public resources is echoed in a later project: "Resources are allocated to public providers on a historical basis. Since they receive allocations that bear only a distant relation to the quality and quantity of services they provide, public hospitals neither have an incentive to provide appropriate care nor to increase the efficiency of service provision" (Health Insurance for the Poor Project Appraisal Document 1999: 4). Performance-based financing and management can, according to the World Bank, ensure that resources are being used appropriately, and efficiently, and to reduce mismanagement of funds. Performance-based financing is viewed by the World Bank as creating positive incentives for better, more efficient care. This strategy was favored in targeted programs, and its important to note that instead of overhauling the public system, to which all Argentinians have access, the government, with the support of the World Bank, decided to pursue the targeted policy of focusing on mothers and children. In this reform it implemented results-based budgeting (*presupuesto por resultados*) in *Plan Nacer* in order to ensure that funding was given per services provided, further incentivizing efficient and targeted, rather than integral, care.

Critics argue that this is problematic because it creates perverse incentives to provide more services, or different kinds of services, rather than treat the patient in a more holistic way concerned not only with immediate symptoms and needs but with the bigger picture of lifestyle, ailments, risks, and issues. However, *Plan Nacer* has generally been considered a success and has tracked better outcomes for mothers and children, especially in rural areas in Argentina.

Private Sector Involvement
The issue of private sector involvement was of concern to both the national government and the World Bank in Argentina. There was an attempt in the mid to late-1990s to allow private insurance to compete with the OS system. In fact the government drafted legislation to allow private pre-paid health plans (*prepagas*) to compete with *Obras Sociales* (Provincial Reform Project II—Tucuman Implementation Completion Report 2000: 18) and looked towards "establishing an effective regulatory framework for the roughly 500 private pre-paid health insurance institutions in Argentina, with a view to the eventual merger of the pre-paid and Obras systems" (Health Insurance Reform Loan Project Information Document 1995: 2). This policy however never came to fruition, according to the World Bank this was largely prevented by the trade unions:

> Trade unions, traditional private health insurance companies and other interest groups threatened by the changes tried to slow or stop the move toward an open, unified, competitive and more professionally supervised regulatory system. Resisting introduction of competition, OS lobbied for regulations and supervisory practices that would create disincentives for people to transfer between OS (Health Insurance Technical Assistance Project Implementation Report 2002: 10).

Other accounts note that private insurers were not particularly excited about this plan either (McGuire 2010). Indeed, some *prepagas* had already been able to penetrate the *obra social de gestion* sector (which is a subset of the OS sectors consisting OS that provide more comprehensive and higher quality services to managers and executives) without submitting to regulatory constraints. Some OS already "essentially served as fronts for private health insurers" (McGuire 2010) which also allowed them to evade a tax on *prepagas* that had been introduced in early 1999. However, the government did legislate, with support from the

World Bank, that private insurers were also required to offer the same basic package of services, the PMO (though as described previously this requirement was little enforced).

Therefore, both the national government and the World Bank would have liked to see a more transparent and open involvement of private insurers to compete with the *Obras Sociales*. However, the complex bureaucratic structure of the *Obras Sociales* and its interface with the government made this unappealing not just to *Obras Sociales*, hesitant to cede even a little control over the system, but also to private insurers. Such open competition would actually mean *more* oversight by regulatory agencies over private insurers rather than the current participation with little regulation on the part of private companies, as they had done by sneaking through the back door of some *Obras Sociales*.

Primary Health Care Approach
The emphasis on primary health care is central to several World Bank projects in Argentina. There is often allusion to this policy instrument working in the interest of both equity and efficiency, but more often efficiency, though it seems to have fallen out of favor since Alma Ata, and more recently seen a resurgence: "During the 1980s, primary healthcare programs were ostensibly given the highest priority at the federal, provincial and municipal level. However, there is little tangible support for primary health care" (Maternal and Child Health and Nutrition Project Staff Appraisal Report 1993: 11). Indeed, one of the primary goals of the maternal and child insurance support provided by the World Bank was "to avoid the overuse of hospitals" (Maternal and Child Health and Nutrition II Project Implementation Report 2006: 2) on the grounds that this was more expensive and less efficient than drawing on lower level clinics and health centers.

The World Bank noted that the maternal and child nutrition project "directly supported the CAS' [Country Assistance Strategy] objectives of reducing poverty and improving efficiency and targeting of social services. By addressing primary health care, the project was seen as a centerpiece of the Bank's strategy in the health sector in Argentina" (Maternal and Child Health and Nutrition II Project Implementation Report 2006: 7). Primary health care should work in tandem with targeting to increase both equity and efficiency in the World Bank's view. The Argentinian government was also centrally concerned with primary health care, framing it in terms of efficiency: "the primary care strategy is extremely positive in its cost-effectiveness" (Argentinian Federal Health Plan for 2004–2007, 2004: 21). The national health plan's text, however, continues by noting that there have been obstacles to implementing a primary health care centered strategy. The primary challenge was that the system is very hospital-centric and that designing, implementing, and evaluating primary health care strategies is expensive. The existing structure of the health system and the expense of such an overall primary care reform has prevented local (state and municipal governments) from implementing these reforms. The lack of a well-developed primary system also came up in interviews, for example, one researcher who regularly serves as a consultant to both the Ministry of Health and international organizations notes: "we have a very weak primary care system, very weak. Primary health care centers that depend on the provinces or municipalities that are often understaffed in terms of doctors and nurses and cannot retain these people. Because of this people, very intelligently and rationally, don't go to the health centers but rather to the hospitals that can attend to them" (Interview #51). An emphasis on primary care can be seen as a neoliberal, cost-cutting tool in that it can increase efficiency and prevent people from seeking care from more complex, expensive facilities for simple ailments. However, it is also fundamentally an issue of equity—since there are many more clinics than hospitals increasing access and quality of care at these clinics turns out to be not only the more inexpensive choice but the one that may reduce health inequities by being more accessible to those in remote and rural locations.

Deconcentration and Separation of Functions
There is also, albeit briefer, mention of the two remaining instruments. Separation of functions more generally is discussed in the context of provincial rather than national government and not very often. One of the few mentions of separating functions is in the context of the province of Tucuman:

> Health reforms will also improve efficiency and equity in the health sector, notably by separating the provision and the financing of public health services (Provincial Reform Project II—Tucuman Implementation Completion Report 2000: 45).

Deconcentration is discussed at length in the context of the government enacting policy that allows hospitals more autonomy—the self-managed hospitals described previously. Largely, both deconcentration and separation of functions are seen as improving efficiency:

> improvements in allocative efficiency could be facilitated by introducing cost-effectiveness criteria in the definition of priorities in resource allocation at the provincial level and through gradually separating the financing and delivery functions at such level to avoid the perverse incentive on the provincial level to continue financing a hospital regardless the cost-effectiveness of its interventions (Provincial Health Sector Development Project Staff Appraisal Report 1995: 6).

In Argentina, the health and political system is already highly decentralized. The merits and drawbacks of having such a decentralized system are discussed by both World Bank and the government alike. While decentralization is not further pursued as a policy instrument the Argentinian government pursues the deconcentration of health facilities most notably with the introduction of self-managed hospitals.

CRITIQUES OF WORLD BANK ACTIVITY IN THE HEALTH SECTOR IN ARGENTINA

Overall, the role of the World Bank in health reforms is seen as positive by government personnel at the time—funding important programs such as *Plan Nacer*. However, there are also several critiques of the World Bank that arise during this time. The first is a commonly echoed critique: that the World Bank promotes a one-size-fits-all approach to policy (Chorev 2013; Stiglitz 1998). The Argentinian government criticized the World Bank's work in the health sector in Argentina for its lack of sensitivity to local conditions which hindered successful program implementation. It also criticized the high World Bank personnel turnover:

> Aside from the generally good opinion about the Bank's technical expertise provided during project implementation, the borrower pointed out one specific issue in which the Bank could have improved its performance, specifically related to the frequent changes in Bank staff and consultants participating in supervision missions. In the opinion of the borrower, these changes implied several redefinitions of emphasis and priority areas for the project, particularly related to the activities targeting the various vulnerable groups involved in the program. In addition, the borrower was left with the impression that missions too often based their judgments and advice on their

own experience in different countries without taking into account the soci-oeconomic and legal framework prevailing in Argentina (Aids and Sexually Transmitted Diseases Control Project Implementation Report 2004: 18).

In addition, the World Bank encouraged the use of decree laws that need only to be signed by the President without Congress' approval (McGuire 2010; Montoya and Colina 1999; Negretto 2004). However, while often an effective tool this strategy sometimes backfired as lack of wide-spread political backing meant that the contents of decrees were not fully implemented, as is the case with the PMO or basic health care packages.

Generally, the national government sees the World Bank as a sig-nificant partner in getting some important programs off the ground in the face of an inflexible, bureaucratic behemoth of a health system, consisting of several important actors, across sectors, often at odds with each other. For example, when discussing the Fourth Social Protection Project, a multisectoral project implemented between 1998 and 2006 which among other advances helped finance small infrastructure improvements to health facilities, the national government notes that:

> The World Bank has played a key role in the planning and implementation of this program, beyond acting as funding agency. These national policies and their instruments resulted from the interaction between international finan-cial institutions and the national government. It is maintained that the design of FOPAR [Participatory Fund for Social Invesments, *Fondo Participativo de Inversión* Social—which financed these sub-projects in health as well as other sectors, for example, community-network building, construction of community centers, etc.] displays this interaction between conceptions of social policy and exemplifies the possibilities that the national government has to procure lines of financing from international agencies in the interest of implementing its policies (Social Protection Project IV Implementation Report 2006: 29)

This quote also indicates that the government takes ownership of its pol-icy decisions, a far cry from foreign imposed directives. A letter from the Ministry of the Economy pertaining to the Provincial Maternal-Child Health Sector Adjustment loan also describes the positive effect of Bank financing of health projects. It notes that:

> Towards the ends of implementing and being able to sustain these policy priorities [for providing vaccination, programs dealing with AIDS and TB, sexual and reproductive health and other health programs], we have

requested that the World Bank, an entity that has helped us with a large number of objectives in the protection of the poorest and most needy... allow us to launch this group of policies and structural changes in the health sector (Provincial Maternal-Child Health Sector Adjustment Loan Program Document 2003: 65).

While these official reports should be taken with a grain (or several) of salt as indeed, the second quote is in the context of the national government asking for additional monies from the World Bank, this sentiment of a generally positive effect of IFI financed projects is echoed by national policymakers as well. As an official from the Medical Confederation in Argentina, COMRA:

[I] believe that they [the NACER and Remediar projects] are positive for the population because it facilitated access to the health of the newborn infants and pregnant women, improved the quality of care in that area... they knew how to use it, to strengthen primary health care, and given a greater impetus, at the time, to the training of staff who worked in primary care and facilitated collecting epidemiological data from a segment of the population that previously there was no data for (Interview #66).

This is not to say that World Bank activity is universally viewed in a positive light. For example, some have argued that creating several programs reinforces fragmentation because each has its own monitoring system and financing stream as pointed out by a Pan-American Health Organization (PAHO) official (Interview #73). There is also extensive criticism of the general economic policies of both the IMF and the World Bank (that is, not those pertaining to the health sector), but in terms of health financing and projects, the opinion is generally favorable. That is, the World Bank is doing good things in health if not the best things there are some things that respondents believe would be good policy reforms that the World Bank would not support, e.g. public production of medication (*Plan Remediar*) which was financed by the IDB, as mentioned by a researcher in the national academy of medicine:

[the World Bank will not support] a public production of medicines program, so, I say, they are supporting Argentina, but I think beyond that, there are certain things that they won't get into, no? that does not change, but the truth is that they support [Argentina's public health policies] (Interview #79).

This underscores the fact that while not exclusively neoliberal in its approach to health neither is the World Bank open to all national suggestions, it is still working in the interest of economic growth within the parameters of the global capitalist system.

CONCLUSION

Much of Argentina's health policy reform during this time period was directed towards coping with severe economic crisis: stagflation in the 1980s and 1990s, then in 1989 with hyperinflation, and again starting in 1995 (following the 1994 Mexico crisis) leading to the economic crisis in 1999–2002. In the early 1980s then health minister, Aldo Neri, saw this as an opportunity to unify the health system. Once this initiative failed reforms focused on providing insurance for the poorest mothers and children and introducing limited competition in the *Obras Sociales* social security system. Therefore, while early in this period there was a concerted effort to unify the health system since then the reforms have been more modest in scope, largely in the interest of preserving basic levels of health care in the face of crisis. The World Bank supported government efforts, on the whole. Argentina's health sector reform has been characterized by mixed outcomes, and its emphasis on coping with crisis delineates the direction and intention of health sector reform between 1980 and 2005 which are therefore responsive to these challenges and piecemeal.

Argentina's high state autonomy meant that it was able to formulate a clear agenda for health policy on several occasions during this time period; However, low state capacity has prevented it from carrying out an extensive overhaul of the health sector as well as some smaller reforms. That is, my analysis indicates that while World Bank projects in the country often supported or remained neutral about the Argentinian government's wishes, both the economic conditions and the power of trade unions often impeded full implementation of these goals. The World Bank was active in Argentina's health sector during the 1980s, but especially in the 1990s and 2000s. The World Bank's approach was supportive of Argentina's goals to increase coverage, especially for mothers and children, and while it prized efficiency, as expected, it also saw equity as an important goal throughout this time period. While it used neoliberal tools that prized market mechanisms (results-based financing, targeting) it did so in the service of extending access and enhancing both equity and efficiency, contrary to expectations of its work as a strictly neoliberal agent in health. As the following chapters on Peru and Costa Rica demonstrate, the World Bank's approach also varied cross-nationally, signaling a need for more nuance in understanding its approach to health across developing countries and challenging its image as a neoliberal hegemon.

References

Báscolo, E. (2008). *Cambios de los mercados de servicios de salud en la seguridad social en Argentina*: CEPAL.

Belló, M., & Becerril-Montekio, V. M. (2011). Sistema de salud de Argentina. *salud pública de méxico, 53*, s96–s109.

Belmartino, S. (2000). The context and process of health care reform in Argentina. *Reshaping health care in Latin America. A comparative analysis of health care reform in Argentina, Brazil and Mexico. Ottawa: International Development Research Centre*, 27–46.

Cavagnero, E. (2008). Health sector reforms in Argentina and the performance of the health financing system. *Health Policy, 88*(1), 88–99.

Cavagnero, E., Carrin, G., Xu, K., & Aguilar-Rivera, A. M. (2006). Health financing in Argentina: An empirical study of health care expenditure and utilization. *Innovations in Health Financing: Working Paper Series* (8).

Chorev, N. (2013). Restructuring neoliberalism at the World Health Organization. *Review of International Political Economy, 20*(4), 627–666.

Devoto, F., & Cetrángolo, O. (2002). Organización de la salud en Argentina y equidad: una reflexión sobre las reformas de los años noventa e impacto de la crisis actual.

Giovanella, L., Feo, O., Faria, M., & Tobar, S. (2012). *Sistemas de salud en Suramérica: desafíos para la universalidad la integralidad y la equidad*: ISAGS.

Interview #50.

Interview #51.

Interview #66.

Interview #68.

Interview #73.

Interview #74.

Interview #79.

Iriart, C., Merhy, E. E., & Waitzkin, H. (2001). Managed care in Latin America: The new common sense in health policy reform. *Social Science & Medicine, 52*(8), 1243–1253.

Lloyd-Sherlock, P. (2000). Population ageing in developed and developing regions: Implications for health policy. *Social Science and Medicine, 51*(6), 887–895.

Lloyd-Sherlock, P. (2005). Health sector reform in Argentina: A cautionary tale. *Social Science and Medicine, 60*(8), 1893–1903.

McGuire, J. W. (2010). *Wealth, health, and democracy in East Asia and Latin America.* Cambridge: Cambridge University Press.

Montoya, S., & Colina, J. (1999). *La reforma de Obras Sociales en Argentina: avances y desafíos pendientes.* Centro de Investigación y Desarrollo de la Educación (CIDE).

Munck, R. (1998). Mutual benefit societies in Argentina: Workers, nationality, social security and trade unionism. *Journal of Latin American Studies, 30*(03), 573–590.

Negretto, G. L. (2004). Government capacities and policy making by Decree in Latin America The cases of Brazil and Argentina. *Comparative Political Studies, 37*(5), 531–562.

Stiglitz, J. E. (1998). *More instruments and broader goals: Moving toward the post-Washington consensus.* UNU/WIDER Helsinki.

Teixeira, S. M. F., & Fleury, S. (2000). *Reshaping health care in Latin America: A comparative analysis of health care reform in Argentina, Brazil, and Mexico.* Idrc.

Tobar, F. (2001). Breve historia de la prestación del ser-vicio de salud en la Argentina. *Ediciones Isalud.*

CHAPTER 5

Peru: Slow, Steady Health
Reform in a Weak State

"When there is an endogenous process, and from the outside they help, you channel that. I find it interesting, and indeed in Peru, there is a will, there is a need to extend social coverage, coverage of health to the most marginalized sectors… one of the most serious problems is the financing. Because the expansion of services, and the expansion of resources needs to be accompanied by an increase in funding, in a sustained manner."
— interview with Dr. Manuel Jumpa Santamaría, then Head of the Office of Decentralization in the Peruvian Ministry of Health, formerly an official advisor to two Deputy Ministers of Health and a Minister of Health in 1991, 2001 and 2008 respectively on the problems facing the Peruvian health care system. (Interview #34)

Peru's health system faces several interrelated challenges, as long time Ministry of Health manager Dr. Jumpa Santamaria identifies: leaders have often lacked both a comprehensive vision and resources, and sometimes both, needed to effect major reforms (Interview #34). Peru has relied on external resources and advice in shaping its health sector, as a country with traditionally low autonomy and capacity in health, rendering it especially open to World Bank recommendations and funding. Since the 1980s, the Peruvian government actively pursued expanded coverage via targeted programs, implementing health projects that focused on extending access geographically, and focusing service

© The Author(s) 2017   119
S. Noy, *Banking on Health*, DOI 10.1007/978-3-319-61765-7_5

provision on the poor as well as mothers and children. The national agenda was influenced by an international discourse on development and health, and the Peruvian government received monies for these programs not only from IFIs such as the World Bank and the IDB but also USAID and other bilateral agencies. Its categorization as a weak state made it more susceptible and open to IFI influence, it was also able to successfully attract the technical and monetary resources that these institutions offered. These resources have translated positively for health indicators and access but may have resulted in a further fragmentation of the system (Interview #45). This continues the historical tradition of vertical programs in Peru, that is, programs that focus on one or several particular health conditions with little institutional coordination. However, the Peruvian government, with assistance from the World Bank and other international organizations, is heading in the direction of national insurance in an attempt to better coordinate national health efforts.

GOVERNMENT AUTONOMY AND CAPACITY IN HEALTH IN PERU: A CLASSICALLY WEAK STATE

Peru is characterized by low autonomy in the health sector where the government has not been able to establish a clear agenda for the health sector in the past several decades. This is partly due to high political instability during this time period. That is, even when governments had some initiatives in mind for change, these were quickly abandoned (and even opposed and directly countered) by subsequent governments and even health ministers within the same presidency. The issue of turnover is perhaps due to nominees' qualifications, as an academic who was served as a consultant to many international organizations on health projects in Peru explains: "The main problem is the selection of the [health] minister. This is not the only central problem, but it is central. [Presidents] will instate their family doctor. Fujimori instated a fish specialist in 1993. In 1998, it he appointed his daughter's gynecologist [as health minister], what I mean is they'll appoint anyone. It's really a problem" (Interview #27). This personally motivated appointment to leadership positions seems to extend to the lower levels of governance as well, in the 1980s especially, as a social security manager notes: "[the appointment of administrators] was irregular, let's say. The oldest doctor was made the director [of the hospital or health services] even if he didn't know how to add, as an exaggeration" (Interview #39).

In addition to this issue with leadership, more broadly there is little coordination within the Ministry of Health, the official regulator of the Peruvian health sector (Cotlear 2006). This posed a challenge even to the international organizations seeking to invest in health in Peru, as one World Bank document notes:

> The organizational culture of the central MOH was appropriately described as "feudal," with little cooperation between internal offices. The lack of leadership over several changes of health ministers resulted in failure to mandate institutional collaboration with externally-financed projects, with no arbiter to coordinate the different strategies developing in parallel form. (Basic Health & Nutrition Project Completion Report 2001: 12)

In addition, the sheer fragmentation of the health system more broadly prior to 1980 and beyond, coupled with political instability, made it a particularly difficult sector to corral. Peru is also characterized by low capacity in health. However, unlike Argentina, this is not because there is a strong labor union which opposes increased government control over the health sector but rather due to a lack of resources. That is, the government has neither the institutional nor financial resources to widely implement those reforms that it did decide to pursue.

Existing academic accounts of social sector reform in Peru, especially in the 1990s, highlight the comparatively small direct role played by international actors. For example, Weyland (2006) notes that IFIs were instrumental largely through advice and availability (rather than resources and conditions), while Brooks (2005) notes that economic liberalization changed the incentives faced by these same governments (which in the case of pensions, she argues, led to a willingness to implement market-oriented reforms in the interest of reducing reliance on foreign capital). I argue this account does not extend to the health sector given the important role of international actors in health in Peru. As highlighted by Ewig: "international organizations became embedded within the Health Ministry itself, blurring the line between 'Peruvian' and 'global' actors but also further cementing the shared ideational basis of this epistemic community" (2010). Global actors were important to Peruvian health sector reform via ideas, resources, monetary, and technical assistance, but were also deeply implanted in the Peruvian health apparatus in the 1980s and beyond.

I argue that this is why it is particularly important to consider the ways in which state autonomy and capacity shape IFIs involvement in health sector reform. The World Bank and other international organizations have played a variable role in national health sector reform, and unpacking states' ability to construct a coherent agenda for health reform and their resources to implement it is central to our understanding of how and where the World Bank and other IFIs were influential in health. In Peru, the World Bank and other health organizations enmeshed themselves among health personnel in a state with low autonomy in health. Because the Peruvian government seldom had an overarching, coherent agenda for health reform, these same organizations were able to influence the reform process even in its planning phase. Even then, however, plans seldom came to fruition, because of weak capacity. This weak autonomy in health evident in the power wielded by the Ministry of the Economy on health as detailed by a WHO functionary in Peru: "Actually the true Minister of Health is the Ministry of Economy and Finance, because it [the Ministry of the Economy] decides how much money will go towards what issues and where. The Ministry of Health doesn't decide that. And interaction is managed by the [international] banks [the World Bank and the Inter-American Development Bank]" (Interview #22). The Ministry of Health, due to its weakness within the Peruvian state, is therefore not allocated much funding, and the World Bank and other international agencies become intermediaries in its interaction with the Ministry of the Economy. In Peru, the World Bank's increased attention to health strengthens the Ministry of Health's position vis-à-vis the Ministry of the Economy in the financing of health projects. However, in the long run, the Ministry of Health remains weak, as its bargaining position depends on World Bank's (and other IFI and bilateral agencies') cooperation and support. Despite this, Peru's health sector reform has slowly moved in the direction of increased access and universalism, albeit via the use of classically neoliberal tools such as targeting.

PERU'S HEALTH SECTOR: HISTORY, STRUCTURE, AND CHALLENGES

The Peruvian health sector, like that of Argentina, has three primary components: a public sector, a social security agency, and a private system. Personnel in the police and armed forces have their own facilities. In contrast to Argentina, the Peruvian social security system is significantly less powerful in the context of the national health system than the *Obras Sociales* in Argentina; it provides lower coverage and is not managed by unions.

The Public Sector

Government involvement in the health sector has a storied past in Peru with the establishment of the precursor to the current Ministry of Health, a public health authority, as early as 1903. Throughout its early years, international involvement heavily shaped the development of the Peruvian health system. The Rockefeller Foundation supported anti-yellow fever and anti-malaria programs in the 1920s and 1940s, followed by involvement by PAHO and UNICEF efforts to eradicate malaria beginning in the late 1950s (Ewig 2010). In 1957, the Ministry of Health developed a basic health plan and began establishing a network of clinics connected to a hospital in an effort to provide basic primary and hospital care. However, these efforts were derailed with the military coup in 1968. The coup resulted in little attention to health and coupled with an economic crisis, and by 1980, the health budget was 3.5% of the general budget, compared with 17% in 1968 (Ewig 2010). The Ministry of Health (*Ministerio de Salud*, MINSA) and its establishments have traditionally provided services to those without insurance in Peru. Estimates from 2008 indicate that approximately 58% of the population did not have health insurance and relied on MINSA health posts (Alcalde-Rabanal et al. 2011). A growing proportion of the population (estimated at over 30%) relies on a national health insurance scheme established in 2001 that is growing in size: the Integral Health Insurance (*Seguro Integral de Salud*, SIS).

Social Security: EsSALUD

Peru's social security agency in health, EsSALUD (*El Seguro Social de Salud*) serves approximately 20% of the population: those formally employed, both current and retired, as well as their families. It has centers in urban areas and is financed by payroll contributions (of 9%). EsSALUD's predecessor, the Peruvian Institute for Social Security (*Instituto Peruano de Seguro Social*, IPSS), was established in 1980 when social security health insurance was combined with pensions by the military government at the time. Its origins date back to 1958, with the establishment of an Employee Social Security (*Seguro Social de Empleado*) (Salaverry and Delgado 2000). Since 1996, the IPSS has been known as EsSALUD and is responsible solely for health insurance, whereas before 1993, the IPSS administered both health and pensions (Cruz-Saco and Mesa-Lago 1999). Finally, members of the police and armed forces and their family members receive services from health establishments designated for their use. While there is not an exact figure for the percent of the population that benefits from insurance via the armed forces and police, it is estimated at less than 4% as of 2008 (Alcalde-Rabanal et al. 2011).

Throughout the end of the 1970s, the quality of social security provided health services was very low. This owed to a large rise in inflation which limited the value of the financial resources available to the then IPSS (now EsSALUD). This period was followed by an economic recession in the 1980s, which led, by the middle of the 1980s, to the social security being "regarded as seriously deficient both administratively and in the delivery of an acceptable quality of health care services" (Fiedler 1996). Social security is then limited in scope, coverage, and quality, and does not represent a particularly powerful actor in the Peruvian health sector, certainly not in comparison to Argentina's *Obras Sociales*.

The Private Sector

The private sector is comprised of private clinics known as *Entidades Prestadoras de Salud* (Health Services Entities, EPS) that provide services to those with the ability to pay for expensive private services (though EPS also subcontract with EsSALUD since the late 1990s) (Petrera et al. 2013). Approximately, 2% of Peruvians have private insurance (known as *prepagos*). While approximately 41% of total spending is private, only 8% is spending on private insurance, as compared with out-of-pocket expenditure. The private sector also includes non-profits and other organizations that provide additional services (e.g., vaccinations and health education).

HEALTH POLICY REFORM, 1980–2005

Reforms in the health sector in Peru from 1980 to 2005 can be summarized as a concerted effort at increased access since the 1990s. The 1980s were essentially a lost decade in health sector reform. In the context of economic crisis, terrorism, and civil war, health policy was relegated to the backburner. Little interest was taken in it and, in turn, little was done. In the 1990s, the major reforms of Peru's primary-level, public health system were the implementation of fees for services, means-testing, a basic package of health services and extending insurance, and decentralization of the administration of local health clinics. As I discuss below, the intended scope of these reforms was broader than their implementation, because of economic crisis, political instability, and lack of resources devoted to health.

The Lost Decade in Peruvian Health, the 1980s to the Early 1990s

The economic crisis in Peru in the 1980s was coupled with civil war and terrorism, with high civilian casualties which made it an especially bloody conflict (Taylor 1998). This led to a reduction in health spending during this period as well. Some efforts toward decentralization in the health sector were attempted in the very early 1980s, but these were purely bureaucratic transfers of power without any real change until the 1990s (Ewig 2002). Therefore, the 1980s saw deterioration in health facilities, especially in rural areas. Through the early 1990s, the public health system network, run by the Ministry of Health, was the hardest hit (Interview #15).

In 1991, partly in an effort to improve the conditions of public health facilities, then-President Alberto Fujimori introduced fees for services. This act was seen by observers less as a strategic move and more as "a stop-gap measure to help desperate health establishments self-finance until economic stabilization was achieved" (Ewig 2002). In the 1990s, regional health authorities (*Direcciones Regionales de Salud*, DIRESAs) began receiving financing directly from the Ministry of the Economy for regional programs (Arredondo et al. 2005). Despite hopes for decentralization and a movement for deconcentration in health that was begun at the end of the 1980s, "no significant changes were made in the management of hospitals. Because of the nation's fiscal restrictions, the only area that was formalized was fee collections. This was meant to give hospitals a way out to their insolvency problems, but the poor were adversely affected" (Cotlear 2006). This is despite the fact that between 1985 and 1987 and again in 1989, David Tejada de Rivero, one of my respondents and a strong advocate of primary health care and Deputy Director-General of the World Health Organization (WHO) during the signing of the seminal Alma Ata conference of 1978, held the office of Minister of Health.

Expanding and Decentralizing Basic Health Services: Salud Basica Para Todos and CLAS, 1994

Coming out of the economic crisis, by the early 1990s, the economy had begun to stabilize, and the privatization of some state industries allowed the state to begin to increase spending on health (Roberts 1995). In 1994, the "Basic Health for All" or *Salud Básica Para Todos* program introduced a basic package of health services with the goal of extending services to areas with a high incidence of poverty and remote areas more generally. Simultaneously, administrative decentralization proceeded guided by the idea that this would allow greater responsiveness to localized challenges and problems and greater efficiency (Interview #28). This process of decentralization began with an amendment in the 1979 constitution but was never implemented. The next big push for decentralization came in 2002, under then-President Alejandro Toledo through a *Ley de Bases de la Descentralización* followed by a *Ley Orgánica de Gobiernos Regionales*. This reform came in conjunction with an attempt to decentralize the administration of health services via the *Comités Locales de Administración de Salud* (CLAS) initiative (Ortiz de Zevallos et al. 1999). CLAS was established as a non-profit organization responsible for the administration of one or more basic health posts consisting (an odd number of) members of the board that are elected by the community and work with the regional (or sub-regional) Health Ministry-appointed director. The program aimed to expand coverage and improve the efficiency via community participation. In doing so, it effectively decentralized the management of health services and was tied financially to the "Basic Health for All" initiative.

Under the CLAS program, local clinics were administered by a board led by the clinic head doctor where the community elected three additional board members and the doctor selected three more. Both of these programs were funded exclusively using national monies. However, the

World Bank and IDB provided consulting services as well as monies for programs which interfaced heavily with these, chief among them the Basic Health and Nutrition Program (*Programa de Salud y Nutricion Basica*) and Project to Strengthen Health Services (*Programa de Fortalecimiento de Servicios de Salud*) between 1994 and 2000 as well as USAID's Project 2000 (*Proyecto 2000*) which worked parallel to "Basic Health for All" in different geographic regions (Interview #43). As such, these national programs were heavily guided and influenced by international organizations including the World Bank (Interview #69).

Populist Presidentialism: Sub-contracting in the Social Security Sector and the Establishment of the Seguro Escolar Gratuito and Seguro Materno Infantil, 1996–1998

In the early 1990s, the Peruvian government considered a policy allowing the participation of private insurers (*Entidades Prestadoras de Salud*, EPS) in the social security system by competing with the state system. While legislation to this effect was passed in 1991, it was not implemented "due to strong opposition from organized labor, retired persons, and health care professionals" (Ewig 2010). In 1997, the Modernization of Health Social Security Law (*Ley de Modernizacion de Seguridad Social en Salud*) passed. It did allow, in practice as well as legislation, for EPS to compete with the state social security system to provide health insurance for companies. According to the World Bank, these reforms served to end EsSALUD's "monopoly on service delivery, instead allowing competition with other providers, including the private sector, and a greater degree of user selection" (Health Reform Project Phase I, Project Appraisal Document 1999: 8). That is, rather than rely solely on EsSALUD's facilities, private sector providers could also compete to provide services, which would allow affiliates to choose where they received their services. The idea was that this would push EsSALUD toward greater efficiency and possibly provide users with better quality service. However, this system was operated according to employing company rather than by employee and covered only primary and secondary care where more complicated procedures were handled by tertiary care facilities (full hospitals) in the public system. As such, according to this law, only one-fourth of the employer's 9% contribution to social security goes to the EPS, which in turn has to provide a minimum set of services (Ewig 2010). This same law also created a regulatory agency to oversee the participation of these private providers: the Superintendency for Private Providers of Health (*Superintendencia de Entidades Prestadoras de Salud, SEPS*) which was responsible for authorizing EPS and keeping track of information about their operations (Interview #26).

In the late 1990s, the government established two different schemes, also run by the Peruvian Ministry of Health: the Maternal Infant Insurance (*Seguro Materno Infantil*, SMI) and the Free School-Children Insurance (*Seguro Escolar Gratuito*, SEG). These programs targeted pregnant women, mothers, and children in public schools. The SEG was implemented nationally, and free health care coverage via the public health system was available to children between the ages of 3 and 17 enrolled in public school. According to Ewig (2002), the reform was implemented in order to encourage parents to enroll their school-age children in school and further asserts that not only was this not an initiative of the Ministry of Health, but that Ministry of Health personnel only found out about it during Fujimori's speech announcing it. As Jaramillo and Parodi (2004) elaborate: the SEG did not address any public health issue; morbidity among this age group is quite low and therefore cannot be said to have a public health policy objective. Rather, while perhaps a positive policy, it was a populist effort to shore up public support.

The SMI, Maternal Infant Health Insurance, was implemented as a pilot program in two geographic regions (called departments in Peru) in 1998, covering pregnant women as well as children younger than 4 years old, expanding nationally by 2002. Yamin (2003) notes that this reform was not just to boost presidential popularity and an effort to improve Peru's poor indicators in maternal health but also to deflect from Peru's poor record in family planning, given the international uproar over forced sterilization and other abuses. As such, this reform was geared toward improving health outcomes in Peru, but also outward-looking in terms of its international image and reputation in family planning.

While both the SEG and SMI were financed with public monies, the SMI also received funding from the Inter-American Development Bank (IDB) and the World Bank whereas SEG was funded only through the national treasury though UNICEF was marginally involved in later years. The SMI, unlike the SEG, was in keeping with the 1997 General Health Law (*Ley General de Salud No 26842*) which noted that state health initiatives should subsidize, wholly or partially, medical attention to populations with fewer resources and that are not beneficiaries of other (public or social security) insurance schemes. In addition, this same law noted, the focus on women and children was warranted as the poor have higher fertility.

State Health Insurance for the Poor with a Focus on Mothers and Infants: Seguro Integral de Salud (SIS), 2001

In 2001, the incoming government decided to combine these two programs: the Maternal Infant insurance (SMI) and the Free School-Children Insurance (SEG), creating the "Integral Health Insurance" or *Seguro Integral de Salud* (SIS). This program deviated from previous public insurance schemes in two main ways: first by expanding maternal coverage nationally, and second by no longer requiring minors to be enrolled in school. That is, everyone below the poverty line can be covered by SIS (Parodi 2005; Interview #12). The SIS program has pursued a strategy of incorporating groups of Peruvians together, rather than individuals, though this insurance is also available to individuals. For example, the SIS has extended coverage to groups, such as women that work in nurseries and kindergartens and leaders of community kitchens ("comedores populares") (Alcalde-Rabanal et al. 2011). The central offices of the SIS are already covered under the budget of the Ministry of Health where SIS pays a fee for each service rendered to its beneficiaries enabling it to circumvent "the 'corporation' by paying directly to front-line providers and by doing it as payment for services effectively provided (and involving a system of audits), instead of following the traditional route that would add resources to a budget line provided to the ministry" (Cotlear 2006).

Along with support for the SIS, the World Bank supported health sector reform via the Program for the Support of Health Sector Reform, *Programa de Apoyo a la Reforma del Sector Salud* (*PARSalud*) which was implemented in 1999. *PARSalud* is focused on maternal and child health and is implemented in seven geographic regions; it finances community outreach and health education but also purchasing of equipment and medicines as well as other support. This program utilized the newly decentralized structure of health and other social services, working via regional governments: "Its implementation involved coordination between program management and the regional governments, which, under the new decentralization laws in Peru, have assumed a more prominent role in the execution of health policies" (Rubio et al.

2009). Of the 75 million for the program cost, 28 and 27 came from the IDB and World Bank, respectively, 14 million from the public budget, and 6 million from the Peruvian–Canadian Fund. This was its first phase, with the second phase, *PARSalud* II having begun in 2009 which also addresses tuberculosis in addition to *PARSalud* I's foci. The current focus is therefore in line with previous programs: the SIS is focused on extending access, particularly to the poor, and in particular on the infant, child, and maternal health.

ENDS AND MEANS IN WORLD BANK HEALTH PROJECTS IN PERU, 1980–2005

Health sector reform in Peru over this time period was influenced by the World Bank: both from within, via consultants, and overlapping employment for Ministry of Health and other government employees in international organizations, but also externally via loans and technical assistance. Peru is the weakest state of the countries examined in this book, with low state capacity and autonomy in health and characterized by political and economic instability (through Argentina arguably weathered the worst economic crises). Of the three cases, the Peruvian one does indeed display the most utilization of neoliberal tools in a quest for efficiency (targeting enforced via means-testing) but also a keen interest in extending access, at least to basic health care, especially among poor segments of the population. My analysis suggests that this outcome is the result of several factors: first, as in the Argentinian case, the World Bank did not seek to implement purely neoliberal means and ends. Second, and related, the overlap between World Bank and other international organization personnel and Ministry of Health personnel, via consultancies and people moving between these institutions in their jobs, served to limit the aspirations of the World Bank and sensitize it to local needs, rather than attempting to transplant foreign approaches to the Peruvian context. Finally, the high fragmentation and low autonomy did not allow the World Bank to co-opt the state apparatus and influence policy as strongly as it might have liked to. Unlike in the case of Argentina, this is not because of powerful labor unions, but rather demonstrates the strength of weak states. Ironically, weak states may be, to a certain extent, impervious to long-term, deep-seated capture and coercion, because there is little to capture given high volatility in leadership and pervasive fragmentation.

The World Bank was involved in several health projects and programs in Peru, especially in the 1990s. In all, the World Bank began 19 health-related projects in Peru between 1980 and 2005. Between one in four and one in five (23.17%) of the projects financed by the World Bank in Peru during this time had a health component, and the average cost of these projects was $91.04 million (with total project costs at $1729.70 million). Of this amount, the World Bank contributed approximately 72% of the financing to these projects (a similar ratio as in Argentina), with the national government and other aid agencies covering the remainder of the costs of these projects (see also Methodological Appendix Table A.4). All World Bank health projects in Peru during this time period and their accompanying documents are listed in Methodological Appendix Table A.5. The IDB was also involved in several initiatives. However, unlike in Argentina (and Costa Rica), USAID was also heavily involved in health sector reform and several programs and most notably in the 2000 Project (*Proyecto 2000*) which worked in parallel to "Basic Care for All" in different geographic regions (and indeed, Oscar Ugarte, the health minister between 2008 and 2011 was a former USAID employee and in charge of the World Bank and IDB-financed *PARSalud* project) (Interview #41; Interview #35). While the funding for SEG and "Basic Health for All" was entirely domestic, SEG, while formally under the charge of the health ministry, was more an education intervention than a health one, with little input from public health professionals in its construction and implementation. Even for the "Basic Health for All" plan, the World Bank and IDB were involved in consulting, and certainly for subsequent programs such as the SIS. The following sections identify, using evidence from archival research and interviews, the paradigmatic goals and instruments utilized in health policies implemented during this time period and detailed above.

Paradigmatic Goals: Problem Definition and National Priorities

While Peru too went through economic crises and inflation in the 1980s, in later periods these were less severe than in Argentina. However, Peru was characterized by political instability during this time period, with

both civil war and periods of dictatorship and democracy. Of the three
cases, the pro-growth and anti-poverty approach espoused by the World
Bank during this time period (elaborated in Chap. 1), and the relationship between promoting growth and eradicating poverty, was most
explicitly and consistently discussed in the context of health in Peru (as
compared with Argentina and Costa Rica):

> The achievement of broad-based growth is the first element of the pov-
> erty alleviation strategy for Peru …. The second prong of the poverty alle-
> viation strategy is investment in the human capital of the poor in order
> to enable them to participate fully in the expanding economy and benefit
> from it. This means increasing use of both health and education services
> and improvements in the quality of those services. This is a priority for the
> rural population, among whom the incidence of poverty is high. Nearly
> half of the rural population living in the mountains are extremely poor.
> Within these groups, mothers and children are at particular risk. (Basic
> Health and Nutrition Project Staff Appraisal Report 1994: 2)

As in Argentina, the World Bank was focused quite heavily on targeting
of women and children during this time period. This echoes the government's strategy with the SMI and SEG, implemented in the 1990s.
There is very little official information about the state's goals in health as
the Peruvian government's published only one official health plan during this time period regarding its goals for health and a political parties
agreement in health signed in December 2005, the end of my analysis
period. The national plan attempted to outline health goals between
2002 and 2006 but was very general and did not discuss specifics. For
example, it talks about equity. It also discusses how the SIS should contribute to equity but in very general terms:

> The principle of equity seeks to reverse the trend of an expanding gap
> between the poor and rich in society. This means prioritizing actions which
> favor of lower income sectors as an expression of a profound sense of
> solidarity and social justice. Part of it will be policies to promote a better
> nutritional status of the population and the prevention of the most com-
> mon communicable diseases. A commitment to equity is also to facilitate
> access to health services for parts of the low income to medium income
> populations through the comprehensive health insurance (SIS). (Sectoral

Policy Guidelines for 2002–2012 and Fundamental Principles for the
Sectoral Strategic Plan 2001–2006 1993: 29)

Therefore, the Peruvian government is committed to equity, and in the
health sector this is to be accomplished via the SIS which would help the
poor in particular. Similarly, the World Bank is concerned with issues of
poverty and human capital promotion; in this way, efficiency in the interest of a deeper and broader labor pool is the goal, in addition to poverty
alleviation in the interest of equity. The World Bank is also concerned
with efficiency more generally, especially given economic crisis and limited budgets apparent during this time period.

Policy Instruments and Levels

The World Bank and the Peruvian government utilize several policy
instruments in the promotion of equity and efficiency. These policy
instruments were often promoted in tandem in World Bank activity in
the health sector. That is, projects often incorporated many of these
instruments together, and these were seen to work in complementarity
to one another, more so than in either Costa Rica or Argentina. For
example, in the early 1980s, the World Bank praises the new government's commitment to

> economic efficiency, decontrol of the economy (including divestiture
> of some of the state-owned enterprises), promotion of the private sector
> (including foreign investment), and policies aiming at a more equitable
> sharing of the benefits of development through job creation and spe-
> cifically targeted social programs. (Primary Health Project Report of the
> President of IBRD 1982: 4)

I focus on targeting separately as it was a big component of policy
reform and World Bank activity in Peru. I then examine decentralization,
primary health care, and separation of functions together, as these were
often discussed in tandem in the service of both equity and efficiency.
Finally, I examine how the World Bank discusses performance-based
management and private sector involvement as these are seen as working in the service of efficiency, though when coupled with decentralization are also viewed as promoting equity in health care across geographic
regions in Peru.

Targeting

The World Bank promoted targeting in health in Peru quite broadly, focusing on the poor as well as women and children. While these programs improved both access and health outcomes, this strategy stands in contrast to a more universalistic expansion of services. Furthermore, this gendered approach has a long history in Latin American health systems, which developed around a male breadwinner model, and some have argued that this focus comes at the expense of universalism (Ewig 2010; Gideon 2014).

Indeed, all health programs during this time period were targeted toward particular segments of the population, though the SIS aspires to achieve universal coverage in the future. While SEG for school children was an education rather than a health program, as explained above, the SMI scheme for mothers and infants was a central health program during this time period. The World Bank pushed this approach, and one of my respondents indicated that while the government was sometimes interested in a more integral approach to health care than the World Bank, it was able to expand the scope of some projects at the implementation stage:

> we [the Peruvian government] were part of a basic health and nutrition project of the World Bank, its formulation was good because it followed a logic of integral attention to health, at the primary level, but the Bank insisted on a maternal and infant scheme that was very fragmented and focused on only some services. And well, we were stubborn and determined in our insistence on an integral approach to primary care in the health posts and in the end the Bank gave in after lots of pressure and because the project had had some successes. (Interview #12)

This indicates that despite not having a strong agenda overall for health talented leaders within the Ministry of Health did sometimes propose different directions than that of the World Bank, and were able to influence implementation. This speaks to the fact that there are well-developed health professionals within the Peruvian Ministry of Health, with clear goals and ideas; though, overall, the health sector and the Ministry are each so fragmented, government technocrats do not always have input into government policies and projects in health.

While the "Basic Health for All" and CLAS were funded using national monies, the World Bank did provide a 34 million dollar loan to finance "The Basic Health and Nutrition Project" between 1994 and 2000. The focus was on poverty alleviation and "increasing the use of maternal and child health and nutrition service by extending access and improving the quality of services" (Basic Health & Nutrition Project Completion Report 2001: 2). According to the World Bank, this loan allowed them to work synergistically and improved the "Basic Health for All" project which they note "had a very positive effect on project implementation by placing health infrastructure and MOH staff in isolated rural areas, greatly facilitating improvements in the coverage of services in project areas" (Basic Health and Nutrition Project Completion Report 2001: 9–10). This further strengthens the assertion that there was significant synergy and overlap between World Bank and government activities, even in policies where the World Bank was not involved in direct financing; it was important for both planning and sometimes implementation.

Decentralization, Primary Health Care, and Separation of Functions
The process of decentralization is an ongoing effort in Peru's health sector. While the 1979 constitution establishes a decentralized political system and while regional health authorities had existed previously, only in the 1980s and 1990s did they begin to receive the responsibility for health programming (*Decreto Legislativo 70*). The power of regional authorities in health care was further codified in *Decreto Legislativo 584* (April 16, 1990) passed under President Alan Garcia. It furthered a separation of functions between health care provision and planning. Regional governments now became responsible for health care provision while the national Ministry of Health is still responsible for establishing a national health agenda. As of the early 1990s, regional governments received their budget directly from the Ministry of Economy and Finance. This meant that while the national Ministry of Health remained the normative leader in national health, it had no resources and little power to implement its recommendations and plans.

However, with the implementation of the "Basic Health for All" initiative in 1994, the financing of health was once again recentralized as funding came from the Ministry of the Economy to the Ministry of Health, and only then to regional health authorities. This stuttering stop-and-start process of decentralization in health has not always mirrored the broader organization of governance in Peru. While Peru's regional governments (with the process still in progress in the metropolitan region of Lima) have assumed responsibility for their territories, it is only since 2003 that they have been democratically elected. In addition, while the Ministry of Health has published general directives for the organization of regional health authorities in 2005 (*Resolución Ministerial No 566-2005/MINSA*), each region has its own organizational model.

Decentralization, therefore, both in the case of "Basic Care for All" and the CLAS project begun at similar times, was tightly coupled with discussions of improving and strengthening primary health care. However, unlike the decentralization in the "Basic Care for All" framework where the decentralization was to regional health authorities, in the case of CLAS, decentralizing the actual administration of health facilities included community members. The CLAS then became legally autonomous but depended on regional health authorities for its financial resources and budget. While CLAS has since disbanded, with only few centers remaining, it was an important policy innovation at the time and supported by international organizations, namely, the IDB and USAID. The World Bank supported decentralization as a means to more efficiently allocate resources and tailor programs to regional health needs, an especially salient concern given the diversity of climates, topography, and health challenges in Peru (with the *Sierra*, the *Selva*, and the *Costa*, or mountains, rainforest, and coast). CLAS was more closely aligned with a quest for equity via community involvement, though it too was justified on the grounds of efficiency and achieving health goals such as vaccination and checkups for lower cost and at higher rates.

Together with decentralization, the World Bank encouraged an emphasis on primary care and separation of functions during this time period. Indeed, one of the World Bank's earliest health sector projects in Peru, signed in 1983, was the Primary Health Project which focused on the "construction of additional primary health care infrastructure" (Primary Health Project Completion Report 1993: ii). This program too encountered issues, with a government change between when it was signed (1983) and when implementation began (1985). Because of the weak institutional capacity of the Ministry of Health, a separate agency was appointed to oversee the project. This had the result of marginalizing the project "from the normal workings of the Ministry [of Health] and [the project had] negligible impact on Ministry capacity" (Primary Health Project Completion Report 1993: iii). The *PARSalud* project, begun in 1999, focused on maternal and child health and decentralization and was financed by both the IDB and the World Bank, also supported decentralization efforts and primary care efforts.

These policy instruments were seen to work in the interest of equity, by making locally administered health units more responsive to local needs, but especially in advancing efficiency with the idea that resources would be used more effectively if decision-making was decentralized and administration of services separated from their financing. With all three of these policy instruments, there was both forward movement and back-tracking, largely the result of low state autonomy, high turnover among health ministers, and a lack of continuity in already weak health adminis-tration.

Performance-Based Management and Private Sector Involvement
Performance-based management is a policy instrument that was closely coupled with decentralization as well, like all of the policy instruments utilized in health sector reform in Peru. Before the 2002 decentraliza-tion process, the Ministry of Health assigned all of the medical person-nel to health facilities across the country but this changed, and was tied to the move toward "budgeting for results" which was promoted by the World Bank (Interview #21). Performance-based management was also closely coupled with decentralization, and the push toward both decen-tralization and performance-based financing in the early 2000s was part of a broader strategy of poverty alleviation and heavily motivated by the international discourse surrounding the Millennium Development Goals (MDGs): "By focusing on results, such as access of the poor to social services, it strengthens several mechanisms such as performance agreements and accreditation that aim towards achieving the MDGs" (Accountability for Decentralization in the Social Sectors Project Information Document 2004: 3). Together with decentralization and the separation of functions, performance-based management was seen as a way for regional authorities to set their own goals while committing to certain aims of the national Ministry of Health, for example: "each region signs Annual Management Agreements (Acuerdos de Gestión) with the central Government in which they agree to meet certain tar-gets with respect to specific health results which include the prevention and treatment of communicable diseases as well as other prevalent health problems" (Health Reform Project Phase I Completion Report 2007: 18). Regulation and a separation of functions were clearly on the World Bank's agenda for reform in Peru:

> Public social expenditures grew substantially during the 1990s. However, pre-existing and newly created programs were scattered across multiple agencies in an ad hoc and uncoordinated fashion, each having its own objectives, targeting criteria, institutional arrangements, and bureaucratic and beneficiary interests. Many lacked a clear strategy, monitoring system, or criteria for evaluating performance. (Programmatic Social Reform Loan Project Implementation Completion Report 2002: 6)

While linking teacher salaries to students' performance was implemented in education in the 2000s, this has only more recently been proposed in the context of health:

> In November 2006, after the declaration of effectiveness of the Project, the Bank approved a Fiscal Management and Competitiveness Development Policy Loan, the first of a series of four Development Policy Loans (DPL) supporting, among others, the Government's policy for the gradual implementation of Performance-Based Budgeting (PBB) throughout the public sector, including sub-national Governments. (Institutional Capacity for Sustainable Fiscal Decentralization Implementation Completion Report 2011: 2)

That is, the focus on performance-based management is expected to increase in World Bank activities across sectors, including health, in Peru. The World Bank notes that in the 2000s, "performance agreements have also been introduced between MINSA [Ministry of Health] and the Regional Health Departments to establish and hold authorities accountable for achieving agreed targets" (Programmatic Social Reform Loan Project II Implementation Report 2003: 12). However, these performance agreements are not actually tied to budgets (as these are delegated by the Ministry of the Economy), and there do not appear to be real consequences for not meeting these targets.

In the future, the focus on performance-based financing and management more broadly should include, according to the World Bank, more involvement of the private sector, not only in health but across social sectors:

> New transfers should be results-oriented and results-conditioned. Further use and strict enforcement of inter-government service delivery arrangements is recommended. They might include incentives to form public-private partnerships or outsourcing. Transfers might also be

establishment-based (like transfers by school according to student enroll-
ment) while keeping monitoring and coordinating capacity at the local
level. ... In the medium term, civil service reform at local and regional
governments is needed. New labor relations in the public sector also
need to be performance-based. Otherwise mayors or governors will have
no room to reorganize production functions, demonstrate higher efficiency or respond to their electorate. It is not recommended to transfer health and education services before labor contracts can be properly
managed at regional or local levels. (Programmatic Decentralization and
Competitiveness Structural Adjustment Loan Implementation Completion
Report 2007: 57)

Performance-based budgeting and financing, particularly insofar as concerns the relationship between the national and provincial governments,
was also coupled with privatization. These instruments are discussed often
in terms of efficiency but also in the context of equity and sub-national
inequality. Involving the private sector and sub-contracting services in
the future is seen as a way to make sure that these inequalities are not
exacerbated: "Not every service needs to be directly provided by sub-
national governments; creativity for efficiency in service delivery needs to
be encouraged. In the end, certification, inter-government performance
arrangements and results-based transfers will lead to asymmetry in service
responsibilities, with good performers ahead of others" (Programmatic
Decentralization and Competitiveness Structural Adjustment Loan
Implementation Completion Report 2007: 57). The IDB was also actively
involved in providing technical assistance for the Superintendency for
Private Providers of Health (*Superintendencia de Entidades Prestadoras
de Salud*, SEPS) in the late 1990s following its creation. The goal of this
loan was to help the Peruvian government create a regulatory agency to
allow private participation in health. The World Bank is then interested in
increasing private-sector involvement but couches this recommendation in
patient satisfaction and outcome terms, rather than in terms of equity.

CRITIQUES OF WORLD BANK ACTIVITY IN THE HEALTH SECTOR IN PERU

Unlike in Argentina, there is no indication in official documentation
that the government was critical of the World Bank's work in the health
sector. My interviews did reveal some points of contention, where the

World Bank (and USAID) wanted to implement targeted programs more narrowly than the Ministry of Health was interested in doing—it wanted to take a more integral approach by providing a wider range of services to mothers and children (Interview #12). In addition, the World Bank itself was able to learn something from its experiences, and in particular was self-critical in noting that it had perhaps been *too* flexible, at least in the context of the Primary Health Project begun in the 1980s:

> after two years of extremely weak performance, a new government proposed a major modification and expansion of the project which the Bank estimated would set implementation back considerably. Although Bank staff working on the project recognized that this reprogramming would not address the constraints which had led to weak performance to date, the Bank expressed willingness to consider this reprogramming. The Bank should be firm in rejecting reprogramming of an already weak project which would further complicate execution. (Primary Health Project Completion Report 1993: v)

Indeed, even local policy makers identified the fault as largely laying with the national government, for example, one respondent noted that despite how long decentralization had been discussed, when it came time for implementation in the early 2000s, decentralization was hastily implemented:

> [implementation of decentralization] has been very rapid, perhaps too fast, the transfer of functions to the regional governments on the one hand, and the transfer of part of the provision of health services, has also been too rapid which has not allowed for a strengthening of local management capabilities and to understand what role the regional governments, the regional bureaus, as regulatory entities, funders and providers should have. (Interview #12)

These challenges are understandable given the weak state autonomy and capacity of the Peruvian government in health, which results in some problems in implementation, partly because different actors (regional governments, the Ministry of Health, managers, and health providers across facilities) all vie for resources, sometimes with little coordination. However, it also, perhaps ironically, prevents the World Bank from fully controlling the direction and particulars of reform across all projects and policies.

Conclusion

The direction of reforms in health in Peru during this time period was in quest of increased access and coverage in an effort to alleviate poverty; in this way, the reforms were centered on issues of equity as well as efficiency. However, these reforms were conceptualized and indeed implemented via classically neoliberal means (targeting, private sector involvement, and other market mechanisms) and placed a high premium on efficiency. For example, competition via private sector involvement in EsSALUD, targeting in the interest of improving health indicators in keeping with the MDGs, and decentralization in the interest of performance-based management to be more fully implemented and expanded in the future. While these reforms, like in Argentina, were sometimes domestic initiatives (especially the targeted programs of the SEG and SMI), the World Bank as well as the IDB and USAID were involved in these reforms in various stages. These organizations were able and indeed invited to participate in all stages of these reforms due to Peru's status as a weak state in health. While the government had ideas for projects and programs, for example, the populist motivation behind the SEG and SMI, there was little continuity between programs, and implementation was slow because of a lack of capacity, both in terms of resources and also in terms of institutions that were ill-coordinated at the national level and ill-prepared to carry out these programs at the sub-national level.

While the Peruvian government was able to secure resources to extend access, especially to the poor and mothers and children, this has resulted in a still fragmented and weak system. Because decentralization was pursued (relatively) rapidly in its implementation (if not in its discussion), and in the context of a weak central Ministry of Health and state agenda for health, it could exacerbate regional inequalities and perpetuate a model whereby multiple projects proceed with little coordination among them, increasing inefficiency. The creation of the SIS has been an attempt to counteract this trend, and thus far is seen as a positive development though it does little to solve the issue of lack of leadership of the Ministry of Health and clarifying the communication between the central and regional health authorities.

Overall, the World Bank's approach embraced neoliberal ends such as efficiency but also universalistic ends in the form of expanding coverage via several programs and more recently the SIS and a quest for increased equity. Like in Argentina, the World Bank promoted neoliberal tools that focused on market mechanisms and sometimes reinforces gendered approaches to health. However, the Peruvian state's largest weakness in health may also be perversely considered a type of strength. Because of its low autonomy and capacity, it was only able to implement piecemeal, staggered reforms; however, this also prevented a takeover by international organizations, possible given the state's vulnerable position during much of this time period, both politically and economically. There was no state apparatus of co-opt, and fragmentation means that even if one part of government pushed back or wholesale adopted World Bank and other organizations' recommendations, it was not likely that other parts of the health sector would fully cooperate. In addition, there is little evidence, like in Argentina, that the World Bank consistently nor aggressively tried to influence change in a neoliberal direction in ends. These two features help explain why the system remains fragmented, the World Bank remains heavily involved in health in Peru, and yet changes have not materialized in a consistently neoliberal direction, as least in terms of ends. Instead, the SIS is attempting to universalize health insurance coverage for Peruvians.

<h2 style="text-align:center">REFERENCES</h2>

Alcalde-Rabanal, J. E., Lazo-González, O., & Nigenda, G. (2011). Sistema de salud de Perú. *salud pública de méxico, 53*, s243–s254.

Arredondo, A., Orozco, E., & De Icaza, E. (2005). Evidences on weaknesses and strengths from health financing after decentralization: Lessons from Latin American countries. *The International Journal of Health Planning and Management, 20*(2), 181–204.

Brooks, S. M. (2005). Interdependent and domestic foundations of policy change: The diffusion of pension privatization around the world. *International Studies Quarterly, 49*(2), 273–294.

Cotlear, D. (2006). *A new social contract for Peru: An agenda for improving education, health care, and the social safety net.* Washington, DC: World Bank Publications.

Cruz-Saco, M. A., & Mesa-Lago, C. (1999). *Do options exist?: The reform of pension and health care systems in Latin America.* Pittsburgh: University of Pittsburgh Pre.

Ewig, C. (2002). The politics of health sector reform in Peru. In *Paper presented at the Woodrow Wilson Center Workshops on the Politics of Education and Health Reforms*, April 18–19, 2002, Washington, DC.

Ewig, C. (2010). *Second-wave neoliberalism: Gender, race, and health sector reform in Peru.* University Park: Penn State Press.

Fiedler, J. L. (1996). The privatization of health care in three Latin American social security systems. *Health Policy and Planning, 11*(4), 406–417.

Gideon, J. (2014). *Gender, globalization, and health in a Latin American context.* Berlin: Springer.

Interview #12.

Interview #15.

Interview #21.

Interview #22.

Interview #26.

Interview #27.

Interview #28.

Interview #34.

Interview #35.

Interview #39.

Interview #41.

Interview #43.

Interview #45.

Interview #69.

Jaramillo, M., & Parodi, S. (2004). *El Seguro Escolar Gratuito y el Seguro Materno Infantil: Análisis de su incidencia e impacto sobre el acceso a los servicios de salud y sobre la equidad en el acceso* (Vol. 46): GRADE.

Ortiz de Zevallos, G., Eyzaguirre, H., Palacios, R. M., & Pollarolo, P. (1999). La economía política de las reformas institucionales en el Perú: los casos de educación, salud y pensiones. Inter-American Development Bank.

Parodi, S. (2005). *Evaluando los efectos del Seguro Integral de Salud (SIS) sobre la equidad en la salud materna en el contexto de barreras no económicas al acceso a los servicios.* Lima: Grupo de Análisis para el Desarrollo.

Petrera, M., Valdivia, M., Jimenez, E., & Almeida, G. (2013). Equity in health and health care in Peru, 2004–2008. *Revista Panamericana de Salud Pública, 33*(2), 131–136.

Roberts, K. M. (1995). Neoliberalism and the transformation of populism in Latin America: The Peruvian case. *World Politics, 48*(01), 82–116.

Rubio, M., Díaz, J. J., & Jaramillo, M. (2009). El impacto de PARSalud sobre la calidad de la atención de salud materna entre la población indígena. *Banco Interamericano de Desarollo, IDB-TN-209.*

Salaverry, G., & Delgado, G. (2000). O, Historia de la Medicina Peruana en el siglo XX. *Tomo II, 1ra. Ed. Fondo Editorial de la UNMSM.*

Taylor, L. (1998). Counter-insurgency strategy, the PCP-Sendero Luminoso and the civil war in Peru, 1980–1996. *Bulletin of Latin American Research, 17*(1), 35–58.

Weyland, K. G. (2006). *External pressures and international norms in Latin American pension reform*. Citeseer.

Yamin, A. E. (2003). *Castillos de arena en el camino hacia la modernidad: una perspectiva desde los derechos humanos sobre el proceso de reforma del sector salud en el Perú, 1990–2000 y sus implicancias en la muerte materna*: Centro de la Mujer Peruana Flora Tristan.

CHAPTER 6

Costa Rica: The Challenges of Maintaining Universalism in a Strong State

Countries have the ability, even if there is pressure from above, if you have sufficient and conclusive information you can better negotiate ... we have to break the technical dependence and defend what belongs to us ... but defending does not mean staying the same, sometimes.
— interview with a former Minister of Health, responding to a question about the impact of the World Bank on health reforms in Costa Rica. (Interview #82)

Costa Rica is hailed as a health success story of "health without wealth." Despite its status as a developing country, it has achieved high life expectancy and low levels of infant mortality comparable to those of many developed countries (Sáenz et al. 2011; Ancochea and Franzoni Martínez 2013). Costa Rica, in contrast to Argentina and Peru, is a strong state, both generally and in its management of the health sector. The Costa Rican government is able to formulate goals for the health sector—high autonomy—and has historically been able to implement this agenda—high capacity in health.

During the period between 1980 and 2005, the Costa Rican government declared two key goals for its health sector: first, a renewed focus on primary care, and second, the government sought to subsume all public provision of health care under the auspices of the parastatal social security agency, the CCSS (*Caja Costarricense de Seguro Social*), with subsidization by the government for the unemployed and those living in poverty. Both of these goals were achieved during this time period.

© The Author(s) 2017
S. Noy, *Banking on Health*, DOI 10.1007/978-3-319-61765-7_6

In implementing these reforms, the government sought to maintain universal access but also make it equitable, with all citizens receiving care from the same facilities, and to cope with the growth of the private sector.

A lack of sweeping neoliberal changes in the Costa Rican health sector during this time period is the result of two interrelated factors: first, as with Argentina and Peru, the World Bank took a varied, rather than aggressively neoliberal approach to health sector reform. Second, because the Costa Rican government had high autonomy and capacity in health, while it did introduce some neoliberal tools (e.g., targeting), these operated in the context of a strong public system, and against a backdrop of and in the service of universalism.

Government Autonomy and Capacity in Health in Costa Rica: A Strong State

Costa Rica can be categorized as a strong state both generally but also in terms of its involvement in the health sector. It has a clear agenda for health and, indeed, provides a comprehensive public record of this agenda via national development plans. A social development plan is published every four years and includes information about plans for the health sector and a brief assessment of previous policies. In terms of state capacity in health, Costa Rica is an outlier both in Latin America and in the developing world more broadly. Costa Rica abolished its military in 1948, freeing up finances to devote to the social sector. It has set up a universal system and its performance in terms of health indicators is much higher than all other countries (save Cuba) in the region, and it offers universal coverage. In the face of much political instability among its Central American neighbors (with civil wars and violence in El Salvador, Guatemala, and Nicaragua), Costa Rica sees investment in the social sector as critical to its political stability and a defining feature of its national character.

This is not to say that Costa Rica's health system has not faced challenges: given its universalist orientation, and the rising cost of health care owing to an aging population and rising prices in medical technology, it faces financial pressures like all other health systems. Immigration, particularly from Nicaragua, has also challenged the universality of this system (Noy and Voorend 2016). Finally, the system reflects additional inequalities, such as the marginalization of indigenous people in Costa Rica more generally. All of these have led to reform efforts to deepen coverage and cut costs while maintaining the high level of quality of the system (Interview #84).

Costa Rica's Health Sector: History, Structure, and Challenges

The Costa Rican health sector, like Peru and Argentina's health sectors, is comprised of three main parts: the public, social security—a parastatal agency, and private sectors. The public sector operates through general funds to provide health care to the general population. However, since the 1970s, the role of the public sector in the provision of health services has declined as public hospitals were transferred to the Costa Rican social security agency, the *Caja* or CCSS. Primary care and health posts, especially in rural areas, remained the responsibility of the Ministry of Health until the 1990s. The social security sector is a semi-autonomous system providing a full range of health services. It is funded by compulsory insurance contributions, and the government subsidizes care for those who cannot afford to pay. Everyone is eligible for care from the CCSS facilities, so this sector is a hybrid of social security and public system in that its services are not limited to those covered by insurance. Finally, the private sector provides supplementary care for those that choose to pay for it in the form of health insurance and fee-for-service. The private sector is small, but growing rapidly.

The Public Sector

The public sector consisted, until the 1970s, of Ministry of Health indirectly controlled public hospitals in addition to other health posts. All hospitals save four CCSS hospitals were public and were administered by Social Protection Committees (*juntas de protección social*). These quasi-public bodies were overseen by the Ministry of Health and funded by proceeds from the national lottery and various taxes and transfers from the central government (*Ley 1153*). Legislation passed in 1973 transferred all public hospitals to the CCSS. The Ministry of Health retained control over health posts (Unger et al. 2008). The goal was to further separate functions to streamline the system and increase efficiencies (Interview #92). The Ministry of Health eventually assumed authority for the leadership and stewardship of the health sector, while maintaining responsibility for first-line and preventative care while the CCSS ultimately assumed control of all the hospitals.

A Public Social Security Agency: CCSS

The main provider of health services is Costa Rica's social security agency, the CCSS, established in 1941. It originally provided health services to formally employed workers and then expanded to include their families in 1961. It has since extended its coverage to the whole population and effectively covers over 85% of Costa Ricans. The Costa Rican model is distinct from all other Latin American countries: in 1973, Costa Rica began integrating CCSS with Ministry of Health facilities resulting in a system managed by the social security program and financed by employers, employees, and the government (Kaufman and Nelson 2004; Sáenz et al. 2011). Under this reform, Ministry of Health hospitals were transferred to the CCSS, and the Ministry of Health retains an oversight role in the sector, functioning as its steward.

The CCSS health system is divided into three levels: the tertiary level is comprised of high complexity hospitals that allow for hospitalization and have equipment and surgeons for advanced surgeries. The second level constitutes a network of clinics, regional hospitals, which can provide emergency care and specialist consultations. The primary level is made up of public clinics and was reformed in the early 1990s. While it is a single agency, the CCSS is comprised of multiple actors who are sometimes in disagreement about the appropriate direction of reforms (Interview #107).

The CCSS insurance consists of three regimes of health social security: the Sickness and Maternity Insurance (*Seguro de Enfermedad y Maternidad*), the Disability, Old Age and Death Insurance (*Invalidez, Vejez y Muerte*), and a non-contributive insurance for those living in poverty. The CCSS relies on tripartite financing, from employers, employees, and the state. The employer pays 14.16% of the employee's salary, the employee contributes 8.92%, and the state contributes 0.50%. The self-employed contribute on a voluntary basis based on their declared income, between 10.5 and 13.5%. Therefore, 15% of the population, consisting largely of agricultural laborers, informal sector workers, self-employed professionals, and business owners, lives without CCSS health insurance. Uninsured people, however, do use CCSS (previously public) health facilities despite not being officially insured, especially hospitals (Unger et al. 2008; Kaufman and Nelson 2004).

The Private Sector

Approximately, 2% of the population in Costa Rica relies on private insurance (Saenz et al. 2011). However, citizens are not allowed to purchase insurance directly from providers, but rather all insurance must be purchased through the National Institute of Health (*Instituto Nacional de Seguros*, INS) (Clark 2002). In addition, the CCSS subcontracts services from non-profit cooperatives which are considered private entities.

HEALTH POLICY REFORM, 1980–2005

Reforms in the health sector in Costa Rica from 1980 to 2005 consisted of a quest to increase efficiency and contain costs while maintaining universalism. The reforms sought to unify the system all the while maintaining its universal character, enhancing equity and limiting the role that the private sector plays in the provision of health services. Together, these efforts resulted in an increased focus on primary care and a rationalizing of the system in the form of separation of functions within the unified system.

Extending CCSS Coverage and Experiments in Public–Private Partnerships, 1980s

The 1980s in Costa Rica saw two seemingly conflicting trends that both had their roots in economic crisis: expanding coverage to the poor and other groups and attempts at mixed models of medicine, that is, private–public partnerships. First, there was a move toward universalism in 1984 when the state implemented an insurance scheme to cover those living in poverty. Under the "Program of the Insured by the State" (*Programa de Asegurados por Cuenta del Estado*), people living in poverty were now affiliated with the CCSS and the cost of their care covered by the state. Around the same time, insurance requirements were applied to independent workers as well as those in unions (Sáenz et al. 2011). This was done in response to the drop in employment in an attempt to ensure that health care was available to the self-employed and that the state subsidized these services for the poor (Unger et al. 2008).

At the same time, patients were complaining of long wait lists and waiting times and an overloaded system (Interview #94). More patients were incorporated which strained the system. The overload on the system was also the result of the rising cost of health care (due to technological improvements and an aging population) coupled with the foreign debt crisis. Together, these factors resulted in a reduction in spending in real terms. Finally, the CCSS suffered from evasion "by private employers, large arrears from unpaid state contributions (on behalf of its own employees), and over-investment in low yield government bonds throughout the same period" (Clark 2002).

In the 1980s as a response to these challenges, CCSS officials set out to make the public system more efficient by incorporating some private market mechanisms through the introduction of mixed models. First, in 1982, patients could make appointments with physicians from a predetermined CCSS list in order to get more rapid service. Patients paid out-of-pocket for the office visit, while the public system provided lab services and medication accompanying this care. This program was not popular, in part because it required an ability to pay for the appointments, because there were extensive paperwork requirements, but also because the public system's inefficiency in medication and in laboratories persisted even for those that chose this option. Second, and related, for a time firms could chose a CCSS doctor to serve their employees on a per company basis. But again, the long wait times for medication and labs rendered this option still largely inefficient for anything but the most minor health needs of users. Finally, in 1988, the CCSS signed a contract with a cooperative of doctors which operated a clinic. While this seemed successful in terms of patient satisfaction, it was not implemented more widely. As Fernando Marin Rojas, one of my respondent and among the architects of this first cooperative, notes this was because the CCSS feared it would lose its control and power in the medical system and because it was deemed more expensive (per patient) than the public system (Franzoni Martínez 2006; Interview #101).

Refocusing on Primary Health Care, Early to Mid-1990s

In an effort to make the system more efficient, the government took the approach of focusing on primary health care in order to reduce waiting times (Interview #88). This would also allow users to receive preventative care in an effort to prevent them from reaching hospitals for more complex treatment as their conditions worsened without treatment. A loan from the World Bank in 1993 supported this effort. The World Bank pushed for competition with private health insurers, but this proposal was rejected by both CCSS and Ministry of Health personnel (Interview #89). While there had been a domestic discussion of improving primary health care for several years, "the approval of the World Bank loan was the backbone of this process of reform in terms of the management model and changes in the model of care" (Interview #107).

Since 1995, basic health services are provided via "Teams of Integrated Health Care" called EBAIS (an acronym for *Equipos Básicos de Atención Integral de Salud*) under the auspices of the CCSS which took over all direct medical functions previously provided by the Ministry of Health. While the hospitals were transferred from the Ministry to the CCSS in the 1970s, the transfer of health posts took longer. Each EBAIS includes a medical team: in urban areas, these are typically clinics but in rural areas these are sometimes mobile teams, which enables them to cover a larger territory. Most EBAIS are CCSS owned but a few are sub-contracted (Bixby 2004). Each "health area" has at least one EBAIS, based on population—one per approximately 4000 people—and there are over a hundred health areas in the country (Clark 2002; Rodríguez Herrera and Bustelo 2008). Implementation of this reform took several years partly because there were negotiations with health personnel unions over their transfer from the Ministry of Health (which had previously staffed these health clinics and outposts) to the CCSS (Interview #89).

Rationalizing the CCSS and Management Contracts, Mid to Late-1990s

Originally, the CCSS managed both pensions and health insurance which were part of a single fund. In the 1990s, pension and health funds were separated. The health system within the CCSS was further subdivided administratively into units responsible for each of health financing, purchasing, and provision where the CCSS purchases health services from its operational units.

The mid to late-1990s were marked by an increased effort at rationalizing the CCSS—increasingly seen as an unwieldy, bureaucratic behemoth. While no one wanted to dismantle the CCSS, the World Bank would have liked to see private insurers and providers competing for CCSS contracts. The CCSS leadership, however, was opposed to this. They compromised on the establishment of performance contracts where hospitals receive a budget in return for medical services rendered while meeting certain quality standards which were first applied in 1997 (Interview #89). These reforms have only been partially implemented. Budgets are still partly historically assigned, and there are no real ramifications for inefficiency on the part of operational units.

Decentralization of Health Facilities and Sub-contracting of Services, Late-1990s and 2000s

Decentralization of administrative authority within the CCSS was one of the main components of health sector reforms in the 1990s and is related to both the creation of the EBAIS and to performance-based measurements and management contracts. A law passed in 1998 (Ley 7852) pursues deconcentration in two ways: first, there is a redistribution of management from the central administration to the clinics and hospitals providing services. In terms of geographic decentralization, the EBAIS were the main vehicle for this implementation. Second, perhaps the most important administrative reform during this time period was the creation of over 100 health committees/councils (*juntas de salud*). These committees are comprised of seven members: two from employers' organization, two from community organizations, and three elected by CCSS affiliates. Each hospital and major clinic has a health committee whose members are elected every two years. However, these were not always successful due to limited participation. Directors of these hospitals and clinics were originally allowed to sub-contract with private clinics and private doctors for services. This practice of sub-contracting has been limited following pressure from medical unions since the early 2000s (Interview #95).

ENDS AND MEANS IN WORLD BANK HEALTH PROJECTS IN COSTA RICA, 1980–2005

In Costa Rica, unlike in Argentina and Peru, the government consistently publishes national development plans, with a section devoted to each sector, including the health sector. These plans, indicative of high autonomy in health, provide a detailed account of goals and an assessment of previous policies. The World Bank was involved in several facets of health sector reform in Costa Rica. My interviews and other accounts of health sector reform in Costa Rica (rather than policy documents from national government or the World Bank which make no mention of this) reveal that the Costa Rican government was able to convince the World Bank to scale back its more ambitious privatization and rationalization measures: private sector involvement and performance-based management (Clark 2002; Interview #89). The World Bank supported the Costa Rican government's focus on primary care in the form of the creation of the EBAIS system in the 1990s and continued to assist with the pursuit of separation of functions. All of these were seen as working in the interest of efficiency given the universal system in Costa Rica, which the government was insistent on maintaining. A list of World Bank projects and accompanying documents in Costa Rica during this time period is provided in Methodological Appendix Table A.5. Altogether, the World Bank began eight health-related projects in Costa Rica between 1980 and 2005. Health was a strong component of the World Bank's work in Costa Rica during this time, 38.09% of World Bank projects in Costa Rica during this time had a health component, and the average project cost of these projects is $46.81 million (with total project costs at $374.50 million). Of this amount, the World Bank contributed approximately 95% of the financing to these projects (much higher than in Peru or Argentina, with rates of 72% in each), with the national government and other aid agencies covering the remainder of the costs of these projects.

Paradigmatic Goals: Problem Definition and National Priorities

Efficiency features as a primary aim in health in Costa Rica since the 1980s. Many of the reforms detailed above, initiated by the Costa Rican government and often supported by the World Bank in their planning, financing, and implementation, were motivated by an effort to increase CCSS efficiency. As early as its 1978–1982 development plan, the Costa Rican government questions the sustainability and suitability of such large government involvement in the social sector. High state involvement is questioned on grounds of efficiency and is seen as contributing to the debt crisis:

> In sum, it's true that historically state intervention was the means of pro-
> moting economic development and resolving social problems, but its
> growth has surpassed the original necessity. The public sector has grown
> and taken shape in a way that makes it difficult to discover a rationale and
> justification for its growth. This has generated negative effects for both
> its efficiency and other variables which affect the rest of the economic-
> social system, and is probably the principal cause of the crisis of values
> that has immersed the country. (Plan Nacional de Desarrollo, 1978–1982
> "Gregorio Jose Ramirez", Tomo 1: 57)

This plan, importantly, discusses the challenges of institutionalizing development goals: "The most difficult task to achieve is that while integrated development programs are institutionalized, development is at the service of man [sic] and not man at the service of development" (Plan Nacional de Desarrollo, 1978–1982 "Gregorio Jose Ramirez," Tomo 3: 1). The issue is that once agencies and programs are created, they are in danger of forgetting their original goal—the improvement of citizens' well-being. Such "mission drift" (Moore 2000) is especially likely in larger organizations and bureaucracies such as the CCSS.

In its 1982–1986 national development plan, the Costa Rican government recognizes the successes of the country in advancing health but notes that the population's diseases are now characteristic of the developed, rather than the developing world. Despite these notable advances, there "are certain social groups and geographic areas whose health indicators are worrisome and who do not have sufficient access to services" (Plan Nacional de Desarrollo, 1982–1986: 34). Equity in health access is an important goal during this time period. This is reiterated in the 1986–1990 development plan, which sets the goals for health sector as maintaining existing health achievements and levels of health indicators. The emphasis is on the most vulnerable groups in the population: mothers, children, and adolescents (Plan Nacional de Desarrollo, 1986–1990).

The 1990–1994 national development plan reiterates the importance of focusing on primary health care but also notes that the health sector and its institutions need to "modernize and develop guided by the principles of integration, decentralization and democratization [in access], so that they may assume their roles efficiently and without duplication" (Resumen Plan Nacional de Desarrollo, 1990–1994, "Desarrollo Sostenido Con Justicia Social": 13). These goals are directly echoed in the 1993 staff appraisal report for the World Bank project on health sector reform (written before the loan is signed, and containing the World Bank staff's appraisal of the possible contribution of the project) for the Health Sector Reform Project. The Health Sector Reform Project of 1993 was "the first free-standing Bank-supported health sector project for Costa Rica" (Staff Appraisal Report 1993: 16) which makes it of particular importance for examining parallels between government and World Bank priorities and the dynamics of its implementation. This project involves the creation of the EBAIS with a redefined model of primary care. It also involved the transfer of all responsibilities from the Ministry of Health to the CCSS (though hospitals were transferred over in the 1970s, the Ministry of Health retained responsibility for providing primary care services—especially to rural areas, *Ley 5349*).

The implementation report, published in 2003, 10 years following the project's initiation, provides important information about which components were and were not implemented but also the World Bank's assessment of the project. The implementation report notes that the general strategy of the World Bank for Costa Rica is to:

> ensure macroeconomic stability, reform the public sector, integrate the economy with world markets, strengthen infrastructure, enhance competitiveness and efficiency of the financial system, improve coverage and efficiency of social programs to further reduce poverty and improve environmental management. The loan was the first Bank operation to Costa Rica in the health sector and was seen as an important vehicle to strengthen the social sector policy dialogue with the Government (Health Sector Reform Project Implementation Completion Report 2003: 3)

This quote indicates the World Bank's focus on poverty amelioration and efficiency, but also notes the World Bank's involvement in this reform serves the general purpose of strengthening ties between itself and the Costa Rican government. This goal is not necessarily related to health but more to the World Bank positioning itself as an important advisor and partner to the government in social policy more generally. The World Bank does this partially to claim a stake in the successes of the strong Costa Rican state in health and other social sectors; by highlighting its involvement, it can point to its role in successful health reforms, both in terms of cost-effectiveness and outcomes. In terms of institutional changes, the World Bank notes several major achievements: "the project also demonstrates important progress in terms of the introduction of the PHC [Primary Health

Care] model, the separation of functions, changes in financial resource management, and the introduction of performance-based payment systems" (Health Sector Reform Project Implementation Completion Report 2003: 7).

The 1994–1998 national development plan highlights health inequities, with a section entitled "from a Costa Rica divided by sickness, to a Costa Rica united in health." While recognizing, again, the excellent levels of health of almost the entire population, the plan notes that:

> unfortunately, in the recent past, the health of the population has deteriorated. The health policies implemented in recent years have been unable to prevent Costa Rica from dividing in two: a minority that lives in healthy environments, with excellent access to medical services, and a majority that is increasingly poor and less healthy, with deficient access to services and that lives in unhealthy environments. (Plan Nacional de Desarrollo, 1994–1998, "Francisco J. Orlich")

Again, there is a discussion of the importance of an integral approach to health, the importance of EBAIS in relieving pressure on hospitals, and the modernization and strengthening of the Ministry of Health.

The 1998–2002 national development plan continues its focus on administrative reform: the creation of the EBAIS and the shift in the attention model to the primary health care model as well as the Ministry of Health assuming the role of steward or guiding body of the health sector (Plan Nacional de Desarrollo Humano, 1998–2002 "Soluciones Siglo XXI"). The 2002–2006 national development plan concludes, after discussing the achievements of the health sector, that the health system must respond in a more timely manner and with more flexibility to the changing epidemiological profile. However, it recognizes that this a daunting task given the restrictions on public spending due to fiscal constraints (Plan Nacional de Desarrollo, 2002–2006 "Monsenor Victor Manuel Sanabria Martinez").

Both the government and the World Bank are concerned with issues of efficiency in the health system in Costa Rica. For the World Bank, this is largely related to financing and evasion of payment. The World Bank's solution is market-oriented: increased rationalization (and bureaucratization) in the form of separation of functions between providers, financing, and purchasing functions. In addition, efficiency is to be achieved

through the use of sub-contracting to private providers and cooperatives or public–private partnerships. Services remain under the purview
of the CCSS which is an autonomous agency of the government so this
involves private sub-contracting, and essentially outsourcing some health
services. This effort is realized in two ways: the opening up the insurance
market, that is, private firms can now provide insurance, but also in terms
of service provision by cooperatives sub-contracted by the CCSS.

The data indicate that the World Bank and the Costa Rican government seem to be largely in agreement about the main problems the
health sector faces. These revolve largely around issues of access, particularly in remote and rural areas and the financial sustainability of the
system given increasing health costs. The framing of these priorities and
how they are discussed in conjunction with values, other ends, means,
and strategies for their achievement, however, varies between the Costa
Rican government and the World Bank.

Similarly to Argentina, but perhaps even more often, the two paradigmatic goals of equity and efficiency are identified in the same sentence or
passage in World Bank health project documents in Costa Rica. Indeed,
when equity is discussed independently, it is largely in descriptions of the
government's historic and current emphasis and strategy, for example:
"the present Government which assumed office in May 1990 is aware
that while important progress has been achieved, the reform process
must be deepened and consolidated if it is to provide a solid base for sustained and equitable development into the next century" (Water Supply
and Sewerage Project II Staff Appraisal Report 1993: 1) and "the func-
tional changes in the national health system count on strong support
from across the political spectrum, and also from the beneficiaries who
count on more equitable, quality health care since health service delivery is seen as a key pillar of Costa Rica's public social services" (Health
Sector Strengthening and Modernization II Project, Implementation,
Completion and Results Report 2010: 30).

The handful of times that equity is discussed independently of efficiency and not in describing government priorities, it appears that the
World Bank's interpretation is narrower than the national, sectoral
definition. For example, for the World Bank, achievement of increased
equity would be apparent via a reduction in differences in CCSS per
capita health spending across designated national health areas (Health
Sector Strengthening and Modernization II Project, Project Appraisal
Document 2001: 26). Equity is also operationalized as increased access:

"The vast majority of sub-projects and activities carried out under the Project incorporated the country's indigenous areas. In such areas, equity was interpreted as ease of access" (Health Sector Strengthening and Modernization II Project, Implementation, Completion and Results Report 2010: 18). In some instances, therefore, equity is synonymous with more equitable spending and access across geographic regions and at others, contradictorily, higher spending and targeting of particular regions. Regions with a high proportion of indigenous people, which is in turn correlated with poverty levels, were often targeted. In World Bank documents, access is discussed in the context of an economic logic, as a way to correct distortions in demand (Health Sector Reform Project Staff Appraisal Report 1993: 3). There is mention of quality in access, but in tandem with efficiency: "This component played an instrumental role in achieving the project's overall objective of extending access, increasing efficiency and improving quality" (Health Sector Reform Project Implementation Completion Report 2003: 13). In national documents, on the other hand, equity is most often paired with terms such as solidarity, social justice, and the distribution of "the benefits of development" (Plan Nacional de Desarrollo, 1978–1982 "Gregorio Jose Ramirez": 93) as well as community participation in an integrated health system (Resumen Plan Nacional de Desarrollo, 1986–1990: 32; Plan Nacional de Desarrollo, 1986–1990: 128).

In national documents, discussions of access are frequently coupled with mentions of universalism in access and equity: "...improve coverage, access, opportunity and quality, in addition to the operations of health services in line with the population's needs and the country's economic conditions" (Plan Nacional de Desarrollo, 2002–2006 "Monsenor Victor Manuel Sanabria Martinez"). The government also notes that quality of services is an important component of adequate access, that is, increased access should not come at the expense of quality: "The challenge in this area is to resituate social development in the center of state action, with the ends of assuring, in the context of a framework of equity, solidarity and equality of opportunity, that the entire population has access to fundamental social services, without sacrificing the quality of these same services" (Plan Nacional de Desarrollo, 1994–1998, "Francisco J. Orlich").

In sum, while the national development plans discuss efficiency and issues in financing, equity is also a primary focus. While the World Bank documents do make mention of equity, their idea of equity is formulaic (developing a formula based on regional inequality and poverty in resource allocation) and geographically bound. For the Costa Rican government, the issue of equity is exemplified in a universally contributive social security system. This system espouses solidarity in that it is progressive and redistributive where funds from those earning higher wages subsidize those with lower wages, and the government subsidizes the poor and indigent. Equity is, therefore, a matter both of outcomes (health environments, sewerage systems in rural areas, etc.) but also a matter of access and intricately tied to financing. While both discuss issues of access as a dimension of equity, the World Bank documents emphasize access as an outcome in the context of economic distortions. The Costa Rican government, on the other hand, prioritizes access as it relates to issues of equity and emphasizes the importance of increased access not coming at the expense of quality of care.

Policy Instruments and Levels

As in Peru, in Costa Rica, decentralization and deconcentration are featured heavily as policy instruments throughout this period. Separation of functions, performance-based management, and privatization are discussed in tandem. Privatization, and more accurately, private sector involvement, was promoted by the World Bank much more aggressively than was ultimately implemented in health sector reform.

Decentralization and Deconcentration

As far as Costa Rica's health reform, decentralization and deconcentration are mentioned on several occasions in both national and World Bank documents and come up frequently in interviews. As early as the 1978–1982 national social development plan, there is a discussion of centralized decision-making in the capital, San Jose. This centralized decision-making is seen as problematic for finding diverse solutions to health challenges: it is "prejudicial to a more dynamic and creative leadership on the part of regional agencies of the ministries and decentralized entities. Most of the decisions are made in San Jose, and consequently, the solutions are paternalistic and do not generate a truly active and committed participation on the part of public office, nor of the communities" (Plan Nacional de Desarrollo, 1978–1982 "Gregorio Jose Ramirez" Tomo 2: 72). Decentralization is therefore seen as a more democratic approach to health policymaking (Interview #98).

The Costa Rican government is centrally concerned with patient satisfaction and the quality not only increased access: "to impel processes of administrative deconcentration and empower all levels of care so they can manage their services to maximize customer satisfaction" (Plan Nacional de Desarrollo Humano, 1998–2002 "Soluciones Siglo XXI"). While this certainly speaks to a concern with quality, it also shows a shift in orientation from thinking of patients as users of services to patients as consumers in the late 1990s, even in government plans. In World Bank documents, decentralization and deconcentration were most often coupled with discussions of separation of functions, both within the CCSS and between the CCSS and Ministry of Health: "The project would support a realignment of the CCSS to ensure greater transparency in the use of resources by separating the administration of health care provision, pensions, and financial management and by decentralizing management and operational programming, and budgeting functions to the regional level" (Health Sector Reform Project Staff Appraisal Report 1993: vi).

Separation of Functions, Performance-Based Financing, and Private Sector Involvement

The second central policy instrument discussed is the separation of functions between the Ministry of Health and the CCSS allowing the specialization of each and within the CCSS itself in the quest for increased efficiency (Interview #83). These discussions often happen in tandem with discussions on deconcentration and decentralization but more often in tandem with performanced-based financing and contracts, and privatization. The World Bank focuses on the need to "establish a comprehensive primary health care model which would allow the CCSS to assume all responsibilities for the provision of public primary health care services, which would be transferred from the MOH" and "to promote the separation of purchasing and provision of services, the Health Services Purchasing Department (*direccion de compra*) was formally established [in the CCSS] and staffed to manage the contracting and evaluation process" (Health Sector Reform Project Staff Appraisal Report 1993: 10). In this conception, the Ministry of Health would then become the regulatory, norm-setting institution and be able to focus more of its attention on this: with the project aiming to "promote improvements in quality and fulfillment of consumer rights, as well as the efficiency and effectiveness of the Ministry of Health (MOH) as a regulatory agency, by strengthening the institutional and regulatory framework" (Health Sector Strengthening and Modernization II Project Implementation, Completion and Results Report 2010: 20).

Reconfiguring the CCSS' financing system involves the CCSS developing performance-based management contracts with its own hospitals and clinics. Performance-based management contracts are often discussed in tandem with targeting as enhancing equity. The World Bank argues that this contractual logic would "ensure greater equity and better targeting of resources" (Health Sector Strengthening and Modernization II Project, Project Appraisal Document 2001: 7). Equity is therefore between geographic sub-national regions where lesser financed regions would see higher resource investments in health: "the project would support the development of a formula-based plan for resource allocation, in which population size, risk-adjustment and poverty are taken into account" (Health Sector Strengthening and Modernization II Project, Project Appraisal Document 2001: 9). Equity is also to be achieved via the introduction of market mechanisms: division of functions within the CCSS and the use of contracts for providers with financing linked to performance. Per the report, increased equity would be apparent if reforms resulted in a reduction of the gap in per capita resource allocation among CCSS health areas (Health Sector Strengthening and Modernization II Project, Project Appraisal Document 2001: 26). This seems logically contradictory as targeting may involve disproportionate resource allocation in the short run, and given varied epidemiological challenges, existing differences in resource allocations, and health outcomes differential investments and targeting may well be warranted. However, throughout World Bank discussions, these kinds of neoliberal means were advocated in the interest of deepening universalism, further underscoring the utility of distinguishing between neoliberal means and ends.

The Ministry of Health transitions from a provider of health to a steward of the health sector, and this includes regulation, especially of the increasingly involved private sector: "Private sector involvement is increasing and requires a clear regulatory structure to attract investment and to protect the public" (Health Sector Strengthening and Modernization II Project, Project Appraisal Document 2001: 39). Therefore, while private sector participation can increase efficiency, regulation is required to protect affiliates from possibly predatory private schemes. Deconcentration necessitates a separation of functions in Costa Rica, according to the World Bank:

> The process started by the Ley de Desconcentracion has generated the
> need for institutional transformation of the CCSS. The centralized struc-
> ture that served well for insuring and delivering health care services to
> most Costa Ricans in the past needs to adapt to the new ways of doing
> business. These "new ways" include both the separation of finance and
> provision, and the movement toward greater autonomy at the provider
> level. (Health Sector Strengthening and Modernization II Project, Project
> Appraisal Document 2001: 17)

National documents also make reference to sub-contracting from private
providers in the interest of efficiency. The government talks about this as
easing the burden on an already overstressed system, evidenced by long
wait times for surgery: "the establishment of mechanisms for procure-
ment of support services with private enterprise in order to relieve the
pressure on consultations with specialists and surgeons" (Plan Nacional
de Desarrollo Humano, 1998–2002 "Soluciones Siglo XXI") and "reor-
ganizing the subsystems that make up the national health system, with
the purpose of streamlining the delivery of services and integrating and
coordinating the efforts of government and the private sector" (Plan
Nacional de Desarrollo, 1994–1998, "Francisco J. Orlich"). The country's foremost public university, the University of Costa Rica, manages
an EBAIS. This is an indication that the sub-contracting of some health
care provision by the CCSS was not simply a process of privatization,
though certainly, the CCSS is no longer the only direct provider. The
World Bank too highlights the potential benefits of sub-contracting, but
to private firms.

World Bank documents and interviews indicate that everyone recognized the importance of regulating a growing private sector: "The provision of services under these contracts has shown excellent results in
comparison with the traditional CCSS model, indicating that the private
sector can provide the PHC [Primary Health Care] package at a considerable cost-saving in comparison to the traditional, public model"
(Health Sector Reform Project Implementation Completion Report
2003: 35) and "Because private sector participation was not traditionally considered an important option in the past, there is almost no regulation of the private sector. This is a significant constraint given the
increasing importance of the private sector and the potential for public-
private partnership arrangements for health service delivery" (Health
Sector Strengthening and Modernization II Project, Project Appraisal

Document 2001: 6). This was echoed in interviews; private sector involvement is seen as promoting efficiency (cost saving) but requires close regulation (Interview #97). This contradiction between a neoliberal imperative to reduce the size and role of the state in the market coupled with a call for the state to regulate a growing and increasingly complex private sector has been noted before (Jordana and Levi-Faur 2005). It is apparent in policy prescriptions for the Costa Rican health sector as well. However, I argue that we can better understand these two seemingly contradictory movements by untangling the differences between neoliberal ends and means: the goal is not to reduce state involvement, the goal remains universalism, but in the interest of efficiency, neoliberal tools, in the form of market mechanisms and private sector involvement, are introduced.

In national documents, management contracts are mentioned in the deconcentration law (*Ley 7852*) and briefly in the *Plan Nacional de Desarrollo Humano*, 1998–2002: "strengthening of the plan for the reassignation of resources to health facilities, through the universalization of management commitment." The discussion of management contracts is circumscribed to the Health Sector Strengthening and Modernization Project in World Bank documents. Reference to management contracts appears most commonly in the preparation for the project calling for the government to: "Implement an incentive scheme linked to the evaluation of management contracts" and "shift to an activity and performance-based hospital reimbursement" (Health Sector Strengthening and Modernization II Project, Project Appraisal Document 2001: 11).

Primary Health Care Approach and Targeting
A primary health care model, and in particular the EBAIS, is another important policy instrument during this time period. The EBAIS are seen as advancing equity, increasing access and efficiency in the system thus fulfilling both paradigmatic goals. The primary health care approach and EBAIS are also discursively and in terms of implementation closely tied to targeting. They are also, like all discussions and implementation of policy instruments in Costa Rica, related to decentralization. Costa Rica was an early innovator in its commitment to and emphasis on primary care, beginning its rural health program administered by the Ministry of Health in 1974. Costa Rica has consistently spearheaded innovations in primary care, providing a model for a successful system proving that good health was possible even in a developing country (Interview #97).

The innovation during the 1990s was the reconfiguration of the primary health care system based on population distribution and "health areas." EBAIS promote access for people in all areas, rural and urban, but in particular, the population and geographic-based system enhances equity because it allows resources to be channeled to previously neglected or poorer areas. Indeed, the World Bank recognizes this as one of the most important reforms of the health sector:

> The redefined Primary Health Care Model (PHC model) is probably the most significant achievement of the reform process supported by the project. Coverage was assured by creating 102 Health Areas in the country's territory (98 are already installed or 96%), each of which comprises around ten to fourteen basic medical units called EBAIS. (Health Sector Reform Project Implementation Completion Report 2003: 12)

The World Bank Health Sector and Modernization Project, begun in 2001, focused on the separation of functions within the CCSS into financing, purchasing, and provision (Health Sector Strengthening and Modernization II Project Implementation, Completion and Results Report 2010: ii). In addition, mirroring the national development plan of 1998–2002, it focuses on the EBAIS—"consolidation of the primary care delivery network based on a population-based system"—and issues of efficiency. A separation of functions in primary health care is seen as one of the several ways to "improve the equitable distribution of resources, improve efficiency in the provider payment mechanisms and strengthen the CCSS's capacity to collect payroll contributions" (Health Sector Strengthening and Modernization II Project, Project Appraisal Document 2001: 2). The logic, therefore, is not simply one of efficiency, espoused in previous World Bank projects, but also one of equity. Equity, in this case, is to be achieved by targeting though the goal of efficiency remains primary: recognizing "the importance of improving efficiency; strengthening the referral system; channeling increasing resources to disadvantaged areas and thereby improving equity; and integrating curative and preventive services" (Health Sector Strengthening and Modernization II Project, Project Appraisal Document 2001: 2). Not mentioned in the World Bank documents are debates between World Bank and CCSS personnel about the function and level at which the EBAIS needed to be staffed, with the CCSS finally prevailing with the appointment of a physician, rather than only a nurse or other technical staff, in each EBAIS (Interview #89). While the relationship between the World Bank and CCSS was not overall contentious, there were certainly points of disagreement, and the Costa Rican state, due to its high autonomy and capacity in health, was able to leverage its proven results and outcomes in health together with clear plans, to succeed in ultimately getting their way in these discussions.

In Costa Rica, targeting is seen as an effective policy instrument in the pursuit of equity and access because it operates against the backdrop of a universal system. For example, one project seeks to "Introduce measures to increase the equitable distribution of resources, targeting of public subsidies" (Health Sector Strengthening and Modernization II Project, Project Appraisal Document 2001: 11). Government documents frequently refer to targeting indigenous communities that often have less access and are underserved: "A special effort will be made to extend the coverage of health services to indigenous communities, many of which do not currently have access to basic services" (Plan Nacional de Desarrollo, 1994–1998, "Francisco J. Orlich"). Targeting is tightly coupled with primary health care in Costa Rican reforms during this time period as the EBAIS were seen as fulfilling both goals.

CRITIQUES OF WORLD BANK ACTIVITY IN THE HEALTH SECTOR IN COSTA RICA

The World Bank's work in Costa Rica, like in Argentina, was critiqued for its more general structural adjustment policies during this time, but not as much regarding its behavior in health. As an academic and sometime consultant in health notes when asked about his opinion of World Bank influence on health policy in Costa Rica during this time period: "Not negative, I think that [the World Bank] has had an impact and has been a necessary impact at that time. Or, to me, something logical, it seems logical to me. I wouldn't say negative because we had [needed] to rearrange some things" (Interview #81). This harkens back to the quote at the beginning of this chapter, with the Costa Rican government understanding that it needed to reform its health sector to address some serious issues, but insisted on doing so while maintaining solidarity and universalism. While there were some disagreements between the World Bank and the CCSS and Ministry of Health, as with the example of how the EBAIS should be staffed (with the World Bank suggesting only a nurse and CCSS and other Costa Rican policymakers insisting on doctors due to patient expectation among other reasons), the World Bank ultimately ceded to Costa Rican demands due to its proven track record in health and its strong state autonomy.

The largest critique appears to be the World Bank's pushing for means-testing in the access of public health facilities. As one World Bank document notes:

> there is a need for developing appropriate means testing and to distinguish between the poor, the insured and the non-insured; a conservative estimate is that the CCSS provides unlimited services to nearly 15% of the population without their having contribute their required share to the plan. (Health Sector Reform Project Staff Appraisal Report 1993: 11)

Therefore, the concern of the World Bank is with evasion, cost recovery, and efficiency, while the Costa Rican government is primarily concerned with reaching the entire population. While the negotiations were serious and the World Bank attempted to push privatization, the government was able to block these initiatives by virtue of a strong agenda and proven capacity. It had established one of the most successful health care systems in Latin America, and hence could point to its accomplishments, even during economically troubled times. In addition, its previous success helped bolster its credibility: Costa Rica was a success story that the World Bank wanted to stake a claim in. Unlike in other Latin American countries, the World Bank did not propose policy tools as often nor as strongly but rather supported local initiatives because Costa Rica had already established that it could build a strong and effective universal health system.

CONCLUSION

Costa Rica's status as a strong state in health means that while it was faced with many of the same challenges as Argentina and Peru, at least economically, during this time period it was able to rebuff some of the more neoliberal tools proposed by the World Bank. Governments over this time period recognized that the system certainly needed reform as it had grown unwieldy, unresponsive, and inefficient—with long wait times and people seeking attention at high complexity facilities that could more cost effectively be treated at lower complexity facilities, but worked to maintain the system's emphasis on universalism. The World Bank's influence on health, in particular its support of the separation of financing and provision functions and the development of a rationalized primary health system, was seen as overall positive by the CCSS and the Ministry of Health. The reforms were all aimed at increasing efficiency in the context of a universal, largely equitable system in that facilities were the same for all users rather than segmenting social security and public facilities. This system had proven itself in its success at attaining high coverage and good health outcomes in Costa Rica, and the World Bank recognized that not only would it not be able to push the state to privatize, that this was likely not in their best interest, as the system had functioned well in the past.

Like in Argentina and Peru, what is perhaps more surprising is that the World Bank's stated goals were not as misaligned with those of the Costa Rican government as the narrative on coercive, neoliberal pressures on the part of international financial institutions suggests. Certainly, there are differences, with the Costa Rican government discourse including issues of social development and citizen's rights in a different way than the World Bank's. World Bank documents focus on efficiency, and interviews reveal an emphasis on cost cutting and other rationalization measures. However, both the national government and World Bank are concerned with cost-effectiveness and equity in the form of regional access. The World Bank, in financing its projects and providing loans, was able to financially and technically support the Costa Rican government's initiatives. Costa Rican governments over this time period were able to both clearly formulate, as a result of strong autonomy in health, and implement health reforms, given the state's high capacity in health, in the direction of universalism. They did so with the help of the World Bank and other international organizations despite economic, financial, and demographic pressures over this time period.

REFERENCES

Ancochea, D. S., & Franzoni Martínez, J. (2013). *Good jobs and social services: How Costa Rica achieved the elusive double incorporation*. Berlin: Springer.

Bixby, L. R. (2004). Evaluación del impacto de la reforma del sector de la salud en Costa Rica mediante un estudio cuasiexperimental. *Revista Panamericana de Salud Publica, 15*(2), 94–103.

Clark, M. A. (2002). Health sector reform in Costa Rica: Reinforcing a public system. In *Woodrow Wilson Center Workshops on the Politics of Education and Health Reforms*, Washington, DC.

Franzoni Martínez, J. (2006). ¿Presión o legitimación? Poder y alternativas en el diseño y adopción de la reforma de salud en Costa Rica, 1988–1998. *Hist. ciênc. saúde-Manguinhos, 13*(3), 591–622.

Interview #81.

Interview #82.

Interview #83.

Interview #84.

Interview #88.

Interview #89.

Interview #92.

Interview #94.

Interview #95.

Interview #97.

Interview #98.

Interview #101.

Interview #107.

Jordana, J., & Levi-Faur, D. (2005). The diffusion of regulatory capitalism in Latin America: Sectoral and national channels in the making of a new order.*The Annals of the American Academy of Political and Social Science, 598*(1), 102–124.

Kaufman, R. R., & Nelson, J. M. (2004). *Crucial needs, weak incentives: Social sector reform, democratization, and globalization in Latin America.* Washington, DC: Woodrow Wilson Center Press.

Moore, M. H. (2000). Managing for value: Organizational strategy in for-profit, nonprofit, and governmental organizations. *Nonprofit and Voluntary Sector Quarterly, 29*(suppl 1), 183–208.

Noy, S., & Voorend, K. (2016). Social rights and migrant realities: Migration policy reform and migrants' access to health care in Costa Rica, Argentina, and Chile. *Journal of International Migration and Integration, 17*(2), 605–629.

Rodríguez Herrera, A., & Bustelo, C. (2008). *Costa Rica: Modelos alternativos del primer nivel de atención en salud.* CEPAL.

Sáenz, M. D., Acosta, M., Muiser, J., & Bermúdez, J. L. (2011). Sistema de salud de Costa Rica. *Salud pública de méxico, 53,* 156–167.

Unger, J.-P., De Paepe, P., Buitrón, R., & Soors, W. (2008). Costa Rica: Achievements of a heterodox health policy. *American Journal of Public Health, 98*(4), 636.

CHAPTER 7

Banking on Health: Variable Approaches and Contingent Outcomes

INTRODUCTION

Health includes not just financial and monetary management but also stands at the core of citizen–state contracts, welfare politics, and national and individual identities, and is, therefore, a more complex field of analysis. All countries are looking for cost cutting, efficiency-enhancing measures with burgeoning health care costs and aging populations. This is especially true in the developing world, where health systems are subject to powerful internal and external pressures. Social protections are under threat from the forces of globalization, and in particular neoliberal ideologies and practices. Global actors such as the World Bank may be pushing for limited state involvement in health. However, researchers have long argued that economic development and democratization fuel popular demand for the expansion of welfare state, including health, protections. State support for the provision of health care is also buttressed by a shift in development thinking. Related, ameliorating poverty and investing in education and health are increasingly seen as enhancing human capital and the labor force's productivity. This book addresses the question of how and whether these contradictory forces manifest in health sector reform in developing countries.

In particular, I ask: what accounts for the World Bank's inability to uniformly pressure countries to pursue privatizing, neoliberal reforms in health in Latin America? The answer is twofold: first, on the supply side, the World Bank's approach to health is different across countries,

© The Author(s) 2017
S. Noy, *Banking on Health*, DOI 10.1007/978-3-319-61765-7_7

challenging existing understandings of it as a neoliberal, monolithic, exclusively coercive institution, at least in health. Second, on the demand side, countries' autonomy and capacity in health as well as existing institutional arrangements in the health sector pattern how and whether the Bank is involved in health sector reforms and how its programs and recommendations are received, negotiated, and implemented.

The results of the analysis presented in this book are somewhat surprising: *first*, I do not find any large or statistically significant negative effects of the World Bank on public health expenditure, even when using a new measure of the primary mechanism associated with the imposition of neoliberal reforms: World Bank conditions on health loans. *Second*, I argue that the lack of an effect of World Bank conditions on regional health expenditures owes to its variable approach to health sector reform across different countries in Latin America, as evidenced in my country case-studies of Argentina, Peru, and Costa Rica. The variability of the World Bank's approach to health is reflected in the number, timing, and spacing of projects but also in the substantive content of these projects. I also find that variation in state capacity and autonomy in health and existing institutional arrangements help account for differences in how the World Bank participated in and influenced health sector reform in these countries.

The World Bank was actively involved in several important projects in health sector reform in Argentina, Peru, and Costa Rica. It is important to reiterate that in this book, health sector reform does not necessarily refer to a major overhaul of the system, but rather to changes in or the creation of new policies, programs, and agencies. Indeed, there are no dramatic overhauls of the health systems of any of the three countries since the 1980s. This in itself is interesting given that all three countries experienced a serious recession in the 1980s and again in the early 2000s. These crises meant that these countries were particularly needful of World Bank and other external loans and resources. As a result, these governments should have been more willing to reform their health sectors in accordance with World Bank recommendations and neoliberal tenets. The expectation, given the literature on coercive IFIs as neoliberal agents and the reality of a state in crisis, would be increased privatization, a reduction in public financing of health, a reduction of union involvement in social security, and a host of other neoliberal reforms. Some reforms moved in that direction, but much of the expected state retrenchment and neoliberal shifts did not materialize. Below, I briefly summarize the findings of the empirical analyses and reflect on their implications for our understanding of health sector reform, the World Bank's work in health, globalization and global governance, and development.

REGIONAL TRENDS IN HEALTH EXPENDITURE

The data indicate that overall spending on health, both per capita and total expenditure as a percent of GDP, has been increasing since 1980 in Latin America and the Caribbean (see Fig. 3.1). Public expenditure has also increased: both as a percent of GDP and as a percent of total health expenditure while private spending as a percent of GDP has remained relatively flat. Therefore, the overall growth in health spending as a percent of GDP is due to growing public and relatively constant private spending as a percent of GDP.

While public health spending as a percent of government expenditure has decreased slightly, the proportion of overall health expenditure that is public has actually been increasing in Latin America and the Caribbean. This finding contradicts "race to the bottom" allegations of globalization and is inconsistent with the idea of coercive pressures from the World Bank and other IFIs driving down public social spending. Indeed, the public share of health spending increased even as overall spending levels were rising. This increase signals a renewed public commitment to health.

TIME-SERIES CROSS-SECTION MODELS
OF HEALTH EXPENDITURE

What is driving this increase in public commitments to health in Latin America? I find that the proportion of the elderly population is an important predictor of total per capita spending as well as total, public, and private spending as a percent of GDP. Democratization, on the other hand, is associated with more public health spending as a percent of total health spending and as a percent of GDP. This is consistent with ideas of democratic governments devoting more resources to social spending, including health. In terms of the World Bank, I do not find that World Bank conditions on all loans or on health loans specifically affect health expenditures in the region. This finding is in contrast to the expectation of strong downward pressures by IFIs on public health expenditures in the region.

My regional quantitative analysis provides some interesting insights into trends, patterns, and the correlates of health expenditure in Latin America and the Caribbean in the 1990s and 2000s. I am able to identify overall increases in health spending. This is important as it provides an indication that the cost of health is rising. Additionally, because most of the health expenditure is public and it too is increasing, it appears that the public system is financing over half of health care in the region. While we do see a reduction in public health spending as a percent of total public expenditure, it is important to note that this includes not just social spending (but rather all public spending, including infrastructure) and indeed shows a slightly curvilinear (U-shaped) trend over this time period. Altogether, this evidence is mismatched with allegations of globalization as creating a "race to the bottom" at least as regards health spending and the World Bank applying downward pressures on public spending. However, it is not inconsistent with more recent discussions of the World Bank (and other IFIs) promoting investments in health and education in the interest of human capital investment and economic growth.

The results of the regional regression models support these conclusions. Democratization is related to higher public health spending while it is largely demographic and economic domestic conditions (GDP, unemployment, and elderly population) that are driving changes in overall spending. This indicates that overall spending in health is increasing, likely due to the increased price of medical care (due to technological advances in medicine) but also chronic diseases (more common as countries develop, as infectious diseases are on the decline and chronic illness is more common in the elderly). The presence of high autocorrelation indicates that there is significant persistence in countries' spending levels over time.

This regional analysis, therefore, uncovers at least as many questions as it answers. Given discussions of the pernicious effects of the World Bank (and other IFIs) on health and additional downward pressures on on social spending, how is it that we do not find these effects on health expenditures in this region so especially vulnerable to neoliberal influence? And what is it about national institutions, together with political and health systems that account for the remarkable persistence in expenditures in the face of these homogenizing pressures? My comparative, case-study analyses help answer these questions.

CASE-STUDY ANALYSES OF THE WORLD BANK'S INFLUENCE ON HEALTH SECTOR REFORM IN ARGENTINA, PERU, AND COSTA RICA

Given the emphasis on efficiency in the literature on neoliberalism and IFIs, as discussed in Chap. 1, I expected few discussions of equity in World Bank documents and little concern with equitable outcomes. However, this expectation was not met. The World Bank often discussed poverty amelioration and other dimensions of more equitable distribution of access and outcomes in health. This resonates with discussions of the tenets of a post-Washington consensus, at least in the World Bank's approach to health. However, I find a shift in emphasis from neoliberal ends to neoliberal means, sometimes in the service of universalism and with increased attention to equity. In addition, the World Bank did not take a monolithic, strictly uniform approach to health sector reform across these three countries. Rather, it worked with governments to support their initiated reforms. While cross-national differences in the World Bank's approach accounts for some of the variation in health sector reform in those three countries, it does not begin to comprise the entire story.

The case-study analyses suggest several conclusions. *First* and foremost, I do not find that World Bank influence is constant across these three countries. Certainly, the World Bank has focused on efficiency and a promotion of several policy instruments: decentralization and deconcentration, separation of functions, performance-based financing, private sector involvement, primary health care, and targeting, but the emphasis on efficiency and the utilization of these instruments is not uniform. *Second*, I find that state autonomy and capacity in health condition how the World Bank seeks to influence and is involved in health sector reform in these three countries from 1980 to 2005. In particular, neither of them works in a standardized way to pattern the World Bank's involvement in health sector reform. *Third*, and finally, I find that existing institutional arrangements in health (actors, interests, and stakes) together with state capacity and autonomy in health shape the direction of health sector reform. These arrangements in the health sector are related to state capacity and autonomy but are not synonymous with them. For example, the fact that the *Obras Sociales* are important providers and actors in the Argentinian health sector is related to the fact that the state has had low capacity in health, but is not synonymous with it. Similarly, the fact that health has been marginalized among government priorities in recent decades in Peru is related to the state's lack of autonomy in health, but does not necessarily follow from it.

THE IMPORTANCE OF STATE CAPACITY AND AUTONOMY IN HEALTH

I have argued that both autonomy and capacity in health shape the interactions between national governments and the World Bank, but in sometimes unexpected ways. My analysis is a departure from previous treatments of state capacity and autonomy in two ways: *first*, I argue that we can and should consider state capacity and autonomy across sectors, rather than as a unitary measure for the entire state. *Second*, existing analyses have focused on internal country dynamics and how the state behaves vis-à-vis other national actors such as civil society and in relation to industry. That is, state capacity in particular has been examined as a domestic, internal feature of states. I argue that state capacity and autonomy in health are just as important for understanding how countries interact with external actors. We might expect that only countries with strong agendas (high autonomy) might be able to resist World Bank and other IFI prescriptions when they are out of line with those agendas. However, this is not necessarily the case: Peru demonstrates the possible strength of weak states. Overall, I find that the World Bank's agenda was not as out of line with national goals as expected. When there were discrepancies, autonomy was one of several factors that enabled governments to contest World Bank invectives.

Argentina, the planner state, had a strong agenda for health reform via the creation of national health insurance in the early 1980s under the leadership of Health Minister Aldo Neri. This reform failed because of the government's lack of capacity for implementation due to political opposition on the part of union-based health insurance schemes (*Obras Sociales*). The World Bank was not involved either way, though in theory (in intention rather than in any practical way), it was seemingly supportive of this initiative. Subsequently, the World Bank worked with the national government to legislate user choice among OSs. Some larger reforms were thwarted by the state's low capacity in health: both the government attempt to create a national health insurance (by Neri in the 1980s) and government attempted, and World Bank supported, farther reaching privatization measures (allowing private insurance to compete with OS in the 1990s) were blocked by the opposition of the *Obras Sociales*. The World Bank also worked with the government to create several national programs in coordination with provincial health ministries. These programs focused on providing basic maternal and infant care and helping ensure the provision of basic medicines by public health facilities, though the IDB was most heavily involved in the latter. The World Bank was therefore not pushing a strongly neoliberal agenda of privatization, though it did back market-based mechanisms, such as competition between OS and self-managed hospitals. The World Bank supported the government's focus on increasing efficiency within the OS system and providing basic care in the service of improving health indicators. These reforms served the goals of poverty reduction, especially in the face of severe and repeated economic crises.

In Costa Rica, the government's high autonomy and capacity—its status as a strong state in health—were together instrumental in preventing more far-reaching neoliberal reforms in that it was able to demonstrate that its system had worked in the past. The Costa Rican government sought to implement primary health care outreach on the part of the CCSS system which would be effective rather than rely more extensively that it did on public–private partnerships and other private sector actors as was suggested by some Costa Ricans in the 1980s and revisited by the World Bank in later years. Costa Rica's health system was and remains characterized by a universal system dominated by its social security agency, the CCSS. However, there were already some domestic efforts at public–private partnerships in the 1980s, before the World Bank had engaged in any health sector reform projects in Costa Rica. The goal of the experiments with private sector involvement was to increase efficiency in an over-extended system. The impetus of these early reforms was domestic, and the actors within the Costa Rican government were searching for solutions. The principles of neoliberalism offered a palette of prescriptions, some attractive and others at odds with Costa Rica's commitment to social development. The World Bank and the Costa Rican government were able to strike a balance in the subsequent health reforms: the focus on primary care with the creation of the EBAIS was equitable but also cost-efficient. Hospitals were transferred from the Ministry of Health to the CCSS, and management contracts were implemented, leading to a separation of functions in health financing, management, and delivery.

Finally, in Peru, low autonomy and capacity—its status as a weak state in health—coupled with the World Bank's focus on poverty alleviation meant that government initiatives providing care to the poor were supported by the World Bank. However, the Peruvian government had the weakest case of the three countries when it did attempt to oppose World Bank preferences. Though even then, the World Bank conceded in some instances when particular leaders in the Ministry of Health suggested alternatives, for example, in insisting on a more integral approach (rather than only covering a few services) to maternal and child health. The Peruvian government was often without a clear plan for the health sector throughout this time period, and in need of money, the World Bank (and other IFIs and aid agencies) was able to provide both. This lack of state capacity, in Peru due to a lack of resources, coupled with a lack of autonomy, seems to have prevented even an attempt at a neoliberal overhaul of the system. That is, if we expect the World Bank to reduce state involvement in health, we do not observe such a reduction in Peru. In order to dismantle a large public system (although there is no indication that this was the World Bank's goal in Peru), one must exist in the first place. However, the World Bank and other international organizations have shaped the development of public health provision in Peru in distinctive ways.

The World Bank, IDB, and USAID supported Peru first in providing basic health services to those in remote areas (the World Bank's nutrition program worked in parallel to the government's *Salud Basica Para Todos* program, largely in different geographic regions). The World Bank supported the Peruvian government in building a public insurance scheme that works to provide health coverage for the poor and improve health indicators. This insurance scheme, Integral Health Insurance (*Seguro Integral de Salud*, SIS), makes use of some market mechanisms partly in response to World Bank influence. Specifically, it relies on means-testing to ascertain eligibility, reimburses frontline providers rather than providing the Ministry of Health with a budget, and provides a limited number of services. The SIS built on two existing schemes: maternal insurance and insurance for school-aged children. These schemes were implemented by the populist president turned dictator, Alberto Fujimori, in an effort to both improve health indicators and endear himself to the populace. Altogether, there was an unexpected upside to Peru's low autonomy and capacity in health vis-à-vis IFIs: it prevents IFIs from co-opting the central health apparatus and implementing sweeping neoliberal reforms. This is the strength of weak states: there is no durable central mechanism to co-opt. Any involvement, positive or negative, is limited, often to project duration. That is not to underplay the influence that IFIs can have, especially in the short-term, but a pervasive criticism (that for those opposing IFI involvement and reforms is a benefit) is that such influence is not sustainable due to its dependence on foreign funding, that is to say—limited.

In this way, not just state autonomy and capacity but also existing institutional arrangements in health have important implications for the avenues open to future reformers. Therefore, while state capacity and autonomy are important, they are also dependent on the pre-existing system, which is in part determined by them. That is, in a state with low autonomy but high capacity characterized by a large public system, we may have seen more

expansive and more successful pressure to privatize or reduce state involvement. Cooperation with the World Bank and other IFIs in pursuing the
SIS, however, will likely limit the Peruvian government's future options.
That is, while it is striving toward universalism, it is not a single-payer universalism as in Costa Rica nor is it based on a strong public system. It is
unclear if the World Bank would support the creation of an entirely public,
single-payer system in any of the countries that it works with. This does not
mean that is not supporting these countries in providing baseline care and
increasing coverage, in a move toward universalism.

Most countries in Latin America and in the developing world are
likely most similar to the Peruvian state as regards health in that they
are characterized comparatively by low autonomy and capacity in health
(though these are continuums). This case may, therefore, be the most
informative to their experiences. Weak states are much more likely to
be open to World Bank (and other IFI) recommendations, not having a strong agenda in their health system or the capability to carry out
reforms. However, this also means that any co-optation, or influence, in
the enduring reforms may be constrained (over time and in scope) by the
weak state health apparatus as was the case in Peru. However, the cases
of Costa Rica and Argentina are also instructive. They are informative
not only because other countries fall in these state autonomy-state capacity
in health quadrants but also because they demonstrate how the World
Bank interacts differently with governments that have a strong health
agenda and with and without the capacity to carry out their intended
reforms. The case of Argentina may be particularly useful when examining countries with unions which are actively involved in the health sector.
The Argentinian case indicates that unions can simultaneously prevent
government reform, even when not neoliberal, in a bid to maintain
power but also serve to limit the possible influence of the World Bank.
Costa Rica, on the other hand, provides information about how existing public systems can best cope with inefficiencies and rising costs even
without having resources comparable to those in developed countries.

The World Bank, Equity, Efficiency, and Policy Instruments

By leveraging the comparative angle of three cases, and paying close
attention to the policy discourse and framing surrounding equity and
efficiency, the dynamics of the health sector reform process becomes

clearer. The document and interview data have allowed me to examine the paradigmatic goals of efficiency and equity as well as policy instruments: (1) decentralization and deconcentration, (2) separation of functions across and within institutions, (3) performance-based financing, (4) privatization and private sector involvement, targeting, (5) primary health care approach, and (6) targeting, and their suggested levels. I have focused on these policy instruments because they were embraced by the World Bank, apparent in its documents, and encompass the bulk of health sector reform in these countries in an effort to increase either efficiency, equity, or both. While there are differences in the discussion of particular policy instruments and goals, there is also much commonality. As expected, the World Bank is more focused on efficiency, discussing investing in health in largely economic terms, while governments tend to place more emphasis on equity. However, there is much overlap in the discussion of problems and diagnoses of solutions.

Table 7.1 provides a summary of my findings in regard to paradigmatic goals and policy instruments. Because there are very few national documents with stated goals for Peru and Argentina, I focused on World Bank documents and information gleaned from interviews in the examination of policy instruments in my analyses. At some point, all policy instruments were discussed in tandem with both equity and efficiency, so this distinction is less informative, though certainly, there is variation in emphasis. However, the combination in which these instruments were discussed is telling.

Standalone, Coupled, and Decoupled Instruments

Targeting fits in quite differently across these three countries. Instead of overhauling the public system whose hospitals and clinics all Argentinians have access to, as the government tried to do in 1980, it ultimately settled on the pursuit of targeted policies of focusing on mothers and children. Targeting was used in order to maintain basic health levels in the face of economic crisis. This is a distinct approach from that of Costa Rica. In Costa Rica, overall care was maintained and targeting was a tool for *deepening* access and utilization. It is also different than that of Peru, although in Peru, as in Argentina, targeting centered on maternal and infant care. The focus on maternal and infant care was supported by the World Bank in both Argentina and Peru, which represented a decided expansion of services. In Argentina, however, the system already had

Table 7.1 Summary of results for case-study analyses of IFI influence on health sector reform in Argentina, Peru, and Costa Rica

	Argentina	Peru	Costa Rica
Paradigmatic goals	*World Bank documents:* Efficiency > equity *Government documents:* Equity and efficiency (few substantive documents)	*World Bank documents:* Equity and efficiency (tightly coupled) *Government documents:* Equity and efficiency (few substantive documents)	*World Bank documents:* Efficiency slightly > equity *Government documents:* Efficiency = equity (equally discussed)
Policy instruments in World Bank documents	Targeting and performance-based financing Private sector involvement Primary health care approach Deconcentration and separation of functions	Targeting Decentralization, primary health care, and separation of functions Performance-based financing and private sector involvement	Decentralization and deconcentration Separation of functions, performance-based financing, and private sector involvement Primary health care approach and targeting
Main critiques of the World Bank activity in health	Ey government: Insensitive to national circumstance, pushing and peddling foreign models via consultants	By the World Bank: The Bank was too quick to acquiesce to government demands and reprogram when requested due to change of government	By government: Pushing private sector participation and privatization of some health services

high coverage, but in the face of economic crisis and unemployment, some lost coverage while public facilities were overburdened and under-funded. The focus on maternal and child health constituted a measure to buffer the effect of these crises on people's health access. The Peruvian programs were established in the presence of a small and weak public health system—quite different than the well-established public and social security system in Argentina which had relatively high coverage even prior to 1980.

In Argentina, targeting was most often coupled with discussions of performance-based financing, consistent with streamlining an ineffi-cient, overlapping system in the face of economic crises. In Peru, on the other hand, targeting was a central policy goal and was often discussed by itself, as it was seen as a stepping-stone to achieving universalism in health. In Costa Rica, targeting was most closely coupled with a focus on primary health care. These reforms then worked to reduce costs and also more effectively and equitably reach the entire population.

While linked to targeting, primary care as well as separation of func-tions, decentralization, performance-based financing, and private sector involvement were discussed separately in Costa Rica. In contrast, decen-tralization in Peru is closely tied to primary health care, a separation of functions between institutions, and specialization via the implementation of the Basic Health for All initiative and the decentralization of health financing and provision in the mid and late 1990s and early 2000s. In Argentina, too, there was a discussion of deconcentration within pro-vincial health systems along with a separation of functions, even the context of an already highly decentralized federal system. In Argentina, private sector involvement was discussed in the context of allowing pri-vate providers to be sub-contracted by *Obras Sociales*. In Peru, on the other hand, discussions of private sector involvement were often coupled with discussions of performance-based financing and moving toward pro-vider contracts. In Costa Rica, private sector involvement (and in particu-lar, public–private partnerships) was often discussed in conjunction with performance-based financing and the separation of functions upon the advent of the CCSS as the primary provider of health, which created con-tracts with hospitals as well as with private actors, namely, cooperatives.

The more diffuse and separate discussions of these policy instruments in Argentina are in keeping with its fragmented system. Coverage is high but segmented, and different tools are viewed as working for different parts of the system (national, public, *Obras Sociales*, and provinces). This is related to the failure to unify the health sector in the 1980s owing to low capacity, despite a strong government agenda and high autonomy. After this failed reform, the Argentinian government turned its attention to gradual change across the health sector. In Costa Rica, the instruments most closely tied with a rationalization of the system were separation of functions, performance-based financing and management, and privatization, which were often coupled together and highly contested by the government when advanced by the World Bank. In Peru, on the other hand, the separation of functions is related to efforts to decentralize in health, mirroring broader efforts at decentralization in other sectors and a focus on primary health care. Performance-based financing and separation of functions in Peru were also seen as rationalizing and imposing order on a growing system by the World Bank, and were embraced by the national government. Targeting in Peru features prominently as an intermediate measure to ensure that more people have access to health insurance; whereas in Costa Rica, targeting is discussed in the context of an already universal system and is seen as complementing a primary health approach.

Alignment of Policy Instruments and Paradigmatic Goals

Unsurprisingly, private sector involvement, performance-based financing, and separation of functions were most closely aligned with efficiency while primary health care was most closely aligned with equity. Targeting was aligned with both, across countries. Results-based financing was also seen as aligning with both equity and efficiency, especially in Argentina and Peru: performance-based financing was discussed as a way to ensure that precious and limited financial resources were not mismanaged in addition to improving health outcomes and indicators by both national governments and the World Bank. Each of the six policy instruments was cited as contributing to both equity and efficiency. However, sometimes the term equity was tacked on to the discussion of efficiency and was never fully explained by the World Bank in its documents. Their configurations also determine the relative emphases on equity and efficiency. For example, the coupling of targeting and performance-based financing in Argentina meant targeting was discussed more closely with efficiency there than in Peru, where targeting was discussed in tandem with both equity and efficiency, or in Costa Rica, where targeting was discussed primarily in the context of equity as it was coupled with a primary health care approach.

The World Bank's Flexibility in Health

The World Bank, while not uniformly and only neoliberal in its involvement in health, is centrally concerned with efficiency and often promotes market-based mechanisms to increase rationalization. However, it is also, at least in the cases of Argentina and Peru, supporting increased coverage in health by the state. This is noteworthy. The World Bank, reputed to favor market solutions to social provision, advocated an increase in state involvement in some aspects of the health system. This is not to say that market principles were neglected, nor was the pursuit of efficiency ever far from view. Therefore, the World Bank, in places without a strong extant health system, does not necessarily dissuade state involvement in health, but supports a particular type of state intervention: one where financing, provision, and regulation are separated, where funding is allocated based on services rendered, and with a focus on maternal and child health. Interestingly, across all three countries, the World Bank's major programs in health, which involved institutional change (rather than support in provision of services) in Argentina, Peru, and Costa Rica, did not start until the early 1990s, after it had already outlined this focus on human capital and poverty amelioration with its 1993 World Development Report.

The World Bank has been criticized for its push toward the incorporation of private actors in health in Costa Rica, the most classic critique of IFIs' neoliberal approach more generally. In Argentina, we see another oft-repeated critique: the World Bank is not sensitive enough to national circumstances, bringing in foreign models that have little applicability to the local context. Interestingly, in Peru, the major critique that the World Bank levels against its own activities is that it was too willing to change project scope and goals in concordance with changing priorities (sometimes little thought out, another reflection of low state autonomy in health) following changes in governments. In this case, the World Bank wanted to continue its work, and therefore acquiesced to modifications, though in retrospect, it believes it should not have.

These critiques, together with the evidence presented in Chaps. 4, 5, and 6, indicate that both the World Bank's approach and its effects are more fluid than often represented, at least in health. Certainly, its approach is sometimes neoliberal and market-oriented, and heavily influenced by the MDGs, a poverty-amelioration goal, and a human capital approach in health since the 1980s. Together, these may be thought of as a post-Washington consensus approach to health, where there has been a shift in emphasis from neoliberal ends (efficiency, competition, and privatization) to neoliberal tools and policy instruments. This stands in contrast to the neoliberal approach discussed in the context of Chilean, and later Colombian health sector reform. In the Chilean reform, a private insurance market was created in 1979, meant to be dominant, in which benefits corresponded to contributions. I have argued more fully elsewhere that Chile and Colombia, however, may be the exceptions rather than the norm in terms of World Bank influence on health sector reform in Latin America. As such, this book introduces evidence which sheds new light on the World Bank's involvement in health in Latin America and its work in health more generally.

BANKING ON HEALTH

Banking on health means different things in different places and over time to the World Bank. This book has examined both the World Bank's reasons for banking on health and what banking in health entails. Banking in health involves the use of diverse policy instruments and is contingent on national contexts. More generally, the World Bank is banking on health because health reforms and investments are seen as fulfilling its central missions of promoting economic growth and ameliorating poverty, via human capital investment. It has also banked on health because doing so allows it to deepen relationships with national governments, enmesh itself in countries' social sectors, and claim a stake in their health successes. More recently, a rights-based approach and a focus on universalism in health have gained prominence in the Bank's work in health.

This research has important implications for our understandings of global governance and globalization, development, welfare states and regimes, and health sector reform. My research clarifies how neoliberal global institutions, and in particular the World Bank, approach health and are involved in health sector reform in Latin America. My findings indicate that previous scholarship on the World Bank's relatively aggressive promotion of neoliberal policies in the developing world is seemingly not generalizable to the health sector. Theories of neoliberalism and neoliberal actors, therefore, require further refinement in the face of this new evidence. This book addresses the puzzle of why sweeping neoliberal reforms in health did not materialize in the 1980s and 1990s across Latin America. In doing so, I have sought to impose analytic clarity on what neoliberalism looks like in health sector reform, utilizing the policy paradigm and instruments approach to do so. As Chap. 2 demonstrates, the World Bank's approach to health has evolved over time, responding to criticisms and changing information since its official commitment to banking in health in 1980.

The World Bank remains fairly closely aligned with its original goal of promoting economic growth and its more recent goal of poverty alleviation in health. In doing so, the World Bank has certainly espoused private sector participation, competition, and a general promotion of market principles in health. While its goals have shifted to encompass those beyond the strictly neoliberal, as classically conceived (e.g., equity in addition to efficiency, promoting universalism), the tools have often remained market-based and can, therefore, be viewed as neoliberal (e.g., results-based financing and management contracts).

My analysis does not find a distinct shift in paradigmatic goals in health. That is, while previous research has indicated the existence of a post-Washington consensus and a shift from a sole focus on efficiency to a focus on equity, I do not identify such a discrete change. Since the publication of its 1993 World Development Report and its Health, Nutrition and Population strategy papers (in 1997 and 2007), people have pointed to a shift in the World Bank's thinking about health. My case-study analyses suggest this shift is a change in approach rather than a change in priorities. That is, the World Bank has increasingly embraced a primary health care approach and has increasingly considered equity in health, but not at the expense of efficiency. Both equity and efficiency are consistently invoked in the context of providing health care to the poor and extending coverage, priorities which have remained relatively constant over this time period. However, it is important to note that my evidence is limited to these three countries, and that some of them did not have many health projects prior to the early 1990s (indeed, Costa Rica's first World Bank health project begins in 1993).

My analysis underscores that the process of development manifests in demographic and economic changes that have important implications for health expenditures. Health expenditures are seemingly driven more by demographic changes as the result of development rather than global economic ties (trade and foreign direct investment). This is significant for understanding health system reform trajectories. My findings are consistent with conceptions of health sector development that underscore the importance of a changing epidemiological profile and an aging society coupled with the increased price of medical technologies and innovations. The continuity in Latin American countries' public health expenditures over time indicates that the structure of the health system, and in particular the state's involvement in health, is historically contingent and path-dependent though responsive to economic and demographic as well as other global changes.

This analysis also has important implications for theories of welfare state development and social policy reform. Welfare regimes in developing countries have been influenced by international discourse about poverty amelioration and maternal and child health in particular. International priorities for health, such as MDGs, and other social indicators exert powerful pressure on governments, often influencing the direction of reforms. In this way, they influence not only the policy instruments but also the goals that guide governments' health sector reform. As my analysis of health expenditures and my case-study analyses indicate, however, reforms are shaped by state capacity and autonomy and existing institutional arrangements in health and more generally within the state. This is particularly important to understand in times of crisis. This book has examined the duration and aftermath of the lost decade of the 1980s but such times have important implications for other times of economic crisis, including the 2008–2009 global financial crisis. It is during these times that employment-based health systems (such as in Argentina) come under particular strain, but also a time of increased interaction with international financial institutions such as the World Bank, in health and in other domains. These interactions are conditioned by existing state capacity and autonomy in health, existing national institutions, and the World Bank's approach to health, which itself is variable.

This book makes several theoretical, empirical, and methodological contributions. *Theoretically*, it serves to clarify what aspects of existing theory on IFIs and neoliberal globalization bear out in health in Latin America, but also the extent that theories of social protection and welfare state development apply to the field of health care in developing countries. I extend existing understandings of state autonomy and capacity. I propose that state autonomy and capacity in health (which may be different than overall state capacity and autonomy) importantly influence World Bank (and other IFI) involvement in health sector reform, in the form of changes in government policies and the delivery, financing, and organization of health provision. I suggest that it is important to examine capacity and autonomy in conjunction with existing institutional arrangements in the health sector (e.g., how the health care system financed and managed). The existing health system (in my case the health system in 1980, which is essentially "time zero" for my case-study analyses and direct World Bank involvement in the health sector) helps account for the approach that the World Bank takes to health sector reform. Importantly, this approach is not uniform across my three cases. The use of the policy paradigm approach allows me to ascertain how neoliberalism operates in the context of goals (equity and efficiency) for the health sector and but also in instruments (e.g., targeting and decentralization) implemented in health policies and programs.

Empirically, the book also adds to our stock of knowledge via its regional and case-study analyses as well as its discussion of the World Bank's changing approach to health. Chapter 2 provides an overview of the World Bank's approach to and involvement in health in developing countries from the 1980s to the present. Chapter 3 introduces a measure of World Bank conditions on health sector loans, allowing a direct test of this mechanism of influence on health sector reform. This book also provides a detailed, historical account of health sector reform and the World Bank's involvement in these reforms in Argentina, Peru, and Costa Rica (Chaps. 4, 5, and 6). I examine how the empirical evidence stacks up against allegations of neoliberal coercive IFIs and the World Bank's effect on social sectors in developing countries. I introduce new information about health sector reform in these countries. This is a cross-disciplinary contribution to our understanding of social provision, globalization, and policy change but also to Latin American studies as well as the global governance, development, and health sector reform literatures.

Methodologically, the book provides evidence for the utility of using a mixed-methods approach in historical, cross-national, and policy research (see the Methodological Appendix). While my quantitative analyses do not reveal evidence of conditionality reducing public expenditures on health, the case-studies provide insight as to why we do not witness such effects. Through the use of quantitative data and case-study analyses which combine regression analysis and process tracing, using policy documents and interviews, together with the concepts of paradigmatic goals and instruments, I am able to provide both narrative but also analytically comparable accounts of health sector reform across three cases.

As this book has emphasized, it is important to distinguish neoliberal ends from means and to contextualize the World Bank's work in health across countries and over time. This requires a careful treatment of neoliberalism as a policy approach, and an understanding of how national conditions, in particular state autonomy and capacity and existing institutions in health affect the World Bank's involvement. Given the World Bank's centrality as a funder of health in developing countries and a normative authority in global health, understanding both its own approach and how countries respond to its recommendations in their implementation of health sector reform is central to our understanding of the dynamics of development, globalization and global governance, and global health. My analysis suggests that while the Bank's work in health varies across countries, there are some common currents in its approach: the goals of equity and efficiency, and the tools proposed to achieve these goals. With the World Bank's recently renewed commitment, at least in words, to universalism in health, it remains to be seen whether and how the World Bank will seek to promote this goal across the developing world and the outcomes of such efforts.

Methodological Appendix: Comparative, Mixed-Methods Research: Challenges, Opportunities, and Some Practical Tips

Various data are required to undertake a comparative-historical, mixed-methods, cross-national project. This appendix contains additional information about the data gathering and analysis process used in this book. The book's argument relies on an immense amount of data of three primary types: (1) interview data generated from interviews with key informants in four countries (Argentina, Costa Rica, Peru, and the U.S.), (2) policy documents gathered during archival research at the Ministries of Health in Argentina, Costa Rica, and Peru, as well as the Ministry of Planning and *Instituto de Investigaciones Sociales* in Costa Rica together with research at the World Bank archives and the World Bank's website to examine project and program documents, and (3) quantitative cross-national data used in the statistical, regional analyses of health expenditures, from a variety of sources.

The questions and puzzle detailed in Chap. 1 could not be answered using only one method or data source. Indeed, as described in Chap. 2, I fail to find an anticipated negative effect of World Bank loan conditions on public health expenditures. How can this be explained? Does the World Bank have no effect on health in Latin American countries? Or, does it matter differently across countries? If so, how and why? The answers to these questions required case-study analyses and a view both from within the World Bank and from without, an examination of the countries it lends to and works in: the research undertaken in this book. It is only by drawing on the comparative leverage of the carefully chosen country cases, together with the regional statistical analyses, that the question of how and why the World Bank's approach to health has changed over time and varies across countries can be unpacked. In this appendix, I detail the data collection and analysis process and methodological decisions made therein.

CASE SELECTION AND COMPARATIVE RESEARCH

The use of a comparative design strategy reduces selection bias often associated with case-studies because it allows a comparison of analytic dimensions across multiple cases, thereby minimizing threats to validity. In addition, case-oriented, small-N, qualitative research designs allow the researcher to work closely with the data and make certain she is measuring the concepts/processes she intends to study rather than identifying spurious relationships, further increasing validity (Tilly 1984; Mahoney 2004). As Gerring (2004) notes, cross-unit case-studies are particularly well suited to examining covariation and answer "how" and "why" questions—in this case, cross-national case-study comparisons allow me to explore how and why the World Bank's involvement in health sector reform varies across these countries, and in particular how state capacity and autonomy influence the ways in which World Bank discourse and policy recommendations in health are implemented in national policies and programs.

In Chap. 3, I utilize quantitative data on health expenditure in Latin American and allow us to gain a sense of general patterns in expenditure and to the correlates and predictors of spending. This chapter provides a general idea of whether World Bank loan conditionality is associated with changes in health spending. However, this type of analysis cannot provide us with details of the process of health sector reform and outcomes other than spending—policy change, new programs, etc. Case-study analyses, on the other hand, can shed light on precisely these details regarding the role of the World Bank in health sector reform, focusing on particular policies, programs, and institutional change rather than expenditures. The three empirical case-study Chaps. 4–6, each present a country case-study of health care programs, policies, and reforms from 1980 to 2005—from the time of the "lost decade" through the current period while providing retrospective analytic distance. The case-studies represent three countries that occupy distinct positions on the axes of state capacity and autonomy in health as detailed in Chap. 1:

Costa Rica with high autonomy and high capacity, Argentina with high autonomy and low capacity, and Peru with low autonomy and low capacity (Fig. 1.1).

At the beginning of each of the three case-study chapters, I examine how Argentina, Costa Rica, and Peru's existing state capacity and autonomy in health account for how they were able and willing to contest, negotiate, and resist IFI pressures. Autonomy refers to how able the state is to formulate collective goals for the health sector while capacity refers to the state's ability to carry out its proposed agenda. Health sector reform is a particularly compelling site in which to examine how policy change occurs because of the diversity of alternatives and the variation in existing institutional arrangements across countries. While I have categorized my three cases: Argentina, Peru, and Costa Rica as high or low capacity, these dimensions exist along a continuum (see Fig. 1.1 in Chap. 1).

In measuring these analytic concepts, I relied on secondary documents and research when selecting the country cases, and then gathered additional information from national documents and interviews, described below. That is, my own research allowed me to triangulate and supplement sometimes limited accounts of health agendas and health sector reform in existing accounts. I was able to gather information from key actors in health sector reform in these countries. In particular, to capture autonomy, I focused in on examining national policy documents and health plans and asking key informants about the presence of national agendas and goals in health, and how and by whom these were formulated. In terms of capacity, I focused on whether government plans for reforms were implemented and whether there was any opposition (whether on the part of the World Bank or other national and international actors) to these initiatives or other barriers (a lack of resources) that prevented their subsequent implementation, both in the analysis of policy documents but more centrally in interviews.

Analytically, I used process tracing to examine the effect of the World Bank on health sector reform in these three countries. Process tracing is a method which through the detailed analysis of policy documents, debates, and histories helps analysts examine a particular historical process (Campbell 2002). It was originally conceived "as a way to incorporate historical narratives within highly abstract theories and explanations in the social sciences" (Falleti 2006), and while it was originally intended to examine causality within a single case, it has also been used in small-N

comparisons (Tansey 2007). It includes content (or textual) analysis where documents (in this case policy documents and reports) are seen as containing valuable information about actors (who wrote it and who is cited), prominent ideas (e.g., neoliberalism), and reflecting temporally bound understandings, ideas, and views on issues, topics, and actors (George and Bennett 2005). In addition, interviews with key informants allow me to further triangulate information gleaned from the official policy record and existing research on the topic (Tansey 2007). The policy documents allow me to examine and compare the World Bank's public statements and plans across the three countries: were the stated goals and plans the same across these three countries as suggested by arguments that IFIs are monolithic neoliberal institutions? They also allow me to analyze and contrast these with national laws, decrees, plans, and other documents about health. The interviews provide (in addition to factual information and a narrative of the reform process) information and opinions unavailable from the official documents (Schneiberg and Clemens 2006). Expert knowledge and access to details and facts of the case are essential to process tracing, but examining propositions also requires knowledge of the applicable general propositions (Mahoney 2012). For example, my case-study analyses allow me to examine how state capacity and autonomy in health affect how World Bank recommendations are negotiated and implemented in health sector reform.

I used the qualitative software ATLAS.ti (Muhr 2015) to code both my document and interview data, write memos, and notes, and keep track of my ideas and the concepts and patterns I observed in the data. In addition to coding for facts, figures, dates, and other factual information, I used my theoretical framework of state capacity and autonomy in health together with insights from the literatures on global governance, neoliberalism, and welfare and developmental states to guide my research. My approach to the linked processes of data analysis, theory testing, and theory building relies on a combination of, and indeed a movement between, inductive and deductive reasoning. The analysis of documents allowed me to gather historical information and details about countries' health agendas, laws, and policies and World Bank projects and discourse. My interviews provide a more complete picture of participating agencies (e.g., the Ministry of Health and Ministry of the Economy), the different stakeholders (those agencies in addition to local NGOs, labor unions, etc.), and their approach according to the different informants, who come from a variety of local and international organizations.

QUANTITATIVE DATA

Chapters 2 and 3 use descriptive and regression statistical analysis. The examination of development assistance in health (Chap. 2) and health expenditures in Latin America and the Caribbean (Chap. 3) drew on data from several sources. The data on Development Assistance for Health (DAH) used in Chap. 2 to illustrate the World Bank's spending in health globally and compared to other sources of health assistance are from the Development Assistance for Health Database 1990–2015 published by the Institute for Health Metrics and Evaluation (IHME 2016). These data are reported in 2014 US dollars, and the DAH measure refers to "the amount of financial and in-kind assistance that is tracked from source to channel to recipient country, region or health focus area. DAH is funded by the channel's corresponding income, or funds transferred from a source to the channel. Disbursements to specific health focus areas can include transfers between two channels, which can be captured in data from both channels" (IHME 2016).

The countries included in the analysis in Chap. 3 are as follows: Argentina, the Bahamas, Barbados, Belize, Bolivia, Brazil, Chile, Colombia, Costa Rica, the Dominican Republic, Ecuador, El Salvador, Guatemala, Guyana, Haiti, Honduras, Jamaica, Mexico, Nicaragua, Panama, Paraguay, Peru, Suriname, Trinidad and Tobago, Uruguay, and Venezuela. The analysis in Chap. 3 begins in 1995. Ideally, I would have begun this analysis in 1980, the year the World Bank formally committed to health lending. However, I use 1995 as the starting point because prior to 1995, there is no consistent or reliable data on spending for most countries in Latin America. In 1995, the World Health Organization (WHO) began working with countries in an effort to more uniformly capture and report their health spending levels, and give them standardized criteria for this reporting in the Americas. Therefore, while some data are available prior to 1995, it is sparse in terms of countries for which we have data and is both less reliable and less reliably comparable across countries.[1] In addition, the period under study begins as countries were emerging from the so-called "lost decade" of the 1980s during which most countries in the region experienced severe economic crisis (often accompanied by political turmoil). During those years, government spending was sometimes correspondingly erratic and ill-cataloged. Data on the country-years used in Chap. 3 are provided in Table A.1.[2]

In modeling cross-section time-series data, there are several things the researcher should account for, including correlation over time. A test for autocorrelation based on Wooldridge (2002) indicated that the data are serially correlated where the autocorrelation coefficient, ρ, ranges between 0.76 and 0.86 (Table 2.3). Therefore, I used a generalized least squares estimator with a Prais–Winsten AR(1) correction. I elected to model a single serial correlation coefficient for all countries rather than country-specific autocorrelation because of the small sample size and the potential bias due to missing data. I used panel-corrected standard errors as described by Beck and Katz (1995) where coefficients are estimated

Table A.1 Country-years in the sample used in the time-series cross-section models in Chap. 3, $N = 226$

Argentina	1996–2008
Bolivia	1996–1997, 2000–2007
Brazil	1996–2008
Chile	1996–2008
Colombia	1996–2008
Costa Rica	1996–2008
Dominican Republic	1996–2008
Ecuador	1996–1997, 2000–2007
El Salvador	1996–2008
Guatemala	2000–2006
Guyana	2002
Honduras	1996–1999, 2002–2007
Jamaica	1996–1997
Mexico	1996–2008
Nicaragua	1996–2007
Panama	1996–2008
Paraguay	1998–2008
Peru	1996–2008
Trinidad and Tobago	1996–2007
Uruguay	1996–2008
Venezuela	1996–2008

Notes While there are a total of 255 observations available for the analysis because left party and GDP were lagged, the sample size used was 226 country-years

There are no data available for one or more of the independent variables for the Bahamas, Barbados, Belize, and Suriname. Haiti is also omitted from the sample as it had only a single year of full information: 1999 using Prais–Winsten regression but the standard errors are robust to the possibility of non-spherical errors. The calculation of the panel-corrected standard errors assumes that the disturbances are heteroskedastic and contemporaneously correlated across panels. Conventional estimation of the panel-corrected correlation matrix requires balanced data, but because these data are unbalanced, I use pairwise correlations technique that adjusts the standard errors based on all available observations with non-missing pairs.[3] Table A.2 provides the descriptive statistics and source information for all of the variables used in the analyses in Chap. 3.

POLICY DOCUMENTS

The three country case-studies focus on health sector reform since 1980, with particular attention to the role of the World Bank in this process. For those analyses, I examined national policy documents produced by national governments and other national actors (including Ministries of Health) and policy documents produced by the World Bank related to its approach to health and, more specifically, related to its health projects in these countries. I supplement the policy document data with interview data with national policy makers, World Bank and other international organization personnel, civil society activists, experts on the health system, and other non-governmental organization personnel to both triangulate and complement the data from policy documents. First, and most importantly, interviews are a source of information in themselves as many of these health reforms have not been written about previously in great detail. Second, they allow me to triangulate information from the policy documents and secondary literature on health reform in these countries. Finally, while the policy documents provide a "public transcript" of World Bank and government discourse surrounding health sector reform, interviews help contextualize this by providing a "hidden transcript," a more behind-the-scenes look of how these policy reforms were initiated, implemented, and viewed by national and international actors, as discussed in the following section.

I utilize policy documents of three types in my analysis: first, I analyzed health sector plans, national development plans, reports, laws, and decrees published by the national governments and other public organizations (e.g., health ministries and social security offices) in Argentina, Peru, and Costa Rica. Second, I examined documents associated with World Bank health-related projects in Argentina, Peru, and Costa Rica

Table A.2 Descriptive statistics for the variables included in Chap. 3

Description	Source	Mean	Standard deviation	Minimum	Maximum
Dependent variables					
Health expenditure per capita (PPP, constant 2005 international $)	World Bank Health Nutrition and Population Statistics (HNP) (Bank 2011)	492.16	259.21	112.25	1209.73
Health expenditure, total (% of GDP)		6.60	1.60	3.49	13.01
Health expenditure, public (% of GDP)		3.48	1.28	1.24	7.12
Health expenditure, private (% of GDP)		3.12	1.08	0.95	7.28
Health expenditure, public (% of government expenditure)		52.20	13.16	23.20	82.46
Health expenditure, public (% of total health expenditure)		13.45	4.46	4.33	26.09
Independent variables					
GDP per capita in purchasing power parity, in hundreds of current US dollars	World Bank World Development Indicators (Bank 2012b)	72.42	37.12	15.50	252
Unemployment as a percent of the total labor force		9.24	4.15	1.30	20.10
Percent of the population 65 years or older		6.05	2.28	3.46	13.64
Democracy score (from Polity IV)	Polity IV (Marshall 2011)	7.94	1.61	1	10
Percentage of total seats in parliament for Left parties	Latin America and the Caribbean Political Dataset (Huber and Stephens 2012)	5.67	13.39	0	79.84
Trade openness (imports plus exports over GDP)	World Bank World Development Indicators (Bank 2012b)	69.93	32.99	14.90	198
Foreign direct investment, in billions of current US dollars		3.15	5.77	−9.42	29.20
World Bank conditions on all loans	World Bank Development Policy Actions Database (Bank 2012a)	9.63	22.51	0	169
World Bank conditions on health and other social sector loans		1.20	4.49	0	42

Notes Sample size is 226 country-years

for which agreements were signed between 1980 and 2005. Some of these projects are ongoing or were completed after 2005, but all were begun during this time period. Third, I draw from important documents by international organizations identified by previous scholarship as significant and often referenced in the loan projects, for example, the World Bank's 1993 World Development Report. The year 1980 provides an ideal starting point as it marks the beginning of the debt crisis, a time when all Latin American countries were reconfiguring their public sectors and when the World Bank loans and advice were especially sought after by governments of developing countries, and marks the year the World Bank officially begins direct lending for health while 2005 provides retrospective distance, especially as it allows me to examine largely completed (rather than in progress) World Bank projects.

National Documents

For the case-study analyses (Chaps. 4–6), I also utilize government documents, including laws, decrees, and national health and development plans, to examine the national public record on health sector reforms. These documents were collected during field research in Argentina, Peru, and Costa Rica in 2011 and from online sources. To the best of my knowledge, I have obtained access to the entire population of official government health plans and laws and decrees related to health sector reform in these countries. I have ascertained this by visiting each of these countries' Ministries of Health archives/document collections during 2011, as well as asking about relevant plans and laws during my interviews.

The archives/repositories I visited are:

Centro de Información del Ministerio de Salud Costa Rica. Location: San Jose, Costa Rica. Description: It contains documents related to the Ministry of Health's work, both nationally and with international organizations.

Instituto de Investigaciones Sociales (ISS) Document Repository at the Universidad de Costa Rica. Location: San Pedro, Costa Rica. Description: A collection of governmental policy documents and national publications on social policy and social relations in Costa Rica.

Ministerio de Planificación Nacional y Política Económica (MIDEPLAN) Archive. Location: San Jose, Costa Rica. Description: It contains documents published by MIDEPLAN and its predecessor

OFIPLAN (the Oficina de Planificación was founded in 1963 and was under the supervision of the Costa Rican president; in 1973, this was converted to MIDEPLAN). These include national plans and documents, as well as background papers and information national development plans and other government documents.

Ministerio de Salud del Peru Documents. Location: Av. Salaverry 801 Jesús María, Lima, Perú. Description: There is a library of sorts located in the Minister's antechamber in the Ministry as well as across offices, which contain statistical information, reports, and other documents, mostly published.

Ministerio de Salud of Argentina Documents. Location: Av. de 9 de Julio 1925, Buenos Aires, Argentina. Description: The Ministry has several spaces which contain historical documents and reports as well as secondary literature, though this has more recently been consolidated into a web-based library, accessible at: http://bvsalud.org/.

World Bank Group Archives. Location: 1818 H Street, NW Washington, DC. Description: It contains World Bank reports, historical records, memos, and internal correspondence for IDA and IBRD work and offices. Documents are only declassified and available if they are 10 years old or older.

The government policy documents are an integral part of examining health sector reform as they allow me to examine the extent to which World Bank projects and documents shaped national agendas and discourse while leaving open the option for feedback and recursive processes of the organizations learning and using national discourses and initiatives in their other projects.

Argentina has one health plan published toward the end of this time period, in 2004, and has passed many laws and presidential decrees related to the health sector, as detailed in Table A.3. Similarly, Peru also has one health plan from this time, from 2001 to 2006, and laws and decrees related to the health sector, which I have examined in detail in an effort to trace both dates in the process of reform but also examine discourse surrounding health sector reform. Costa Rica provides the most consistent and regular source of government plans for the health sector as the Costa Rican government publishes a national development plan approximately every four years, which contain sectoral goals, assessment of previous accomplishments, and future plans. I procured most of Costa Rica's social development plans (which include the health component) during archival research in 2011, save for the two most recent plans

Table A.3 National documents related to health sector reform including legislation and health plans in Argentina, Costa Rica, and Peru

Name	Date	Source
Argentina		
Decreto-Ley 18610: Obras Sociales, Normas de Funcionamiento [Decree-Law 18610: Obras Sociales, Operating Rules]	February 23, 1970	Congreso de la Nacion
Decreto 19032: Creacion del Instituto Nacional de Servicios Sociales Para Jubilados y Pensionados [Decree 19032: Creation of the National Institute of Social Services for Retired People and Pensioners]	May 28, 1971	Presidente de la Nacion
Ley 23660: Obras Sociales [Ley 23660: Obras Sociales]	January 20, 1989	Congreso de la Nacion
Ley 23661: Sistema Nacional del Seguro de Salud [Law 23661: National Health Insurance System]	January 5, 1989	Congreso de la Nacion
Ley 22373: Creacion Consejo Federal de Salud [Ley 22373: Creation of the Federal Committee for Health]	January 13, 1981	Congreso de la Nacion
Decreto 9/1993: Obras Sociales, Libre Eleccion [Decree 9/1993: Obras Sociales, Free Choice]	January 18, 1993	Presidente de la Nacion
Decreto 1141/1996: Obras Sociales, Deregulacion/ Opcion de Cambio [Decree 1141/1996: Obras Sociales, Deregulation/Option to Switch]	October 9, 1996	Presidente de la Nacion
Decreto 84/1997: Obras Sociales, Cambio [Decree 84/1997: Obras Sociales, Switching]	January 28, 1997	Presidente de la Nacion
Decreto 578/1993: Hospitales Publicos, Registro de Hospitales de Autogestion [Decree 578/1993: Public Hospitals, Registration of Self-Managed Hospitals]	April 7, 1993	Presidente de la Nacion
Decreto 492/1995: Obras Sociales Sindicales, Programa Medico Obligatorio, Reduccion de Aportes [Decree 492/1995: Union Obras Sociales, Obligatory Medical Plan, Reduction in Contributions]	September 22, 1995	Presidente de la Nacion
Decreto 292/1995: Contribuciones Patrimoniales, Distribucion Automatica del Fondo Solidario de Redistribucion, Reduccion [Decree 292/1995: Economic Contributions, Automatic Distribution of the Solidarity Fund of Redistribution, Reduction]	August 14, 1995	Presidente de la Nacion
Decreto 257/1996: Consejo Nacional del Trabajo y Empleo, Creacion/Integracion [Decree 257/1996: National Committee for Worlkand Employment Creation/Integration]	March 14, 1996	Presidente de la Nacion

(continued)

Table A.3 (continued)

Name	Date	Source
Ley 25649: Especialidades Medicinales, Medicamentos Genericos [Law 25649: Medical Specialties, Generic Medications]	September 19, 2002	Congreso de la Nacion
Memoria Salud 2001 del Ministerio de Salud [Health Report 2001 of the Ministry of Health]	2001	Ministerio de Salud
Acuerdo Federal de Salud [Federal Health Agreement]	March 22, 2003	Ministerio de Salud
Bases del Plan Federal de Salud [Basis for the Federal Health Plan]	May 2004	Presidencia de la Nacion, Ministerio de Salud de la Nacion, Consejo Federal de Salud
Acta de Aprobacion del Plan Federal de Salud 2004/2007 [Adoption Act of Federal Health Plan 2004/2007] *Peru*	March 31, 2004	Consejo Federal de Salud
Decreto Legislativo 70: Ley de Organización del Sector Salud [Legislative Decree 70: Health Sector Organization Law]	April 14, 1981	Consejo de Ministros
Decreto Legislativo 584: Ley De Organizacion y Funciones del Ministerio De Salud [Legislative Decree 584: Health Ministry Organization and Functions Law]	April 18, 1990	Consejo de Ministros
Ley 26790: Ley de Modernización de Seguridad en Salud [Law 26790: Law of the Modernization of Social Security]	May 15, 1997	Congreso de la Republica
Ley 26842: Ley General de Salud [Law 26842: General Health Law]	July 15, 1997	Congreso de la Republica
Ley 27656: Ley de Creación del Fondo Intangible Solidario de Salud —FISSAL [Law of the Creation of the Solidary Health Fund, FISSAL]	January 29, 2002	Congreso de la Republica
Ley 27657: Ley del Ministerio de Salud [Law of the Ministry of Health]	January 29, 2002	Congreso de la Republica
Lineamientos de Política Sectorial para el Período 2002–2012 y Principios Fundamentales para el Plan Estratégico Sectorial del Quinquenio 2001–2006 [Sectoral Policy Guidelines for 2002–2012 and Fundamental Principles for the Sectoral Strategic Plan of the 2001–2006]	June 21, 2002	Ministerio de Salud

(continued)

Table A.3   (continued)

Name	Date	Source
Ley 27812: Ley que Determina las Fuentes de Financiamiento del Seguro Integral de Salud [Law that determines the source of financing for the SIS]	August 13, 2002	Congreso de la Republica
Ley 27660: Ley que Declara de Carácter Prioritario el Seguro Integral de Salud, para las Organizaciones Sociales de Base y Wawa Wasis [Law 27660: Law that Establishes the Integral Health Insurance as a Priority, for the Grass-Roots Social Organizations and "Children"'s Houses"]	July 3, 2003	Congreso de la Republica
Acuerdo de Partidos Políticos en Salud 2006–2010 [Political Parties Agreement in Health 2006–2010]	December 20, 2005	
Ley 28588: Ley que incorpora al Seguro Integral de Salud a la población mayor de 17 años en situación de extrema pobreza y pobreza [Law that incorporates people older than 17 living in extreme poverty and poverty into the SIS] *Costa Rica*	July 21, 2005	Congreso de la Republica
Plan Nacional de Desarrollo, 1978–1982 "Gregorio Jose Ramirez"		Oficina de Planificacion Nacional (OFIPLAN)
Plan Nacional de Desarrollo, 1982–1986 "Volvamos a la Tierra"		Ministerio de Planificación Nacional y Política Económica (MIDEPLAN)
Plan Nacional de Desarrollo, 1986–1990		Ministerio de Planificación Nacional y Política Económica (MIDEPLAN)
Plan Nacional de Desarrollo, 1990–1994 "Desarrollo Sostenido Con Justicia Social"		Ministerio de Planificación Nacional y Política Económica (MIDEPLAN)

(continued)

Table A.3   (continued)

Name	Date	Source
Plan Nacional de Desarrollo, 1994–1998 "Francisco J. Orlich"		Ministerio de Planificación Nacional y Política Económica (MIDEPLAN)
Plan Nacional de Desarrollo Humano, 1998–2002 "Soluciones Siglo XXI"		Ministerio de Planificación Nacional y Política Económica (MIDEPLAN)
Plan Nacional de Desarrollo, 2002–2006 "Monsenor Victor Manuel Sanabria Martinez"		Ministerio de Planificación Nacional y Política Económica (MIDEPLAN)
Ley Constitutiva Caja Costarricense de Seguro Social (Ley 17) [Constitutive Law of the Costa Rican Social Security Agency]	October 22, 1943	Asamblea Legislativa
Ley General De Asistencia Medico-Social (Ley 1153) [General Law Of Medical-Social Assistance]	April 14, 1950	Asamblea Legislativa
Ley Para Reorganizar Los Servicios Medicos Preventivos Con Base a la C.C.S.S.(Ley 5349) [Law to Reorganize Preventative Medical Services Based at the CCSS]	October 3, 1973	Asamblea Legislativa
Ley General de Salud (Ley 5395) [General Health Law]	October 30, 1973	Asamblea Legislativa
Ley Orgánica del Ministerio de Salud (Ley 5412) [Organic Law of the Ministry of Health]	November 8, 1973	Asamblea Legislativa
Ley de Desconcentración de Clínicas y Hospitales de la Caja Costarricense del Seguro Social (Ley 7852) [Law of Deconcentration of Clinics and Hospitals of the Costa Rican Social Security Agency]	November 30, 1998	Asamblea Legislativa
Derechos y Deberes De Las Personas Usuarias de Los Servicios De Salud Públicos y Privados (Ley 8239) [Rights and Responsibilities of Users of Public and Private Health Services]	April 2, 2002	Asamblea Legislativa

which are only available online. While each of the three countries produced more laws and decrees pertaining to the health sector (anything from medical school requirements to pharmaceutical regulations) than those included in Table A.3, these are the ones that are central to my examination of health sector reform and the documents I reference in Chaps. 4–6.

World Bank Documents

My analysis also draws from the population of documents related to health sector projects and loans from the World Bank in Argentina, Peru, and Costa Rica. That is, I did not have to rely on a sample of World Bank health projects and loans in three countries but rather I was able to examine the entirety of its activity in these countries. In order to identify relevant projects, I examined all World Bank projects in Argentina, Peru, and Costa Rica from 1980 to 2005 via the World Bank indexed system and looked up projects' summaries and descriptions and included any project which had a health sector component. I confirmed that I had identified all relevant documents by conducting a keyword search of "health" (and variants thereof "health care," etc.) and each of the country names (e.g., "Peru," "Argentina," and "Costa Rica") to locate all relevant documents associated with these projects. It is important to note that my definition of "health related" is broader than that of the World Bank. The World Bank has been categorizing loans and project by sector since the early 1990s. Projects' sector categorizations are defined by the financing allocated to each sector where some projects contribute to several sectors.[4] However, I have included several projects that the World Bank does not categorize as "health" sectoral programs. For example, the first and second structural adjustment programs in Costa Rica are identified in the World Bank's database as relating to "economic management" but because these may have implications for public sector and health spending and because existing scholarship points to their importance in shaping social sector, health, and policy, I include them in my analysis. The World Bank identifying a project as related to health is, therefore, a sufficient, but not a necessary condition for its inclusion in my analysis.

Figure A.1 provides an overview of the health-related projects that I examine in Argentina, Costa Rica, and Peru. As Fig. A.1 demonstrates, projects are variable in length and often overlap substantially in their

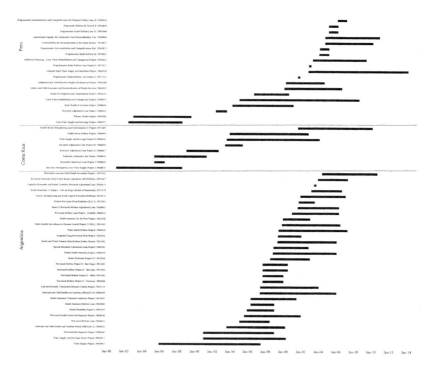

Fig. A.1 World Bank health sector-related projects in Argentina, Costa Rica, and Peru, approved between 1980 and 2005

timing. In addition, there is a variation in the number of health-related projects in each of the three countries: 31 in Argentina, eight in Costa Rica, and 19 in Peru. Table A.4 provides a summary of all and health-related projects in Argentina, Peru, and Costa Rica. Table A.4 indicates that there were 58 projects related to the health sector across the three countries that began between 1980 and 2005 out of a total of 223 projects across all sectors. While some of these projects were exclusively health related, many of them were multi-sectoral, a popular approach at the World Bank. That is, often the health component comprises only a fraction of the monies allocated in these projects, most notably the Structural Adjustment Projects. The average length of projects was between five and seven years across the three countries.

Table A.4 Overview of World Bank projects in Argentina, Costa Rica, and Peru approved between 1980 and 2005

		Argentina		Costa Rica		Peru	
		Total project cost	World Bank contribution	Total project cost	World Bank contribution	Total project cost	World Bank contribution
All projects	Total project costs	32,417	21,228	850	645	8142	5802
	Average project cost	270	177	40	31	99	71
	Number of projects	120		21		82	
Health projects	Total project costs	10,981	7829	392	375	2379	1730
	Average project cost	354	253	49	47	125	91
	Number of projects	31		8		19	
	Total cost of health projects over total cost of all projects	34	37	46	58	29	21
	Average cost of a health project over average cost of all projects	131	143	121	152	126	129
	Percent of all projects that are health projects	26		38		23	
	Average health project length (years)	5		7		5	

Source World Bank projects and operations, http://data.worldbank.org/data-catalog/projects-portfolio
Notes Costs are in millions of US dollars

Table A.5 provides a list of the World Bank documents used in the analysis. The documents are indexed by project, and Table A.5 details their accompanying documents and project start and end dates. And each World Bank loan has between two and 14 associated documents which in turn range between two and 170 pages in length (see Table A.5).

Other International Organization Documents

In order to supplement the information from national documents and World Bank documents, I also examine important documents in health, largely published by international organizations. I examined documents that were mentioned in the secondary literature on international health sector reform, as well as those referenced in my policy documents. For example, I examined documents relating to the Alma Ata conference on primary health care (Report of the International Conference on Primary Health Care, Alma-Ata 1978) and the seminal 1993 World Bank World Development Report "Investing in Health". These documents allow me to examine how other organizations view the issues and sometimes propose solutions to the health problems that they identify in these countries. Most notably, the WHO in the form of its regional arm in the Americas, the Pan-American Health Organization, has worked closely with governments and sometimes IFIs in Latin America in health policy reforms.

Table A.5 Policy documents for World Bank health sector-related projects in Argentina, Costa Rica, and Peru approved between 1980 and 2005

Project name	Project ID number	Associated documents: Year, name, length	Project approval date	Project closing date
Peru				
Lima Water Supply and Sewerage Project	P007977	(1) 1982, Staff Appraisal Report, 117 p (2) 1982, Report of the President of IBRD, 37 p (3) 1991, Completion Report, 28 p	May 11, 1982	June 30, 1988
Primary Health Project	P007982	(1) 1982, Staff Appraisal Report, 101 p (2) 1982, Report of the President of IBRD, 39 p (3) 1993, Project Completion Report, 58 p	November 30, 1982	June 30, 1989
Structural Adjustment Loan Project	P008034	(1) 1991, Grant Agreement, 12 p (2) 1992, Loan Agreement, 1992, 9 p (3) 1995, Completion Report, 118 p	Mar 26, 1992	June 30, 1993
Basic Health & Nutrition Project	P008048	(1) 1993, Japanese Grant Agreement, 13 p (2) 1994, Staff Appraisal Report, 78 p (3) 1994, Loan Agreement, 15 p (4) 1998, Loan Agreement Amendment 1, 2 p (5) 1998, Loan Agreement Amendment 2, 2 p (6) 1998, Loan Agreement Amendment 3, 2 p (7) 2000, Loan Agreement Amendment 4, 1 p (8) 2001, Completion Report, 43 p	February 3, 1994	December 31, 2000
Lima Water Rehabilitation and Management Project	P008051	(1) 1994, Staff Appraisal Report, 127 p (2) 1995, Project Agreement, 12 p (3) 1995, Loan Agreement, 14 p (4) 1996, Loan Agreement Amendment 1, 2 p (5) 1997, Loan Agreement Amendment 2, 2 p (6) 2009, Implementation Completion Report, 56 p	November 22, 1994	June 30, 2008

(continued)

Table A.5 (continued)

Project name	Project ID number	Associated documents: Year, name, length	Project approval date	Project closing date
Social Development and Compensation Fund II	P040125	(1) 1996, Staff Appraisal Report, 88 p (2) 1996, Project Agreement, 6 p (3) 1996, Loan Agreement, 15 p (4) 2001, Implementation Completion Report, 83 p	July 16, 1996	June 30, 2000
Health Reform Project (First Phase: Mother and Child Insurance and Decentralization of Health Services)	P062932	(1) 1998, Japanese Grant Agreement, 9 p (2) 1999, Project Appraisal Document, 91 p (3) 2000, Project Information Document, 4 p (4) 2001, Loan Agreement, 25 p (5) 2007, Completion Report, 74 p	December 16, 1999	June 30, 2006
Indigenous and Afro-Peruvian Peoples Development Project	P060499	(1) 1999, Project Information Document, 8 p (2) 2000, Project Appraisal Document, 75 p (3) 2000, Loan Agreement, 17 p (4) 2004, Completion Report, 40 p	February 10, 2000	June 30, 2004
Programmatic Social Reform Loan Project	P071243	(1) 2001, Loan Agreement, 11 p (2) 2002, Implementation Completion Report, 55 p	June 19, 2001	September 28, 2001
National Rural Water Supply and Sanitation Project	P065256	(1) 1999, Japanese Grant Agreement, 8 p (2) 2001, Project Information Document, 7 p (3) 2002, Loan Agreement, 29 p (4) 2002, Integrated Safeguards Data Sheet, 6 p (5) 2002, Environmental Assessment I (Spanish), 45 p (6) 2002, Environmental Assessment I (Spanish), 54 p (7) 2002, Environmental Assessment III (Spanish),	August 29, 2002	December 31, 2013

(continued)

Table A.5 (continued)

Project name	Project ID number	Associated documents: Year, name, length	Project approval date	Project closing date
		(8) 2002, Project Appraisal Document, 78 p		
		(9) 2006, Amendment 1, 58 p		
		(10) 2006, Amendment 2, 4 p		
		(11) 2010, Loan Agreement 2, 25 p		
		(12) 2011, Procurement Plan, 11 p		
		(13) 2011, Implementation Status and Results, 5 p		
		(14) 2011, Implementation Status and Results 2, 6 p		
Programmatic Social Reform Loan Project II	P073877	(1) 2001, Japanese Grant Agreement, 7 p	September 17, 2002	December 31, 2002
		(2) 2002, Project Information Document, 3 p		
		(3) 2002, Loan Agreement, 25 p		
		(4) 2003, Japanese Grant Agreement, 10 p		
		(5) 2003, Implementation Report, 42 p		
Lima Water Rehabilitation and Management Project, Additional Financing	P081834	(1) 2002, Integrated Safeguards Data Sheet, 3 p	February 25, 2003	March 31, 2009
		(2) 2003, Project Information Document, 9 p		
		(3) 2003, Technical Annex, 38 p		
		(4) 2004, Amendment 1, 18 p		
		(5) 2009, Implementation Report, 56 p		
Programmatic Social Reform III	P078951	(1) 2003, Program Information Document, 8 p	November 11, 2003	December 31, 2004
		(2) 2003, Program Document, 126 p		
		(3) 2003, Loan Agreement, 16 p		
		(4) 2004, Completion Report, 44 p		

(continued)

Table A.5 (continued)

Project name	Project ID number	Associated documents: Year, name, length	Project approval date	Project closing date
Programmatic Decentralization and Competitiveness Structural Adjustment Loan	P082871	(1) 2003, Project Information Document, 6 p (2) 2003, Loan Agreement, 13 p (3) 2007, Implementation Completion Report, 106 p	December 2, 2003	December 31, 2004
Accountability for Decentralization in the Social Sectors	P078953	(1) 2004, Project Information Document, 10 p (2) 2004, Project Appraisal Document, 70 p (3) 2004, Loan Agreement, 28 p (4) 2004, Integrated Safeguards Data Sheet, 9 p	July 15, 2004	December 31, 2009
Institutional Capacity for Sustainable Fiscal Decentralization	P088809	(1) 2004, Project Information Document, 5 p (2) 2004, Project Appraisal Document, 102 p (3) 2004, Loan Agreement, 28 p (4) 2009, Data Sheet 1, 27 p (5) 2010, Data Sheet 2, 2 p (6) 2010, Restructuring Paper, 5 p (7) 2010, Procurement Plan, 12 p (8) 2011, Implementation Completion Report, 47 p	July 15, 2004	September 30, 2010
Programmatic Social Reform Loan IV	P083968	(1) 2004, Project Document, 134 p (2) 2004, Program Information Document 1, 4 p (3) 2004, Program Information Document 2, 4 p (4) 2004, Loan Agreement, 15 p (5) 2006, Completion Report, 44 p	December 7, 2004	December 31, 2005
Programmatic Reform for Growth II	P083949	(1) 2004, Program Document, 218 p (2) 2004, Project Information Document, 5 p (3) 2004, Loan Agreement, 19 p (4) 2007, Implementation Completion Report, 106 p	December 7, 2004	December 31, 2005

(continued)

Table A.5 (continued)

Project name	Project ID number	Associated documents: Year, name, length	Project approval date	Project closing date
Third Programmatic Decentralization and Competitiveness Development Policy Loan *Costa Rica*	P089826	(1) 2005, Project Information Document, 5 p (2) 2005, Project Document, 151 p (3) 2005, Loan Agreement, 17 p (4) 2007, Implementation Completion Report, 106 p	December 8, 2005	December 31, 2006
San Jose Metropolitan Area Water Supply Project	P006921	(1) 1980, Report and Recommendation of the President of the IBRD to Executive Directors, 39 p (2) 1980, Staff Appraisal Report, 101 p (3) 1990, Project Completion Report, 33 p	December 23, 1980	June 30, 1988
Structural Adjustment Loan (SAL) Project	P006923	(1) 1985, Recommendation of the President of the IBRD to Executive Directors, 88 p (2) 1994, Project Completion Report, 76 p	April 16, 1985	June 30, 1986
Technical Assistance Loan Project	P006933	(1) 1985, Recommendation of the President of the IBRD to Executive Directors, 66 p (2) 1993, Project Completion Report, 76 p	April 16, 1985	April 1, 1991
Structural Adjustment Loan Project II	P006927	(1) 1988, Recommendation of the President of the IBRD to Executive Directors, 75 p (2) 1988, Loan Agreement, 11 p (3) 1988, Loan Agreement Amendment, 1 p (4) 1989, Loan Agreement Amendment, 2 p (5) 1992, Loan Agreement Amendment, 3 p (6) 1994, Project Completion Report, 76 p	December 13, 1988	July 31, 1992

(continued)

Table A.5 (continued)

Project name	Project ID number	Associated documents: Year, name, length	Project approval date	Project closing date
Third Structural Adjustment Loan Project	P006952	(1) 1993, Loan Agreement, 14 p (2) 1996, Project Completion Note, 12 p	April 15, 1993	April 30, 1995
Water Supply and Sewerage Project II	P006941	(1) 1993, Loan Agreement, 20 p (2) 1993, Guarantee Agreement, 4 p (3) 1993, Staff Appraisal Report, 123 p (4) 1996, Amendment 1, 4 p (5) 1997, Amendment 2, 5 p (6) 2005, Implementation Completion Report, 59 p	June 17, 1993	December 31, 2003
Health Sector Reform Project	P006954	(1) 1992, Grant Agreement 10 p (2) 1993, Loan Agreement 18 p (3) 1993, Project Agreement 6 p (4) 1993, Staff Appraisal Report, 170 p (5) 1996, Amendment, 3 p (6) 2003, Implementation Completion Report, 66 p	October 21, 1993	September 30, 2002
Health Sector Strengthening and Modernization II Project	P073892	(1) 2001, Project Agreement, 8 p (2) 2001, Loan Agreement, 12 p (3) 2001, Project Information Document, 9 p (4) 2001, Project Appraisal Document, 95 p (5) 2002, Integrated Safeguards Data Sheet, 4 p (6) 2010, Implementation, Completion and Results Report, 94 p	July 12, 2001	December 31, 2009
Argentina				

(continued)

Table A.5 (continued)

Project name	Project ID number	Associated documents: Year, name, length	Project approval date	Project closing date
Water Supply Project	P005945	(1) 1985, Staff Appraisal Report, 66 p (2) 1985, Memo and Recommendation of IBRD President, 36 p (3) 1998, Implementation Report, 43 p	December 10, 1985	June 30, 1997
Water Supply and Sewerage Sector Project	P005977	(1) 1990, Staff Appraisal Report, 77 p (2) 1990, Memo and Recommendation of IBRD President, 16 p (3) 1991, Project Agreement, 12 p (4) 1991, Loan Agreement, 15 p (5) 1995, Amendment 1, 2 p (6) 1997, Amendment 2, 5 p (7) 2001, Implementation Report, 43 p	December 18, 1990	April 30, 2000
Maternal and Child Health and Nutrition Project	P006025	(1) 1993, Staff Appraisal Report, 94 p (2) 1993, Loan Agreement, 9 p (3) 1994, Amendment 1, 1 p (4) 1994, Amendment 2, 3 p (5) 1995, Amendment 3, 3 p (6) 2000, Implementation Report, 51 p	August 3, 1993	March 30, 2000
Provincial Reform Loan	P006035	(1) 1995, Loan Agreement, 12 p (2) 1999, Implementation Report, 66 p	January 24, 1995	June 30, 1998
Provincial Health Sector Development Project	P006030	(1) 1995, Staff Appraisal Report, 70 p (2) 1996, Loan Agreement, 17 p (3) 1998 Amendment 1, 3 p (4) 2002, Implementation Report, 34 p	August 3, 1995	December 31, 2001

(continued)

Table A.5 (continued)

Project name	Project ID number	Associated documents: Year, name, length	Project approval date	Project closing date
Social Protection Project	P035495	(1) 1995, Staff Appraisal Report, 100 p (2) 1995, Loan Agreement, 18 p (3) 2000, Implementation Report, 49 p	November 21, 1995	December 31, 1998
Health Insurance Reform Loan	P040909	(1) 1995, Project Information Document, 4 p (2) 1996, Loan Agreement 1, 10 p (3) 1996, Loan Agreement 2, 12 p (4) 1997, Amendment 1, 2 p (5) 1999, Implementation Completion Report, 63 p	April 25, 1996	December 31, 1998
Health Insurance Technical Assistance Project	P045687	(1) 2002, Implementation Report, 38 p	April 25, 1996	June 30, 2001
Maternal and Child Health and Nutrition II (PROMIN)	P006059	(1) 1997, Project Appraisal Document, 50 p (2) 1997, Loan Agreement, 14 p (3) 1997, Project Information Document, 6 p (4) 2001, Amendment 1, 4 p (5) 2002, Amendment 2, 34 p (6) 2006, Project Implementation Report, 57 p	May 15, 1997	December 31, 2005
AR Aids and Sexually Transmitted Diseases Control Project	P043418	(1) 1997, Project Appraisal Document, 42 p (2) 1997, Project Information Document, 5 p (3) 1997, Loan Agreement, 14 p (4) 1997, Japanese Grant Agreement, 12 p (5) 2001, Amendment 1, 3 p (6) 2004, Implementation Report, 36 p	May 22, 1997	December 31, 2003

(continued)

Table A.5 (continued)

Project name	Project ID number	Associated documents: Year, name, length	Project approval date	Project closing date
Provincial Development Project	P006005	(1) 1990, Staff Appraisal Report, 94 p (2) 1990, Memo and Recommendation of IBRD President, 15 p (3) 1991, Loan Agreement, 16 p (4) 1997, Amendment 1, 3 p (5) 1998, Amendment 2, 2 p (6) 1999, Implementation Report, 87 p	December 18, 1990	December 31, 1998
Provincial Reform Project II—Tucuman	P006006	(1) 1997, Project Information Document, 6 p (2) 1998, Loan Agreement, 11 p (3) 2000, Implementation Completion Report, 60 p	August 26, 1997	December 31, 1999
Provincial Reform Project II—Salta	P051693	(1) 1997, Project Information Document, 6 p (2) 1997, Loan Agreement, 11 p (3) 2000, Implementation Completion Report, 66 p	August 26, 1997	December 31, 1999
Provincial Reform Project II—San Juan	P051694	(1) 1997, Project Information Document, 6 p (2) 1998, Loan Agreement, 13 p (3) 2001, Implementation Completion Report, 55 p	August 26, 1997	June 30, 2000
Provincial Reform Project II—Rio Negro	P051695	(1) 1997, Project Information Document, 6 p (2) 1997, Loan Agreement, 13 p (3) 2001, Implementation Completion Report, 59 p	August 26, 1997	June 30, 2000
Social Protection Project III	P049269	(1) 1998, Project Appraisal Document, 37 p (2) 1998, Loan Agreement, 12 p (3) 2003, Implementation Completion Report, 48 p	June 30, 1998	December 30, 2002

(continued)

Table A.5 (continued)

Project name	Project ID number	Associated documents: Year, name, length	Project approval date	Project closing date
Social Protection Project IV	P006058	(1) 1998, Project Appraisal Document, 58 p (2) 1998, Project Information Document, 9 p (3) 1999, Loan Agreement, 14 p (4) 2000, Amendment 1, 2 p (5) 2002, Amendment 2, 8 p (6) 2002, Amendment 3, 7 p (7) 2006, Implementation Report, 40 p	October 15, 1998	December 31, 2005
Special Structural Adjustment Loan Project	P062991	(1) 1998, Project Information Document, 6 p (2) 1998, Loan Agreement, 13 p (3) 1999, Notice on Request for Inspection, 3 p (4) 1999, Recommendation on Request for Inspection, 64 p (5) 1999, Amendment 1, 7 p (6) 2002, Amendment 2, 5 p (7) 2002, Implementation Report, 48 p	November 10, 1998	October 31, 2002
Social and Fiscal National Identification System Project	P055461	(1) 1999, Project Appraisal Document, 42 p (2) 1999, Project Information Document, 3 p (3) 1999, Loan Agreement, 14 p (4) 1998, Japanese Grant Agreement, 5 p (5) 2006, Implementation Completion Report, 48 p	April 20, 1999	December 31, 2005
Integrated Drug Prevention Pilot Project	P058526	(1) 1999, Project Appraisal Document, 47 p (2) 1999, Project Information Document, 4 p (3) 1999, Loan Agreement, 14 p (4) 2002, Project Completion Report/Cancellation, 6 p	May 5, 1999	December 31, 2001

(continued)

Table A.5 (continued)

Project name	Project ID number	Associated documents: Year, name, length	Project approval date	Project closing date
Water Sector Reform Project	P006046	(1) 1997, Project Information Document, 4 p (2) 1996, Japanese Grant Agreement, 10 p (3) 1999, Project Appraisal Document, 97 p (4) 2000, Loan Agreement, 17 p (5) 2000, Amendment 1, 2 p (6) 2000, Amendment 2, 4 p (7) 2002, Amendment 3, 8 p (8) 2007, Implementation Completion Report, 66 p	June 1, 1999	March 31, 2007
Public Health Surveillance and Disease Control Project (VIGIA)	P055482	(1) 1999, Project Appraisal Document, 82 p (2) 1999, Project Information Document, 10 p (3) 2000, Loan Agreement, 18 p (4) 2000, Amendment 1, 2 p (5) 2002, Amendment 2, 38 p (6) 2006, Implementation Report, 74 p	October 14, 1999	May 31, 2006
Health Insurance for the Poor Project	P063383	(1) 1999, Project Information Document, 5 p (2) 1999, Project Appraisal Document, 59 p (3) 2003, Project Completion Report/Cancellation, 4 p	November 24, 1999	December 31, 2002
Provincial Reform Loan Project - Cordoba	P068344	(1) 2000, Project Information Document, 4 p (2) 2001, Loan Agreement, 17 p (3) 2003, Amendment 1, 15 p (4) 2003, Amendment 2, 56 p (5) 2007, Implementation Report, 68 p	November 22, 2000	March 31, 2006

(continued)

Table A.5 (continued)

Project name	Project ID number	Associated documents: Year, name, length	Project approval date	Project closing date
Santa Fe Provincial Reform Adjustment Loan	P069913	(1) 2001, Project Information Document, 4 p (2) 2001, Loan Agreement, 14 p (3) 2003, Amendment 1, 43 p (4) 2007, Implementation Report, 65 p	July 19, 2001	March 31, 2006
Structural Adjustment Loan I—Federal Provincial Fiscal Relations	P073591	(1) 2001, Project Information Document, 3 p (2) 2001, Loan Agreement, 12 p (3) 2003, Tranche Release Document, 23 p (4) 2005, Implementation Completion Report, 55 p	August 28, 2001	June 30, 2003
Family Strengthening and Social Capital Promotion (ProFam)	P070374	(1) 2001, Project Appraisal Document, 47 p (2) 2000, Project Information Document, 7 p (3) 2002, Loan Agreement, 28 p (4) 2002, Amendment 1, 7 p (5) 2007, Implementation Report, 53 p	November 8, 2001	December 31, 2006
Social Protection VI Project—Jefes de Hogar (Heads of Household)	P073578	(1) 2002, Project Appraisal Document, 66 p (2) 2001, Project Information Document, 7 p (3) 2002, Integrated Safeguards Data Sheet, 5 p (4) 2003, Loan Agreement, 26 p (5) 2004, Environmental Assessment, 31 p (6) 2007, Implementation Report, 74 p	January 28, 2003	July 28, 2006
Argentina Economic and Social Transition Structural Adjustment Loan	P083074	(1) 2003, Project Information Document, 3 p (2) 2003, Program Document, 78 p (3) 2003, Loan Agreement, 19 p (4) 2004, Implementation Completion Report, 31 p	May 22, 2003	August 29, 2003

(continued)

Table A.5 (continued)

Project name	Project ID number	Associated documents: Year, name, length	Project approval date	Project closing date
Provincial Maternal-Child Health Sector Adjustment Loan (PMCHSAL)	P072637	(1) 2003, Project Information Document, 7 p (2) 2003, Program Document, 126 p (3) 2003, Integrated Safeguards Data Sheet, 3 p (4) 2003, Loan Agreement, 23 p (5) 2004, Second Tranche Release, 6 p (6) 2007, Implementation Report, 36 p (7) 2011, Performance Assessment Report, 117 p	October 28, 2003	March 31, 2007
Provincial Maternal-Child Health Investment Project	P071025	(1) 2004, Project Appraisal Document, 82 p (2) 2004, Integrated Safeguards Data Sheet, 8 p (3) 2004, Loan Agreement, 31 p (4) 2006, Procurement Plan, 6 p (5) 2009, Project Brief, 2 p (6) 2010, Indigenous People Plan—Catamarca, 27 p (7) 2010, Indigenous People Plan— Chaco, 17 p (8) 2010, Indigenous People Plan—Formosa, 34 p (9) 2010, Indigenous People Plan—Jujuy, 15 p (10) 2010, Indigenous People Plan—Misiones, 27 p (11) 2010, Indigenous People Plan—Salta, 17 p (12) 2010, Indigenous People Plan—Santiago del Estero, 36 p (13) 2010, Indigenous People Plan—Tucuman, 12 p (14) 2011, Performance Assessment Report, 117 p	April 15, 2004	July 31, 2010

INTERVIEW DATA

Gathering data from policy elites poses particular challenges, among them access and confidentiality. Most of my respondents were comparatively high-ranking current or former policy makers in Argentina, Costa Rica, and Peru. Gaining access to elites is difficult, especially so if you do not embed yourself in a particular organization for a longer period of time. Although that approach comes with its own challenges, in those situations researchers have the benefit of time, slowly earning, and gaining their respondents' trust. In my case, however, I met with respondents for interviews that lasted between 45 and 150 minutes, typically only once. With this in mind, my consent forms allowed respondents to choose to identify themselves fully, only by their position (this could be as broad or specific as they wanted: for example, it could be as the head of a particular office or as a Ministry of Health official), or only by their institutional affiliation (again, this allowed respondents who often had multiple institutional affiliations across their careers to select the one most salient to them in terms of the information they disclosed during the interview). This was key to earning respondents' trust and indeed, while they received and signed the consent forms at the beginning of the interviews, I encouraged them to wait until the end of the interview to indicate how they wanted to be identified, so they were clear on the topics covered in the interviews and knew what information they had disclosed.

Gaining access was another challenge. Recruitment of these key informants proceeded in several stages: I sent a letter to the Ministry of Health and Social Security each, along with World Bank and WHO offices in each of these countries about 4 weeks prior to arrival, requesting an interview. This strategy worked for the international organization offices, but not as well for the government offices. Simultaneously, I had identified important academics and government officials as well as World Bank and other international organization personnel from the secondary literature I had read while selecting my cases. I contacted these people (largely via e-mail but sometimes via phone) and most agreed to be interviewed; similarly, academic colleagues, local to these countries, were very generous and helpful with their time and referrals.

In 2009 and 2011, I conducted 50 interviews in Peru. In 2011, I conducted 30 interviews in Argentina and 28 in Costa Rica. The interviews in 2009 were part of a pilot research trip which was planned for several purposes: to ascertain whether I could gain access to these informants, to see whether the informants would be willing to tell me about their experiences in health sector reform, and finally, in order to improve and refine my interview instrument. I was not able to gain access to all the informants on my initial list based on the secondary literature nor to all those on the list generated by snowball sampling, either because of scheduling or other issues. However, I am confident that I was able to interview the majority of important actors involved in health sector reform in these countries. To ensure completeness of information, I did interviews until I started to encounter heavy repetition. I also asked each respondent to name three people they thought I should interview at the end of the interview. I was able to interview a representative from all agencies/organizations involved in reforms or named by my respondents and was able to interview over 75% of the unique name referrals (some people were named twice or more) I received.

During my in-country stays in Argentina, Costa Rica, and Peru, I spoke with 107 out of 141 unique names I was given for people to interview and those I generated based on the secondary literature. Overall, I conducted 108 interviews with 114 people—accounting for the fact that I interviewed one person on two different occasions (Interview #5), four of the interviews involved two people (Interviews #11, 13, 56, and 103), and one involved three people (Interview #12).[5] Each interview was fully transcribed (either by myself or by local transcribers), and when quoting the interviews, I have translated the responses into English (except for the two interviews conducted in English). In summer 2015, I conducted five additional interviews with World Bank personnel, either via telephone or during my visit to the World Bank archives.

On a practical note, I found retired or semi-retired senior officials to be among my best respondents in the sense that they were willing to talk more freely about their experiences and were more generous with their time, likely because they had more of it available. They were also great at providing me with historical documents (or telling me where I could access them) and referring me to other important actors. Their experience and former positions carried weight, and people were often enthusiastic to speak to me on the recommendation of these people. Another interesting ritual I encountered was the importance and formality of the exchange of business cards. I carried my own business cards (even as a graduate student) and during my pilot trip in 2009 found them to be particularly well received: it almost always immediately prompted the reciprocation of my respondents' business cards which was helpful for follow-up contact, and appeared, at least in my perception, to lend an air of legitimacy to myself and the research. Therefore, I made sure to have more cards printed for my 2011 visits. I am unsure how particular these experiences were to my situation: I was a comparatively younger white woman interviewing mostly Latin American men, many of them highly educated, with distinguished careers, senior officials (past and present) in important positions. While my Spanish is fluent, there were technical terms and acronyms I was not familiar with across the three countries. I found my relatively lower ranked position to be a benefit: my respondents seemed to be more willing to explain everything in great detail, provide lots of background information, be generous with their time, and patiently answer my clarification questions than I think would have otherwise been the case (e.g., if I was an older, local, male). I cannot say how useful this advice or my experiences are across other national or institutional contexts but I offer them in this appendix in the hopes they may help others seeking to conduct high-status key informant interviews, especially cross-nationally.

Altogether, I am confident that my interview sample provides excellent coverage of the institutional actors engaged in health reform in each country, including personnel from all important public health agencies, World Bank and other IFI personnel, policy analysts, and health experts. The informants were policy makers across national governments and agencies, past and present, experts in the field of health care reform in the three countries, World Bank and IDB personnel, other agencies (local and international NGOs and bilateral aid agencies), experts in the health sector, and other relevant informants from civil society. All of the country interviews were conducted in person and all but two were conducted in Spanish. Three of the five subsequent World Bank personnel interviews were conducted over the phone, and all were conducted in English.

Interview #1: Escalante Guzmán, Giovanni. Organizacion Pan-Americano de Salud. July 6, 2009. Lima, Peru.

Interview #2: World Bank Official. July 7, 2009. Lima, Peru.

Interview #3: Regional Governmental Organization Senior Official. July 7, 2009. Lima, Peru.

Interview #4: World Bank Senior Official. July 9, 2009. Lima, Peru.

Interview #5: Castro Quiroz, José Alberto. Director of the Office of International Cooperation at the Peruvian Ministry of Health in 2009 and Official at the Instituto Nacional de Seguros in 2011. July 10, 2009, and May 11, 2011. Lima, Peru.

Interview #6: Peruvian Ministry of Health Senior Official. July 14, 2009. Lima, Peru.

Interview #7: Chiroque Benites, Luis. Primary Health Care Office, EsSALUD (*El Seguro Social de Salud*). July 14, 2009. Lima, Peru.

Interview #8: Inter-American Development Bank Senior Official. July 15, 2009. Lima, Peru.

Interview #9: Seguro Integral de Salud (SIS) Senior Official. July 16, 2009. Lima, Peru.

Interview #10: Peruvian Ministry of Health Senior Official and Regular World Bank Consultant. July 17, 2009. Lima, Peru.

Interview #11: Gutarra Álvarez, Melchor and Álvaro Eduardo Vidal Rivadeneyra. National Medical Union for Social Security in Peru, and Minister of Health between 2003 and 2004, respectively. July 18, 2009. Lima, Peru.

Interview #12: Three Managers from the Seguro Integral de Salud (SIS). July 22, 2009. Lima, Peru.

Interview #13: Two USAID Senior Officials. July 22, 2009. Lima, Peru.

Interview #14: Salinas Rivas, Abel. Advisor to the Vice-Minister of Health. July 24, 2009. Lima, Peru.

Interview #15: Tejada de Rivero, David. Deputy Director-General of the World Health Organization (WHO), 1974–1985 and Minister of Health, 1985–1987 and 1989–1990. July 29, 2009. Lima, Peru.

Interview #16: Former Minister of Health. July 31, 2009. Lima, Peru.

Interview #17: Local Health-NGO Director. July 31, 2009. Lima, Peru.

Interview #18: Researcher. July 31, 2009. Lima, Peru.

Interview #19: Researcher, Universidad Peruana Cayetano Heredia. August 3, 2009. Lima, Peru.

Interview #20: Acosta Saal, Carlos Manuel. Director of Health Management, Ministry of Health. August 4, 2009. Lima, Peru.

Interview #21: Gonzalvez, Guillermo. Organizacion Pan-Americano de Salud Official. May 12, 2011. Lima, Peru.

Interview #22: Arosquipa, Carlos. Organizacion Pan-Americano de Salud Official. May 12, 2011. Lima, Peru.

Interview #23: Rasmussen Ochoa, Alfredo. Director of the Torre Treca Public-Private Partnership between GrupoSalud and EsSALUD. May 16, 2011. Lima, Peru.

Interview #24: Begazo Dongo, Hector. Private Health Organizations Manager (including Protectora Corredora de Seguros.). May 17, 2011. Lima, Peru.

Interview #25: Bocanergra Cotez, Alberto. Superintendencia Nacional de Salud (SUNASA) Senior Official. May 17, 2011. Lima, Peru.

Interview #26: Salinas Rivas, Abel Hernan. Superintendencia Nacional de Salud (SUNASA) General Intendent. May 17, 2011. Lima, Peru.

Interview #27: Academic. May 18, 2011. Lima, Peru.

Interview #28: Granados Torano, Ramon. Organizacion Pan-Americano de Salud Official. May 19, 2011. Lima, Peru.

Interview #29: Gutierrez, Nelson. World Bank Official. May 23, 2011. Lima, Peru.

Interview #30: Seminario Carrasco, Jose Luis. USAID Official. Health. May 23, 2011. Lima, Peru.

Interview #31: Rios Barrientos, Mario. Foro Salud (coalition of health civil society organizations) General Coordinator. May 24, 2011. Lima, Peru.

Interview #32: Ruiz Portal, Jorge. General Director of Stella Maris Private Health Clinic. May 24, 2011. Lima, Peru.

Interview #33: Ministry of Economy and Finance Senior Official. May 25, 2011. Lima, Peru.

Interview #34: Jumpa Santamaría, Manuel. Ministry of Health Senior Official. May 25, 2011. Lima, Peru.

Interview #35: USAID Senior Official. May 26, 2011. Lima. Peru.

Interview #36: Velásquez Valdivia, Aníbal. Ministry of Health Senior Official. May 26, 2011. Lima, Peru.

Interview #37: Bustamante Garcia, Mauricio. President of Salud Internacional Consulting Group. May 27, 2011. Lima, Peru.

Interview #38: La Rosa Huertas, Liliana del Carmen. Director of the Office of International Cooperation at the Peruvian Ministry of Health. May 30, 2011. Lima, Peru.

Interview #39: Barredo Moyano, Alfredo. EsSALUD Senior Official. May 31, 2011. Lima, Peru.

Interview #40: Garcia Torres, Victor Raul. Advisor to the Minister of Health, Coordinator with Parliament. May 31, 2011. Lima, Peru.

Interview #41: Guisti Hundskopf, Paulina. General Coordinator of PARSALUD (Ministry of Health Project with Financing from World Bank and Inter-American Development Bank). June 1, 2011. Lima, Peru.

Interview #42: Castro Gómez, Julio. Former Dean of the Colegio Medico de Peru (Peruvian Medical Union). June 1, 2011. Lima, Peru.

Interview #43: Researcher at Consorcio de Investigación Económica y Social (CIES), Social and Economic Research Consortium. June 1, 2011. Lima, Peru.

Interview #44: Senior Health Sector Official. June 2, 2011. Lima, Peru.

Interview #45: Ministry of Health Senior Official. June 2, 2011. Lima, Peru.

Interview #46: Cordero Muñoz, Luis. Academic, Universidad Cayetano Heredia and former Official in Ministries of Health and Economy and Finance. June 2, 2011. Lima, Peru.

Interview #47: Ricse, Carlos. Consultant, formerly Official at the Ministry of Health. June 3, 2011. Lima, Peru.

Interview #48: Cárdenas Díaz, Max. Former Dean of the Colegio Medico de Peru (Peruvian Medical Union). June 3, 2011. Lima, Peru.

Interview #49: Francke, Pedro. President of the Board of Directors of Sistema Metropolitano de la Solidaridad (SISOL, network of clinics in the Lima metropolitan area). June 3, 2011. Lima, Peru.

Interview #50: Tobar, Federico. Consultant. June 8, 2011. Buenos Aires, Argentina.

Interview #51: Vasallo, Carlos Alberto. Consultant. June 13, 2011. Buenos Aires, Argentina.

Interview #52: Inter-American Development Bank Official. June 16, 2011. Buenos Aires, Argentina.

Interview #53: Redondo, Nelida. National Institute of Statistics and Census of Argentina Official. June 16, 2011. Buenos Aires, Argentina.

Interview #54: Academic. June 17, 2011. Buenos Aires, Argentina.

Interview #55: Cetrangolo, Oscar. Economic Commission for Latin America and the Caribbean Official. June 21, 2011. Buenos Aires, Argentina.

Interview #56: Rios, Marta Enriqueta and Luisa Isabel Diaz. Academics, Universidad de Buenos Aires. June 22, 2011. Buenos Aires, Argentina.

Interview #57: Glanc, Mario. Academic, ISALUD. June 22, 2011. Buenos Aires, Argentina.

Interview #58: Schweiger, Arturo. Academic, ISALUD. June 22, 2011. Buenos Aires, Argentina.

Interview #59: Pippo Briant, Tomas A. Ministry of Health Official. June 27, 2011. Buenos Aires, Argentina.

Interview #60: Mera, Jorge Alberto. Official at Instituto de Obras Sociales (Institute of Obras Sociales). June 29, 2011. Buenos Aires, Argentina.

Interview #61: Surace, Benjamin. Director of Obra Social de la Union de Trabajadores del Turismo, Hoteleros y Gastronomicos (Obra Social of the Union of Workers in Tourism, Hotel/Hospitality, and Catering). June 30, 2011. Buenos Aires, Argentina.

Interview #62: Ventura, Graciela. General Coordinator for REMEDIAR+REDES: FEAPS, Fortalecimiento de la Estrategia de la Atencion Primaria de la Salud (project by the Ministry of Health to increase the accessibility of medications and strengthen primary care in health). July 1, 2011. Buenos Aires, Argentina.

Interview #63: Spinelli, Hugo. Academic, Universidad Nacional de Lanus. July 4, 2011. Buenos Aires, Argentina.

Interview #64: Garavelli, Carlos. Organizacion Iberoamericana de Seguridad Social (OISS, Ibero-American Organization for Social Security) Official. July 5, 2011. Buenos Aires, Argentina.

Interview #65: Bellagio, Ricardo E. Superintendencia de Servicios de Salud (SSSalud, Superintendency for Health Services) Official. July 6, 2011. Buenos Aires, Argentina.

Interview #66: Jañez, Jorge Carlos and Jorge Alberto Coronel. Confederacion Medica de la Republica Argentina (COMRA, Medical Confederation of the Argentinian Republic) Senior Officials. July 7, 2011. Buenos Aires, Argentina.

Interview #67: Sabignoso, Martin. Coordinator for Plan NACER in the Ministry of Health. July 8, 2011. Buenos Aires, Argentina.

Interview #68: Medical Director at a large *Obra Social*. July 11, 2011. Buenos Aires, Argentina.

Interview #69: World Bank Official. July 12, 2011. Buenos Aires, Argentina.

Interview #70: Stolkiner, Alicia Ines. Academic, University of Buenos Aires. July 12, 2011. Buenos Aires, Argentina.

Interview #71: Diosque, Maximo. Ministry of Health Senior Official. July 13, 2011. Buenos Aires, Argentina.

Interview #72: Escudero, Jose Carlos. Academic, Universidad Nacional de la Plata. July 14, 2011. Buenos Aires, Argentina.

Interview #73: Güemes, Armando. Organizacion Pan-Americano de Salud Official. July 15, 2011. Buenos Aires, Argentina.

Interview #74: Neri, Aldo. Minister of Health of Argentina between 1983 and 1986. July 15, 2011. Buenos Aires, Argentina.

Interview #75: Perreiro, Ana Cristina. Ministry of Health Official. July 18, 2011. Buenos Aires, Argentina.

Interview #76: Alvarez, Marcelo G. Academic, University of Buenos Aires. July 19, 2011. Buenos Aires, Argentina.

Interview #77: Maciera, Daniel. Researcher at Centro de Estudios de Estado y Sociedad (CEDES, State and Society Studies Center). July 28, 2011. Buenos Aires, Argentina.

Interview #78: Sonis, Abraam, Academic, Universidad Maimonides. July 26, 2011. Buenos Aires, Argentina.

Interview #79: Barbieri, María Eugenia. Ministry of the Economy Official. July 28, 2011. Buenos Aires.

Interview #80: Soto, Sergio Rueben. Academic, University of Costa Rica. August 24, 2011. San Pedro, Costa Rica.

Interview #81: Carazo Salas, Juan Antonio. Academic, University of Costa Rica. August 26, 2011. San Pedro, Costa Rica.

Interview #82: Former Minister of Health. August 29, 2011. San Jose, Costa Rica.

Interview #83: Rosales, Carlos. Organizacion Pan-Americano de Salud Official. August 30, 2011. San Jose, Costa Rica.

Interview #84: Miranda Gutiérrez, Guido. Former Executive President of the CCSS between 1982 and 1990. August 30, 2011. San Jose, Costa Rica.

Interview #85: Salas Chaves, Álvaro. Executive President of the CCSS between 1994 and 1998. August 30, 2011. San Jose, Costa Rica. August 31, 2011. San Jose, Costa Rica.

Interview #86: Herrera Guido, Roberto. Director of the Hospital Metropolitana (private hospital). September 1, 2011. San Jose, Costa Rica.

Interview #87: Luque, Hernán. Organizacion Pan-Americano de Salud Official. September 1, 2011. San Jose, Costa Rica.

Interview #88: Vargas Brenes, Juan Rafael. Academic, Universidad de Costa Rica. September 9, 2011. San Pedro, Costa Rica.

Interview #89: Senior Official at the CCSS. September 16, 2011. San Jose, Costa Rica.

Interview #90: Sáenz, Luis Bernardo. CCSS Senior Official. September 20, 2011. San Jose, Costa Rica.

Interview #91: Jimenez Fonseca, Elias. MD in private and public hospitals. September 21, 2011. San Jose, Costa Rica.

Interview #92: Vargas Fuentes, Mauricio. Ministry of Health Senior Official. September 21, 2011. San Pedro, Costa Rica.

Interview #93: Villalobos Solano, Luis Bernardo. Academic at the University of Costa Rica. September 22, 2011. San Pedro, Costa Rica.

Interview #94: Weinstock, Herman. Minister of Health between 1974 and 1978. September 23, 2011. San Jose, Costa Rica.

Interview #95: Former President of the Union Medica Nacional (National Medical Union). September 26, 2011. San Jose, Costa Rica.

Interview #96: Cortés Rodríguez, Jorge. General Medical Director of Hospital Clinica Biblica (private hospital). September 27, 2011. San Jose, Costa Rica.

Interview #97: Lopez, Maria Elena. Ministry of Health Senior Official. September 29, 2011. San Jose, Costa Rica.

Interview #98: Piza Rocafor, Rodolfo. President of the CCSS between 1998 and 2002. October 4, 2011. San Jose, Costa Rica.

Interview #99: Sáenz Jiménez, Lenín. Ministry of Health Senior Official. October 5, 2011. San Jose, Costa Rica.

Interview #100: Villegas, Hugo. Organizacion Pan-Americano de Salud Official. October 11, 2011. San Jose, Costa Rica.

Interview #101: Marín Rojas, Fernando. President of Instituto Mixto de Ayuda Social (IMAS, Mixed Institute for Social Assistance private–public institute to assist people in extreme poverty). October 11, 2011. San Jose, Costa Rica.

Interview #102: Pardo-Evans, Rogelio. Minister of Health between 1998 and 2002. October 19, 2011. San Jose, Costa Rica.

Interview #103: Robles Monge, Mario and Cristina Bonilla Alfaro. Officials at Ministerio de Planificacion (MIDEPLAN, Ministry of Planning). October 21, 2011.

Interview #104: Arias Sobrado, Jorge. Former Ministry of Health and CCSS Senior Official. October 21, 2011. San Jose, Costa Rica.

Interview #105: Montero, Jorge E. Former Inter-American Development Bank Official. October 28, 2011. San Jose, Costa Rica.

Interview #106: Vargas González, William. Ministry of Health and CCSS Official. October 31, 2011. San Jose, Costa Rica.

Interview #107: Martinez Franzoni, Juliana. Academic, University of Costa Rica. November 21, 2011. San Pedro, Costa Rica.

Interview #108: Former Senior World Bank Official. May 25, 2015. Washington, DC, USA.

Interview #109: Former Senior World Bank Official. May 29, 2015. Washington, DC, USA.
Interview #110: Levine, Ruth. Former World Bank Official. June 9, 2015. Telephone interview.
Interview #111: Senior World Bank Official. June 12, 2015. Telephone interview.
Interview #112: Senior World Bank Official. June 22, 2015. Telephone interview.

Since I interviewed people with different roles across reforms in each of the three countries and in the World Bank, I utilized a semi-structured interview format. I opted for open-ended questions that allowed respondents to discuss reforms and issues that they viewed as important, and probed based on their answers and specific to their circumstances and involvement in health sector reform. My interview instrument for the country case-studies consisted of the following questions (which I translated as almost all interviews were conducted in Spanish) though not all respondents were asked all of these questions since sometimes their answers to subsequent questions emerged earlier, or due to time constraints, or because they gave me CVs, for example, which covered some of their biographical backgrounds.

Respondent Background
I want to ask about your background and position in [agency]
What is your position in this [agency]?
How long have you worked at [agency]?
What has been your role/position in [agency] during your time there?
And what is your educational background?
Did you study, work, or otherwise receive any training internationally?

General Questions about Health Care in Country
Now I want to ask you about the [country] health care system.
What government agencies are responsible for the provision of health services in [country]?
What are the responsibilities of the Ministry of Health compared with the social security office?
What types of programs exist?
How are the government programs complemented by non-government organizations' (NGOs) programs?
What are the main international organizations that the Ministry of Health and other relevant government agencies work with? [I then asked about the World Bank specifically if they did not elaborate as all of my

respondents mentioned it, and sometimes probed about other agencies mentioned in response to this question as well if they did not elaborate about their role]

Health Care Reform and Historical Perspective

I want to ask you about social security in [country] in recent decades, and especially since the 1980s.

What have been the major reforms in the [country] national health care system in recent decades?

What other organizations/agencies and/or people have participated in this reform?

How active has [government agency] been in the provision of health services in [country]?

What role has [government agency] has in reforms to the [country's] health care system?

And you specifically?

What do you think about these reforms and changes in the [country's] health care system?

Issues and Priorities in Health Care

In your opinion, what are the main problems with the current health care system in [country]?

What would you consider to be priorities for health care in [country]?

What do you think these will be/how do you think these will change in the next 10 years?

What have been the major successes and failures in the provision of health services in [country] and in the health care system?

Do you think that the international community has an impact on health policies in [country]?

What type of impact?

How do you think the field of health care in [country] will change in the next 20 years?

Comparative Questions

Now I want to ask you about the [country] health care sector in comparison with other sectors in [country].

How do you think the public expenditure on health compares to public expenditure in other sectors, for example, on education? Why?

Now I would like to ask you about the [country] health care sector in comparison to health care systems in other countries.

Different countries have different ideas about the best way to structure social policy and particularly, health services.

Do you think that there is any particular country that [country] should imitate/follow in terms of health care? Why?

Final Questions

Is there anything else you want to tell me or you think I need to know about health care in [country]?

Finally, can you name three people who you consider especially important in the field of health care in [country] who you believe I should speak with?

Interviews with World Bank personnel not stationed in country offices varied because they were done after I completed the country visits, and depended more specifically on these people's experience at the World Bank. I asked about their background and experience; I also asked questions specific to their involvement in different reforms and reports, and some general questions, including the following:

International Organizations' Role in Global Health

What do you think is the ideal role of international organizations in national health care reforms?

What international organizations do you think have been most important in influencing countries' health reforms? Any specific examples you can think of?

Questions on the World Bank's Approach to Health

What do you think is the World Bank's current approach to health?

What do you think about this approach?

Do you think this approach has changed over time? If so, how?

What do you think of these changes?

How do you think the World Bank's approach to health differs from or is similar to its approach in other domains, for example, education?

Comparative, and in particular cross-national, mixed-methods research is an immense undertaking. Despite its challenges, however, mixed-methods, comparative research yields data second to none. It allows the researcher to take both a bird's-eye view (national, regional, and over time trends) and dig into the meat of their case-studies (via detailed accounts gathered from interviews and content analyses). It has allowed me to triangulate information and move between the details and the trends. Most importantly, it has allowed me to answer the questions that motivated this research about the World Bank's involvement in health in Latin America. I have offered some practical tips for recruiting key informants, and some particularities of my own experiences which I hope may be helpful to others. I'll offer a final bit of advice: if you're interested in puzzles and questions that require extensive, comparative, mixed-methods data, do not be daunted: the rewards (both in answering the research questions and in personal experiences) far outweigh the trials.

NOTES

1. This information about the reliability of the data comes from an interview with a WHO functionary in Costa Rica (Interview #100). An examination of these same indicators in the World Bank's HNP dataset (World Bank HNP Stats) shows the very limited and patchy nature of these data. In previous research, I used data dating back to 1980 from CEPAL (Noy 2011), used in the Huber and Stephens data. Since, however, in addition to the information above I was advised by an interviewee in Argentina I was told that their estimates for public health spending were incorrect, which I confirmed by comparing the official Ministry of Health figures to those published by CEPAL and used in the Huber and Stephens dataset, see Huber et al. (2008). The WHO Global Health Expenditure Database, part of the National Health Accounts database, has collected and systemized health expenditure data only since 1995. The HNP World Bank data which I use draw on these data (as both the WHO and the World Bank are part of the United Nations system). I opted to download them from the World Bank database as that allowed me to simultaneously gather data from the World Development Indicators compiled by the World Bank on my independent variables for the time-series cross-section regression models—GDP, elderly population, etc.

2. The Bahamas, Barbados, Belize, and Suriname are not included in the time-series cross-section analysis because they do not have data on democratization (in addition to many years with missing unemployment data). Haiti has only a single data point after accounting for missing data on the independent variables, and therefore, it is excluded from the analysis (due to the fact that in lagging GDP and left seat share, I require at least two full data points for those variables). Since all of the data on democratization are missing for the Bahamas and Barbados, it is not possible to impute. In addition, there are several country-years for which there is no data on one or more of the independent variables. These observations are therefore excluded from the analysis. The final sample includes 226 observations for 21 countries.

3. I use the *xtpcse* command with the *pairwise* option in Stata12.1. As an additional check for robustness, I re-estimated all models using conventional panel techniques that prioritize within-country correlation rather than between-country contemporaneous correlation. A common concern in panel models is how to account for the unobserved, permanent, country-specific error component. If the unobserved errors are correlated with the covariates, a fixed effects estimation can remove this source of bias (that is, the "within" panel estimator), however at the cost of efficiency in the regression model (Wooldridge 2002). If the unobserved panel-specific component of the error is uncorrelated with the covariates, both OLS and fixed effects are unbiased, and a random effects model is preferred because it is more efficient. In order to adjudicate between the fixed and random effects models, researchers typically use a Hausman test or regression-based Mundlak test (Wooldridge 2002). Because serial correlation remains a problem even after adjusting for country-specific errors, I used random effects and fixed effects panel models with a first-order correlation correction, AR(1). I used the Mundlak tests to decide between the fixed and random effects (Wooldridge 2002). I present these results and shade the preferred models (according to the Mundlak test) in gray in Appendix A in Chapter 3 in Tables 3.A.1 and 3.A.2.

4. Details on the sectors for each project are available in the World Bank's Projects and Operations database.

5. Because I started with people who featured in secondary and primary documents, their names were also frequently mentioned by one of my respondents as people I should speak to. I received 63 unique names in Peru and interviewed 49 of them (for a total of 50 interviews), in Argentina I received 37 unique referrals and interviewed 30 of them (for a total of 30 interviews), and in Costa Rica received 41 unique referrals and interviewed 28 of them (for a total of 28 interviews). As noted, this was not an organized roster, so sometimes respondents would indicate I should talk to someone at some institution (rather than naming as specific person) that was involved in reform efforts at a particular time (for example, a local NGO or a government agency), and I was able to talk to someone at each of these (indeed, often a specific name for someone at said agency was recommended by a different respondent).

WORKS CITED

Bank, W. (2011). World Bank Health Nutrition and Population Statistics (HNP). http://data.worldbank.org/data-catalog/health-nutrition-population-statistics. Accessed October 6, 2011.

Bank, W. (2012a). World Bank Development Policy Actions Database http://web.worldbank.org/WBSITE/EXTERNAL/PROJECTS/0,,contentMDK:22209407~pagePK:41367~piPK:51533~theSitePK:40941,00.html. Accessed April 12, 2012.

Bank, W. (2012b). World Bank World Development Indicators. http://data.worldbank.org/data-catalog/world-development-indicators. Accessed April 19, 2012.

Beck, N., & Katz, J. N. (1995). What to do (and not to do) with time-series cross-section data. *American Political Science Review, 89*(03), 634–647.

Campbell, J. L. (2002). Ideas, politics, and public policy. *Annual Review of Sociology, 21*–38.

Falleti, T. G. (2006). Theory-guided process-tracing in comparative politics: Something old, something new. *Newsletter of the Organized Section in Comparative Politics of the American Political Science Association, 17*(1), 9–14.

George, A. L., & Bennett, A. (2005). *Case studies and theory development in the social sciences.* Cambridge: MIT Press.

Gerring, J. (2004). What is a case study and what is it good for? *American Political Science Review, 98*(02), 341–354.

Huber, E., Mustillo, T., & Stephens, J. D. (2008). Politics and social spending in Latin America. *The Journal of Politics, 70*(02), 420–436.

Huber, E., & Stephens, J. (2012). Latin America and the Caribbean Political Dataset. http://www.unc.edu/~jdsteph/common/data-common.htm. Accessed September 15, 2012.

IHME. (2016). *Development assistance for health database 1990–2015.* Seattle, United States: Institute for Health Metrics and Evaluation.

© The Editor(s) (if applicable) and The Author(s) 2017
S. Noy, *Banking on Health*, DOI 10.1007/978-3-319-61765-7

Mahoney, J. (2004). Comparative-historical methodology. *Annual Review Sociology, 30*, 81–101.

Mahoney, J. (2012). The logic of process tracing tests in the social sciences. *Sociological Methods & Research, 41*(4), 570–597.

Muhr, T. (2015). Atlas. ti (Version 7). *Berlin: Scientific Software Development.*

Noy, S. (2011). New contexts, different patterns? A comparative analysis of social spending and government health expenditure in Latin America and the OECD. *International Journal of Comparative Sociology, 52*(3), 215–244.

Schneiberg, M., & Clemens, E. S. (2006). The typical tools for the job: Research strategies in institutional analysis. *Sociological Theory, 24*(3), 195–227.

Tansey, O. (2007). Process tracing and elite interviewing: A case for non-probability sampling. *PS. Political Science & Politics, 40*(04), 765–772.

Tilly, C. (1984). *Big structures, large processes, huge comparisons.* New York: Russell Sage Foundation.

Wooldridge, J. M. (2002). *Econometric analysis of cross section and panel data.* Cambridge, MA: Massachusetts Institute of Technology.

INDEX